Love and
Democracy

*What we learned
on the road with Granny D
and other American heroes*

By Dennis Michael Burke

Burke

Copyright 2026 by Dennis Michael Burke
All Rights Reserved

L'Enfant Press, Washington D.C.
ISBN 9 781734 586787

First Printing February, 2026

BOOK I 5

- THE HOPE OF AUDACITY 5
- KEN 23
- DORIS 35
- NEWSPEOPLE 43
- YOU'RE GOING TO NEED A BIGGER BOOK 48
- WALKS IN THE WOODS 64
- LOVE SERVED ROUGH 78
- THE EXPLOITED 91
- BIRDS 101
- HELL FREEZES OVER 109
- AMERICAN VALENTINE 121

BOOK II 131

- COEXISTENCE 131
- BISHOP'S GAMBIT 152
- THE POWER OF STORY 165
- WHO THE HOLY F IS THAT? 170
- ASHEVILLE CEREMONIES 183
- FLORIDA'S MERMAID VOTE 193
- GET UP! STAND UP! 210
- TRIANGULATION 225
- LIFE ON THE MISSISSIPPI 236
- ANNOYING SEATMATE 254
- THE CANDIDATE 260
- AND SCENE 280
- THE ORANGE REVOLUTION 288
- THREE NOTES 302

"It happens quickly and moves swiftly. It is nothing for the forces of raw power to discredit the proper law enforcement agencies and set up new ones, run by political cronies, and with prisons and police of their own to suppress and arrest those who dare investigate or protest. It is nothing for raw power to thumb its nose at the interests of world peace or the Earth's environment for the sake of power and plunder. It is nothing for raw power to mistake the flowering of political ideas and dissent in a democracy as a dangerous tangle of garden plots and disloyalties. It can happen quickly. It can happen in America. Open your eyes!"

—Doris Haddock in Tallahassee, 2001

Book I

The Hope of Audacity

Woolly worms, or call them woolly bears, about two inches long, mostly black, fat and fuzzy, cross the green and bloody folds of Appalachia every autumn, taking chances against fast coal trucks, four-wheelers, dirt bikes, rattling pickups and ever more coal trucks. If the caterpillars have rusty midsections, the coming winter will be mild. If the creatures are solid black or nearly so, it will be a hard winter. People who go to college to study bugs will tell you this weather predictor is a myth, but we live by our myths, don't we?

A pink-aproned woman of Belpre, Ohio, wrestling a family-reunion-size coffee tank onto a folding table set hastily beside the road and apologizing for the local weather, mentioned that the woolly worms were black as coal that previous autumn. Her retired husband, delivering cream, sugar, cups and spoons on a rattling Pittsburgh Pirates party tray, jerked a glance toward the slate sky as proof of the wisdom. It was seven days before Christmas, 1999.

"It's going to get a bit more serious from here, weatherwise," he said to his wife and to a 90-year-old woman walking coast-to-coast through their town. The couple had learned about the woman on the TV the previous evening and thought they would help welcome her. They were surprised to see their mayor in the old woman's entourage, and too many people for the coffee on hand.

Dark weather, starting as a tropical depression in the Gulf and now crawling up the Mississippi and Ohio Rivers, would soon hatch into the worst blizzard and deepest snow in forty years.

The elderly walker, Doris "Granny D" Haddock, said she was aware of the forecast. She sipped the gift of coffee and looked at the gradual rise of the Fifth Street Bridge, spanning the Ohio River into West Virginia, just ahead. She whispered to her coffee hosts that she hated uphill stretches, big or little, mountains or humped bridges. Her legs, she said, were strong, but her emphysema and arthritis favored flat roads like all West Texas and long downhill marches into valleys like everything since.

After the bridge it would be one hill after another, trending uphill for 175 miles to the Eastern Continental Divide—the top of the Appalachians. Beyond the Divide, Washington would be only 200 miles more, and all downhill. Peanuts for her, unless the worst blizzard and deepest snow in forty years might stop her. She could imagine walking right up to the U.S. Capitol, having braved a million speeding trucks and a dozen sandstorms and one blizzard. If the woolly worms could make it, taking flight as gypsy moths in the spring, she knew she could spread her wings on the steps of the U.S. Capitol before March.

She had been worried about getting over the Appalachians since starting her walk in California nearly a year earlier, but there had always been something or someone just ahead to keep her going. Presently it was a friend made on the road, Ken Hechler, the Secretary of

State of West Virginia, standing midway on the bridge ahead and beckoning her with the helicopter wave of a white something over his head. She first met him when he came to walk with her behind the Rose Parade in Pasadena on New Year's Day, the start of her journey for political reform. A small notice about her planned walk in USA Today had caught Ken's attention, and he flew to California to be a part of it. He had returned to join her on the road whenever his duties in Charleston allowed.

"What do you suppose Ken's got there?" Doris asked me. I was in a chilly mood and suggested it might be a Welcome to West Virginia shirt for her to wear. She hated that sort of thing. "God!" she said.

There were twenty-five people on the bridge with Ken Hechler, including West Virginia Governor Cecil Underwood and the mayor of Parkersburg, Jimmy Colombo. That would make seventy-five, as fifty volunteers were already walking with her.

West of Cleveland, two female students at Oberlin College, Laura and Mary, were folding their knit caps, mittens and other warm woolens into their backpacks. Concerned for their country and inspired by something their history professor had said, they would hike with Doris through their holiday break.

All along her walk, people had come and gone, some joining Doris for a few minutes or a few days. Secretary Hechler had walked five hundred of her nearly three thousand miles so far. He was tall and elegantly balding and always presented a spectacle as he towered over garden-hatted, 4-foot-11 Doris.

Many other people, perhaps because they heard about her from their local news or on one of the network morning shows, would walk for a while, go home to take a warm bath and relax in front of their televisions, and then feel guilty that Doris "Granny D" Haddock was still out there walking for Democracy. They would often figure a way to find her again on the road or make plans to walk the last miles with her in DC, if she made it.

Also coming and going were book club members and other friends and relatives from her New Hampshire hometown of Peterborough, where Thornton Wilder wrote *Our Town* after looking around and meeting the people.

Doris's son, Jim, recently retired as a top New Hampshire mental health professional, was one of the trail bosses, arranging overnight stays and scheduling volunteers for his mother's walk. I was with Jim on that duty, and Doris was starting to think of me as her second, more manageable, son. I was also there because Ken Hechler had told Doris how he wrote countless speeches for Harry Truman on his presidential campaign train, and Doris would need lots of speeches like that, tailored to the issues of each place she stopped to speak.

She latched onto me for that, as I can research and write and my wife volunteered me when Doris was walking through our Arizona kitchen. I would come and go from her walk, as I was also organizing an anti-gerrymandering ballot initiative back in Arizona after a successful "clean elections" public campaign funding initiative a year earlier.

Some people just waited on the road to meet or applaud Doris as she passed. Women invariably gave her a hug, and the older ones also cried. Local officials wanted to walk with her, sometimes just to get into a local television story or front-page photo. This morning, the mayor of Belpre, Ohio and Ohio's Secretary of State were walking her out of their state, ready to hand her off to their West Virginia counterparts who were flapping like penguins to keep warm on the bridge.

She crossed it, continuing past Parkersburg through light rain that became a series of drenchers by Clarksburg, nearly three difficult weeks later. In the warm living room of a volunteer there, Ken showed up again and gave her a medal he had crafted himself to mark her full year on the road.

I called her that evening about some speeches she would need for the towns ahead. I told her the speech she gave in Lexington about Senator Mitch McConnell was still reverberating against him in his home-state press, after it was reproduced in two full pages in the main paper. She was delighted. McConnell, longtime majority leader of the Senate Republicans, had become the very symbol to her of the corrupt political system, as he was the main roadblock to the passage of the McCain-Feingold bill in Congress, and that negative press must have punched him hard. I asked her what she would have done if he had shown up in front of his office where she gave the speech. Or what would she do if he came to walk with her on the road, just as other politicians had done to avoid being seen as dissing her. What would she say to him?

She said she would talk to him like his mother. She would tell him she was ashamed of his selfishness and his bullying. She went on to describe her whole conversation, after which Mitch starts crying and promising to be good.

"But the evil would still be out there," she told me. "We are always in a struggle between the loving sense of community and the evil of selfish power. It would settle on someone else for us to oppose. The play goes on and on, you know. It's the show we came for in this life."

> *On Saturday, November 6, 1999, Mrs. Haddock walked into Louisville and assembled a rally of 160 people outside the office of Kentucky's U.S. Senator Mitch McConnell. As with most her speeches, it was widely covered by newspaper, radio and three television stations. This speech was run in its entirety in the newspaper, with favorable editorial comment. Senator McConnell's effort to stall the issuance of an event permit was discovered and defeated, allowing the event to take place legally. "We would have done it anyway," she told a reporter. "The Constitution is our permit."*

The next morning in Clarksburg and in the miles ahead she would be walking in a whiteout blizzard. Nick Palumbo, a young volunteer from Chicago who had been driving the support van and organizing her days though quite a few states, suggested they settle in somewhere until the storm passed. Doris reminded him that people in DC were making plans, getting permits, all that. She didn't want to disappoint them. Nick therefore drove slowly along the shoulder so Doris and the two college girls now with her could walk between the headlight beams and not get lost in the ferocious blast of snow and ice. Most other volunteers had fallen away until the storm might pass. It would not.

From her memoir:

> *On January 5, the rain turned to snow with such ferocity that Nick, driving behind me up the grades, had a hard time seeing me, even when I was but a few yards ahead. Laura and Mary, two students from*

Oberlin College, arrived to walk with us, as did Ken and a Japanese TV crew. The fellow walkers were welcome, as I didn't fear wandering off in the snow in the wrong direction. We single-filed through the whiteout like a bunch of good, frozen scouts, with the young eyes in front. Several days later, after conquering the six-mile hill we had been warned about, our slipping and sliding little parade made it into Morgantown. From there, the weather turned remarkably worse. Nick nervously drove the van several feet behind me–it was the first time I had seen him so anxious. If he lagged too far back, he could not see me in the snow; too close, and he feared rolling right over me. It was hard going.

On top of the blizzard, the grades were steep and slippery, and my breathing sounded inside my head like an old tea kettle. It was impossible to go the full ten miles each day. Six was a good day in a blizzard. This was the mountain I had dreaded for three thousand miles. I knew the long year would either have me in shape for this climb, or I would be too worn out to even think about it. One foot in front of the other, Doris. The whiteout of a blizzard is a remarkable environment to experience for long hours. The world is a blank screen all around you, save for the glow of headlights and the faint, pastel shapes of your companions. It's a private space.

Americans were walking with her because they were watching their elections being bought up from under them, and they knew they might be walking in the last days of the American democracy. Doris at least had a plan, and they were with her. People like Ken, and reform lobbyists on the Hill, believed her audacious walk was generating real hope for the passage of the McCain-Feingold bill, which had been stalled in Congress for the last few years. Doris was now providing the grassroots element and national press coverage that had been missing.

> "The big money lobbyists put money out in the troughs each morning on K Street, and then the great oinking starts up on Capitol Hill. Soon, members of Congress are all nudging each other at the troughs. It's enough to make you a vegetarian."
> — *Doris speaking in Morgantown*

It was personal with Ken. He told me on a very long road in West Texas that he had been friends with West Virginia politician Jay Rockefeller, the richest man he ever knew, who arrived in West Virginia as a young back-to-the-land hippie environmentalist but became a supporter of strip mining and its devil child, mountaintop removal mining, just for more campaign support.

"His great-grandfather was John D. Rockefeller," Ken added, "the man who supposedly orchestrated the massacre of striking coal miners in Ludlow, Colorado in 1914. Twenty-one were killed, mostly the wives and children of miners. So, he had that family debt to repay, but he strayed to the wrong side anyway."

"Did you see the movie Chinatown?" Ken then asked. He and Doris and I were walking past oil wells at the time. I often recorded the conversations around Doris, but this is from memory:

"There's a scene when Jack Nicholas…"

"Nicholson," Doris corrected him.

"Yes, Nicholson, playing the detective, Jake Gittes. He is talking to the murderous Mr. Cross…"

Love and Democracy

"John Huston," Doris inserted.

"Yes, he asks him how much money he has, maybe over $10 million? Oh, yes, Huston replies. Then why are you doing it? How much better can you eat? What can you buy that you can't already afford? And Huston replies, The future, Mr. Gittes. The future."

I remember that conversation because Ken looked and sounded so much like Huston when he said that line. And the movie's biggest line, "Forget it , Jake, it's Chinatown," how many times in politics have those words come to mind?

"Why are so many of the rich like that?" Doris thought aloud as we walked.

"When you're famously rich and powerful and you got it by being morally blind you don't care if your grandchildren will have a decent planet or not." Ken said. "You only care about more wealth and power. Heroin must be easier to quit. And political influence is their jackpot."

"The rich are not like us," he added a quarter mile later from a Fitzgerald quote.

Doris reminded him that he was rich, himself.

"Not like they are," he said. "I can buy you a car. They can buy you a car factory."

Ken had, in fact, purchased the used van we were then using for Doris's road support.

The billionaires of interest to Doris were fellows like the master of misdirection Rupert Murdoch and the coal and oil barons who have been tilting our ballot boxes with their million-dollar donations.

And what are they buying? The future? I don't think they care a whit about the future. Financial power is a sickness. It eats its young. It is beady-eyed, scaly, always fluttering its flycatcher tongue for the scent of new victims.

Allow me to carve out a huge exemption for Melinda Gates and George Soros, in case I ever meet them. And Ross Perot, whom I met on the road but won't again in this life. I add him to the good list because, somewhere in Texas, he invited Doris to take a few days off her walk to speak at the Reform Party Convention, which she did to thunderous applause. She had to turn down their floor nomination for vice president—she was an Al Gore Democrat, as she reminded them. But their enthusiasm for her message of campaign reform reminded everyone—including members of Congress—that this was not a partisan issue.

After her speech, Ross told Doris, "Whatever you need, you just call me." She was not walking to bring more billionaire money into the fight and was too shy to ever ask for anything, even when we couldn't afford new tires for the support van and Common Cause said no, but the princely offer was appreciated.

As for other billionaires, I once interviewed Warren Buffett's adult son in his Midwest home. It was a usual day for him but not for me. We did a ride-a-long with the local sheriff because it was Saturday and that's what the younger Buffett liked to do on Saturdays. We took Buffett's SUV with all the best police technology, reading license plates as it drives along, looking for lapsed registrations, stolen cars, maybe lapsed green cards now.

Buffett and the sheriff delivered a summons to a tiny house and pulled over a slightly speeding woman driver to show me how the radar works at long distance. Honoring my entreaty, they just gave her a warning. We got burgers at a Dairy Queen, which his dad owned along with railroads and so much else, but it seems I was the only one with a wallet, so I paid. I told him I would take it from my Burgers for Billionaires fund, which amused.

After lunch we went out to a little fake town that he had built so local police and sheriff deputies could play urban warfare for when it comes to that, like now I suppose. Then we went to his farm where he has a blimp-size hanger full of giant bespoke farm machines built by America's biggest farm machinery company just for him, as he is pioneering some very good sustainable farming practices. He may be used to having major corporations doing his bidding, as earlier that morning I had a very hard time finding his house. He explained, "Yeah, sorry, I'm not on Google."

I was there by his invitation, following up on a story I had come across in Rwanda and Congo. I learned a lot more about that from him, and I admired what he was up to in Africa, but it's another story. But so you know, it has to do with electrifying villages with local-scale hydro power and protecting gorillas and other endangered animals from poaching militias. I first learned about it over breakfast in Uganda with two South African mercenaries, a San Diego surfer and a Belgian prince, which is the kind of breakfast you can easily find yourself having in Africa.

In the years since my meeting with Buffett, he has spent many millions assisting right-wing sheriffs in Arizona and elsewhere to patrol the Mexican border. He has financed the defoliation of whole areas so his donated electronic eyes might better see immigrants hiking in.

Years earlier I met Willard Voit. His company made every inflatable ball you ever played with, plus your fins and snorkel and mask and much more. I was fresh out of college and on his yacht in Newport Beach, on a trip between the Balboa Yacht Club and the Los Angeles

Yacht Club for lunch. Voit had sold his company to a big conglomerate some years earlier. Sitting beside him with probably my first gin and tonic, I asked him what he was doing now with his time and resources. I expected to hear about some philanthropy. In an irritating voice he said some guys were talking to him about a possible new market: little rubber and ceramic disks—billions and billions of them—to be glued on the lane lines of highways to make a sound when you cross them. He was only interested in making another pile. I hear his voice whenever I drive over those highway dots.

He was also busy giving money to far right political candidates from Texas and elsewhere. The abusive moment our democracy is going through right now has had many such sugar daddies, and I don't think they are ever trying to buy the future. They do things to feel powerful and look busy—the future be damned—their grandkids be damned. They want things to talk about on their yachts to make them sound powerful and relevant. And they want bigger yachts.

In that same year, the president of the company I was working for, a co-developer of the first digital computer and its use in finding oil, sent me out for a pack of cigarettes. We were all working very late before a contentious stockholder meeting. He told me to take his Porche to the store, which stunned me. He knew I had my own car, and nobody but him ever drove his custom Porche. I later learned that he was worried someone might have put a bomb under it, as one of the angry investors turned out to be the biggest drug lord in Laos and was expected in town with friends and fellow investors from Air America.

One more: One of my first jobs out of college was working for the CEO of a security products company. He and I were up high in the Pentagon-view condo of a friend of his from World War II, an active-duty Army general who was opening some doors for us in Pentagon and GSA purchasing. He gave us both the business card of his latest side-hustle: an oil partnership. What he said as he passed along that card is something I will never forget. He said, "Quite a few of us have good wells offshore there in Vietnam. If the war continues for a few more years, we'll do very well." It was one of the last shoves I needed to become a Democrat after having been raised by Republicans.

One of the previous shoves had been a long conversation I had with a New York City cab driver, who pulled over, meter off, to answer my questions about his hard life. I was seventeen and traveling alone. What I learned in that hour was that the Republican fantasy I had been raised on—about everyone having a shot at success if they will just work hard and get over the fact that their ancestors were slaves or whatever—is bogus.

I'm getting too far ahead of myself, or too far back, but my point is that they are surely not like us, the rich, most of them. Why deliver warrants and speeding tickets when you could send their kids to college without denting your checkbook? Our future, our lives, our planet, are not important to them. There is an automatic psychological thing that happens when you oppress and abuse and cheat people long enough: you come to hate them as a way of absolving yourself, just as you come to hate the US Government if you are constantly cheating on your taxes.

I think that is part of the reason why some billionaires don't mind what is happening to our world or our democracy. It soon won't be their world, and we are their *other*. The hell with us and the nice little planet we've got here.

The business of hating the people you oppress and disrespecting the institutions you cheat is also understandable on the smaller, non-billionaire scale. My father had a drug store that was competing with incoming chain stores because no one was preventing chain stores from creating essential monopolies—their owners already owned Congress. Any tax dollars Dad could save could make the difference between a profit and a loss. You justify that by thinking the government would just waste your tax dollars on people who don't deserve help.

My son worked during high school for two brothers who owned a little photo shop. They were taking half the money from the till each day to avoid taxes, and each lunch hour they were listening to Rush Limbaugh on the radio. Rush and Fox News were involved in this great slight-of-hand, making good Republicans like Dad come to hate "big government" instead of hating the big corporations putting the family businesses of Main Street out of business.

The biggest corporations were making campaign donations to eliminate regulations, eliminate enforcement of anti-monopoly laws and eliminate their own taxes. Reagan came in and started taking apart the unions and allowing corporate raiders to take over companies that had earlier been happy to offer lifetime employment and make annual profits well under ten percent. But after acquisition with expensive junk bonds, they needed to make twenty. To do that, whole divisions were cut and much of their manufacturing was sent to cheap labor markets in the Far East. A new class of CEOs who could do that cruel work started paying themselves thousands of times the pay of their workers. The pressure on the American middle class pitted race against race, aggravated by Republican messaging, which continues today.

Love and Democracy

Reagan also eliminated the Fairness Doctrine in broadcasting, which allowed the rise of Republican disinformation networks like Fox and the vitriolic AM radio stations.

Why did hard-working Americans cut their own throats by voting to let the superrich do that to them? You can only conclude that there's nearly half the country born every minute, and probably always has been. It's just that, in the past, the Fairness Doctrine helped keep real facts in front of voters, while unions and locally owned companies kept the middle class strong. You must remember how the locally owned newspaper and television station could and would shame any politician who acted shamefully. Shame was more powerful than the law, and it's gone now.

Well, Doris was walking because she could see through the new game very clearly, and it's why people were responding to her—not everyone, of course. She was sometimes in tears when she saw the boarded up little businesses of town after town. We were in the shade of a roadside rest in Arkansas once when a garbage truck pulled in. The driver sat near us and ate his bologna sandwich. Doris asked him what he thought America's biggest political problem might be. He didn't hesitate. "The death tax," he said. This man was listening to right-wing AM radio all day long so the rich could keep him and his grandkids in bologna sandwiches.

The farther she walked, the more people tended to recognize her and want to walk with her. Some honked and waved as they passed. Doris had been on national news repeatedly. *Good Morning America* covered her crossing from California into Arizona. The New York Times was with her in El Paso. The Dallas Morning News changed their official position on the McCain-Feingold Bipartisan Campaign Finance Bill after she talked to them. *The Today Show* and The Washington Post followed her.

She was in the local news of the communities she passed. West Virginians were now learning about her, hearing her message of campaign finance reform, and getting a lesson in the values of authentic personality and personal sacrifice in politics—two critical elements for victory that are usually missing.

Larry Gibson on Kayford Mountain, far in the southern part of the state, heard about her from Ken, as he hadn't quite got the hang of reading and didn't have a TV. He had grown up on Kayford but moved away to Detroit to help build cars for his whole adult life. He had come home to retire, finding his family mountain carved away on three sides by the blasting of mountaintop removal coal mining. He owned the top of the mountain, but it was falling apart because the sides were not his and were being simply removed. He was heartbroken. His family cemetery on the top of the mountain was cracking open, revealing old coffins and bones.

He had been trying to figure how to get other people upset about it. He liked how this Granny D was getting attention for her cause, and Ken Hechler encouraged him to give it a try, himself. Doris was still months away from West Virginia when he started walking back and forth across West Virginia with a state flag to talk about mountaintop removal mining. He had already walked 500 miles by the time Doris arrived at the Ohio River—the same number of miles that Ken had walked with Doris. Larry had a mystical view of Doris. He thought she was the bulletproof coal mine union organizer Mother Jones, come back from the dead. He really did. He told me that every time her name came up, which it did about six times the last time I was with him on his mountain, after the mine people had hung his dog on his porch and run him off the road a few times, once leaving him for dead. They wanted the rest of his mountain.

Jimmy Weekley was on Blair Mountain, west and a little south of Kayford. His family had been up there since Native Americans were among the people you married, and everyone now is proud to have Cherokee ancestors. He had been fighting Arch Coal, trying to save his mountain from the same fate as Larry's. He got thinking, too.

Laura Forman lived near Huntington with her air-traffic-controller husband and their little son. They had recently moved to West Virginia from Long Island, New York and were still getting used to life in this very different culture. Laura was a bird watcher by hobby, which would cause her to meet Janet Fout, who was recovering from a breakup by learning about the birds visiting her backyard feeder in Huntington. This was along the Ohio River, considerably south of where Doris would cross into the state and give everybody good ideas.

Doris had no special political skill other than putting one foot in front of the other and making a few obvious remarks about democracy, representative government, and the bill in Congress they might want to support with a phone call. I don't know how many people she inspired to stand up and do something for their own issues, but I guess it was in the thousands, and it's still going on because those people inspired other people.

In 2025, Demitri Camperos, a young teacher who lost his home in the Los Angeles wildfires, launched a walk of 700 miles to Paradise, California, another town destroyed by fire, raising nearly $10,000 for the victims of both. He cited Granny D as his inspiration.

A week after Doris crossed into West Virginia, Ken Hechler took Larry Gibson out to find her on the road. Larry tried to give her his well-traveled state flag, but Doris told him to keep it a bit longer, as the big wars for justice and beauty are rarely ever over, so you need to keep showing up.

Larry was small in the way that people can get when their families have been isolated in the hills for hundreds of years. His short arms would pump like the rods of a steam locomotive when he got to talking about what they were doing to his mountain and to all the mountains of his state—and Kentucky's—and how coal-fired power plants along the Ohio are poisoning the air and water of the Eastern Seaboard. Larry and Ken had come to find Doris in Ken's red Jeep, which, like federally funded things named for Robert C. Byrd, was seen all over West Virginia. Ken was the person nearly every West Virginian would mention if you asked if there happened to be at least one honest politician in the state.

So, let me start with Ken and the massive explosion three decades earlier that made this now 86-year-old man want to walk five hundred miles with a 90-year-old pilgrim.

Ken

At 5:30 a.m. on Thanksgiving eve, November 20, 1968, a volcano-like explosion of rock, timbers, flames and smoke boomed out of the Lewellan Portal of the Consolidated #9 mine in Farmington, West Virginia, a hundred miles toward Washington from the Parkersburg bridge. Debris and black dust rained down on the area around Farmington for long minutes.

Number 9 spidered so endlessly under the mountain that different entrances were in entirely different towns. The explosion turned the mine into a hundred wind tunnels, rolling loose coal dust up into supersonic balls of fire.

Thanksgiving turkeys were cooked the next day because you need to do something with them and you must stay busy, but they sat uncarved as families prayed and waited, including Pete Kaznoski's wife, Sara, and their children.

Sara hadn't heard the explosion. She heard about it on television. She was watching the Today Show from New York, waiting for Pete to come home for breakfast, when they flashed the news from a few miles away. Ninety-nine men were in the mine. Twenty-one would scramble out alive, some up narrow air shafts. Seventy-eight would perish, nineteen of whom remain entombed there today, including Pete. By the end of that first day, most of the families knew the men still down there could not be alive—too much smoke was still pouring out from every entrance.

Tony Boyle, national president of the United Mine Workers, rushed up from Washington in a limousine for the news cameras. He wore a rose in his lapel and looked like a gangster, which he was. The gathered new widows and townspeople and a thousand area miners who weren't underground at the wrong time expected Boyle to stand up for the miners, but as soon as he opened his mouth they knew better. He complimented the Consolidated Coal Company for its history of safe operations and mused that bad things happen to good companies.

Those gathered were aghast, including union official Jock Yablonski, already angry with Boyle's corrupt connections with coal companies. Jock went back home to his big house across the Pennsylvania line to talk calmly with his wife, Margaret.

He told her it was a breaking point. He had tried to keep things cool between Boyle and the rank and file, but not after this. Both men were tough union organizers. Both men sported bushy, black eyebrows and street brawler looks.

The Yablonski's daughter, Charlotte, a coalfield social worker educated at Morgantown, had been giving Jock a new view into the lives of older and injured miners—lives of great poverty and suffering. Jock was well-read himself, and his wife was a bit of a playwright, but his daughter's dinner-table reports were sitting ever heavier on his shoulders. He watched Boyle living in luxury with funds that should be going to the health, safety and retirement of miners, especially those crippled by roof falls and Black Lung disease. Boyle was not advocating for the mine safety measures every coal miner and every coal family knew were necessary and possible. Instead, he was taking bribes from the mine companies to keep his mouth shut.

Love and Democracy

On the second day after the disaster, Sara Kaznoski started using the energy of grief to create something worth Pete's sacrifice.

Survivors' resolve has driven many of America's reforms. The crucible days of great loss can compel people to create a little beauty from the chaos and injustice.

Sara told the other new widows they should get a congressman to come meet with them right away and push him to work for real mine safety reform. She knew that her own congressman was a coal toady and would be a waste of time, but another part of the state, farther south, had another representative, Ken Hechler. She knew that Ken had been going against Big Coal in Congress, quite unlike any West Virginia Congressman in history. He was publicly appalled by the unsafe conditions. Young West Virginians who shipped off to Vietnam, Hechler said in speeches, had a better chance of living to old age than if they stayed to work the mines.

Ken was moved by Sara's phone call. He asked when he should come, not wanting to impose on their grief.

"Now," she said. "Today."

When he entered Sara's houseful of coal wives, the mine was still afire and they were holding out desperate hope, pressuring the rescue workers to keep searching and keep fighting the fires. The mine operators were calling for all the portals to be sealed with concrete—the only way to put out the fires but a death sentence for anyone inside. The wives weren't quite ready for it, though they knew the score.

Ken thought he was being asked to offer his condolences, but the women did not want to be consoled. Ken was impressed by their command of their emotions and their iron resolve to honor their husbands, dead or alive, by making all mines safer. Over 200,000 men and boys had died in these mines over the years.

Their deep knowledge of necessary reforms amazed Ken. They understood that if you somehow controlled coal dust in the mines you would not only stop the worst explosions and fires, but you would reduce Black Lung at the same time. Safety and health had to be linked in one law, they argued. They sounded like mining engineers and medical experts. They knew every broad feature of the needed law. They had spent lifetimes hearing safety and health horror stories from their coal-blackened mates. They were the national experts.

"You know, if you change the angle of the drill and shoot water at it, like the law now requires in England, you can cut the coal dust to almost nothing," Ken said. He knew the issues, too. In that comment, the women knew they had the right advocate.

Ken had introduced a mine safety bill late in the previous Congress, but it came up too late for passage. Besides, you usually need a crisis or a scandal or a tragedy to get a good reform bill passed. When he was working for Truman, a coal safety bill came through on the heels of an earlier mine tragedy and became law, but it was accompanied by Truman's signed statement that the damn thing was too full of loopholes purchased by the coal lobbyists to do much good. Ken had been paying attention.

He said he would give his full effort to pass the widows' dream bill, but only if they would help. The immense power of Big Coal, the Nixon White House, and even Tony Boyle would be against it, he said. To have a chance of overcoming that, the widows would need to come to Washington to testify repeatedly as his witnesses, countering the coal lobbyists on the Hill.

Love and Democracy

"Many trips, many hours, many hearings and appointments and press conferences," he warned. They worried that they didn't have the money to travel and stay in Washington. Ken said he would foot the bill personally. He in fact did that, all out of his own pocket, sometimes providing private planes to get them to Washington at critical times. He was a best-selling author of books about World War II that he had reported from the front lines, particularly "The Bridge at Remagen," which became a big movie, too. He didn't have a family, so he used that money to do good.

Some of the women said they would not be able to speak in public. "I'm sure you'll find the courage to speak when you remember this week and when you hear lobbyists lying through their teeth in ways that will cost more lives around here," he assured them.

The bill took shape. Ken knocked it out on his typewriter, along with a statement of principles for the coming campaign. A young lawyer named Ralph Nader was involved. John O'Leary at the Bureau of Mines was involved. Cosponsors were found for the bills in the House and Senate. Ken didn't put his own name on the bill and was not a member of the committees that would hear it. That gave him the ability to operate outside the committee rules and courtesies that normally get an important bill watered down to a meaningless lump. He made appointments for the widows and brought them in to roll over the coal lobbyists, which the women did. He convinced speaker McCormack to keep the safety and health measures in a single bill, as "divide and conquer" was always Big Coal's strategy.

Boyle sent fifty thugs into Ken's office on the Hill to belly-bounce him and try to scare him. He stood up to them, argued his case with them, got them to sit down, and before they left, they agreed with him.

Jock Yablonski took sides with Ken against his own boss, Boyle. Ken and Jock held rallies throughout the coalfields, countering Boyle's misinformation and getting the rank and file behind the bill. They were joined by three coalfield physicians who moved the issue through West Virginia's coal communities and finally through the state legislature.

Ken and Jock organized a coal strike that shut down the industry throughout the state. That got national attention, keeping the issue alive after Farmington and transferring that energy to Ken's battle in Congress. Jeanne Rasmussen, the journalist wife of one of the three black lung physicians, kept the national reporters supplied with good contacts and inside stories.

Yablonski went hard against Boyle, uncovering a massive fraud in the United Mine Workers pension fund. In May of that year, 1969, Jock declared against Boyle for the union presidency, turning the rallies into events for union democracy as well as for the bill.

When the very big-coal-friendly West Virginia medical association put out a bogus report downplaying the health conditions in mines, Ken told a rally crowd in the overflowing Charleston Convention Center that he wanted to show them the report. He held up a 12-pound bologna to their cheers and laughter. At that same event, he read a letter from Nader encouraging the miners to dump Boyle.

Ken arranged nonstop meetings between Members of Congress and the widows. He and his staff arranging continuous transportation and hotels, briefing the widows and the press on the latest movements of the bill. Big Coal simply could not compete, even with all its money.

Love and Democracy

Every week the bill got stronger, not watered down. As Christmas approached, it passed Congress and headed to Nixon for his signature. The bill was now so tough that Nixon indicated he might not sign it. Ken threatened to organize a nationwide coal strike. Nixon relented, but he childishly refused to let the widows be present as he signed the bill into law. As Nixon signed and then headed to his helicopter and a Christmas vacation, the widows waited in a room in the White House and Ken waited in the snow outside. But it was accomplished.

A few weeks earlier, December 9th, Jock Yablonski won the union presidency, but a very irregular vote count gave it to Boyle. Yablonski triggered a federal investigation and a recount.

That was the last straw for Boyle. He had been talking about having Yablonski killed ever since June. He now transferred $20,000 to several men in West Virginia with the understanding that Yablonski had to go. The men laid in wait along a highway to shoot Yablonski and Ken as they came along after a rally. But somebody was driving fast enough, and the road was curvy enough that they couldn't get a good bead. The gunmen later confessed to that.

On New Year's Eve, the last night of 1969, three men with two guns slipped into the Yablonski home. First, they killed Charlotte, Jock's social worker daughter, with two shots at point blank into her sleeping head. Then they killed Jock as he fumbled for ammunition and killed his wife as she rose screaming from bed. The killers and Boyle would go to prison. Boyle would die there.

The Yablonski's had done a great thing, and their surviving sons, Chip and Ken, would clean up the union, restore pensions to thousands who had been cheated, implement the new Black Lung benefits, and restore democracy to their father's union. I got the details from Chip one long afternoon in his office.

"Does Ken still have that red Jeep?" Chip asked me. "Because it ought to be in the Smithsonian, you know. And someday they can just put Ken in it, too."

That would be quite a display, we agreed. There's no reason to put a good fellow like that underground if you don't have to.

When Ken took you into a coal community, that red Jeep was as welcome as an ice cream truck in summer. People who would never tell their stories to anybody would tell them to you if Ken asked them to, which he did for me.

Pete Kaznoski's son, Pete Jr, was happy to talk to me after Ken called him. He was in the Air Force when his father was killed in #9. After his tour of service, he took a job in a Consolidated mine, like his father. One day, after asking for a new section of roof to be bolted above the working face, and after it wasn't done, it fell. He was at that moment loading drill bits on the supply car to have them sharpened, so he was spared by a few feet.

That was his last day in the mines. His family had given enough for America's energy needs. When his mother, Sara, died, he gave several file cabinets full of her mine safety advocacy to his daughter, as it was important history, and the work is never over.

Sara and Ken had made quite a team. They cut annual mining deaths by 90 percent, and so any Thanksgiving in Appalachia now has a lot more people at the table. You used to see little shacks in all the hollows where men suffered their last years with Black Lung. Now the houses are nice brick ones, and everyone has medical care. That was Ken.

Love and Democracy

There is a monument near the cemented-shut portal of #9. It was a dark night and freezing cold when I was up there. I was directed to it by some fellows coming out of a fellowship hall in Mannington. They pointed the way and seemed happy to have someone care to see it.

Up in the attic of the Marshall University library, where Ken's archives are stored, the memos, clippings, telegrams are all there—the story of people not dying in vain because widows called on Ken.

He had always been a single man. I was curious and asked him about it. I said I might be writing about him someday and wanted to know why. He was often seen dating much younger women, but that doesn't mean anything, as it would have been difficult to be a gay man in West Virginia politics when he started out—I didn't press him on it, in case that's what it was. He said no, it wasn't that; he just "hadn't met the right woman." I think I later figured out why he hadn't, which I'll explain in a minute.

I called on him early one morning in Charleston when his Secretary of State duties kept him from the road. I was in West Virginia to advance the trail for Doris, who was walking in Kentucky at the time.

I parked near the Kanawha River, which flows by the elegant State Capitol building. The morning mists were still on the river. Silently slipping through them were the never-ending coal barges that, quietly as pickpockets, relieve West Virginians of their wealth, leaving them poor and very angry at the wrong people. The barges are forever on their way to power the electrical plants downstream along the Ohio that will pollute the air and water of the Eastern Seaboard. The bright gold dome of the Capitol covers a dish of corruption so long served up that it has passed for honest fare to all but a few steady reformers like Ken.

The next thing the river flows by after the Capitol is a modest apartment building where Ken lived in the basement. He was always on time. Up the stairs from his apartment bounced Ken—six-one or two depending on the news of the day, always looking fit, always with a stiff but princely gait, a big political smile, pink cheeks, and a regal wave. We were to meet Larry Gibson for breakfast, and maybe Jimmy Weekley, too, if the two men were getting along. They both came. Ken told them all about how Doris was rocking politics, and they were interested because they needed to rock it, too. Ken bought breakfast. He always bought. He was putting Larry through school to learn how to read and how to give a good speech so he could better defend Kayford Mountain. Jimmy was defending Blair Mountain and was eager for ideas.

Ken could have afforded the best house in Charleston, but his little apartment was a statement, plus it was a two-minute walk from his office. He had also lived modestly in Washington during his eight terms in Congress, where he pushed the coal bills and Kennedy's space program.

I think Ken's affection for the space program stemmed from his friendship with West Virginian Homer Hickam, whose memoir *October Sky*, later published and filmed as *Rocket Boys*, recounts the popular will behind America's reach into Space. Homer, as a young man, asked a question of Kennedy when Ken took him around to the Cabin Creek area for a speech. Homer suggested that Kennedy, if he won the White House, ought to get us to the Moon. Kennedy thought for a moment and then agreed. I expect we would have reached the Moon even if Ken hadn't taken Kennedy around to Cabin Creek that

Love and Democracy

day, but it's fun to think about. Ken did take occasional credit for the moon shot.

His book and film money, and some more from the sale of his family's Long Island farm, allowed him to spend his House salary to bring those coal widows to Washington, but also to bring high schoolers from his district to see their government in action. His "Week in Washington" program opened the eyes and the lives of hundreds of West Virginia kids, many from rough coal camps and many who have ever since been serving their state and their communities.

Each student got to choose a current issue of interest and meet with national experts on those issues. Before the students went home, they had to report to Ken and give their advice on their issues and how Ken should vote when they came up. If every Member of Congress had a bunch of idealistic kids watching over their shoulders, imagine what a different country this would be.

One more thing about Ken: As a college professor he treated his students as equals. They had to call him Ken in class, as if they were in an adult meeting. In those classes, he often called up current or former government officials on a speakerphone. When a student once asked Ken why Kennedy said a certain thing in a particular speech, Ken called up fellow speechwriter and friend Ted Sorensen so they could all hear the answer from the man who wrote the speech. I happened to sit in the back of his classroom a day after the 9/11 attacks and watched him walk the students through the long history of American and Western involvement in the Middle East. To the horror and anger of the day was added perspective and wisdom.

Years earlier, in 1960, Ken introduced John F. Kennedy and Jackie all over West Virginia, certainly playing a major role in Kennedy's primary victory in that state, which was essential to his nomination. Ken taught Jack how to pronounce place names like the Kanawha River, which is Ka-NAW. The young senator didn't have any trouble calling the mountain canyons *hollars*, as he naturally tended to put an R after everything ending in a vowel sound. Ken got to know Jackie. He had a signed photo of her in his teaching office at Marshall. He didn't have other pictures, and Jack Kennedy was not in the picture—just Jackie and a warm inscription in her hand. When I saw that, I realized why he was single. She had set the bar too high.

Let me skip ahead to tell you that he did get married. He got married when he was a month shy of 99 and still had a few years left for a good married life. He found his Jackie, by the name of Carol Denise Kitzmiller. She was less than half his age, but Ken always did favor younger women, which is the one thing Doris didn't like about him. At all.

Love and Democracy

Doris

"The problem with Granny D is that she makes the rest of us look like such schlumps." —Molly Ivins

I got my first look at Doris in Twentynine Palms, California when she was just two weeks into her walk. I was there because I received a call in Phoenix from the head of Common Cause in DC, explaining that an 89-year-old New Hampshire woman had recently flown to Los Angeles to walk from there to Washington, DC. She was doing it in support of the McCain-Feingold Bipartisan Campaign Finance Reform Bill. Fearing an accusation of elder abuse, Common Cause was not sponsoring or endorsing her walk, but they asked if I would please not let her die on Arizona's desert, as that might embarrass Arizona's Senator McCain and hurt the bill's chances for passage.

I had been organizing in Phoenix for McCain's bill, recruiting volunteers to camp around the clock in front of the Phoenix office of Jon Kyl, Arizona's other U.S. senator, whom we were pressuring to support McCain's bill. We were also writing letters to editors, doing news interviews and the other things you do.

I started calling around New Hampshire until I found the woman's retired son, Jim Haddock, in Dublin, New Hampshire. I warned him that even young hikers die in the Mojave Desert and asked him how his mother was going to get across. He delivered the best three-word organizing speech I have ever heard: "You tell me!" he said, laughing his woodsy New England mushroom-hunter's laugh.

He told me there was no stopping his mom, even if it killed her, maybe especially if it killed her, because her life after the loss of her husband, Jim Sr., and then of her best friend, Elizabeth, had been impossibly hard, and she needed something meaningful to do, maybe so they would be proud of her when she got to heaven, which she thought imminent. He told me that she had gathered thousands of petition signatures in favor of the McCain bill at the behest of Common Cause, sometimes standing in rainy and snowy parking lots, but ultimately decided that it had all been a waste of time—probably just a list-builder for the organization's fundraising. The McCain bill and the issue generally—political corruption via campaign donations—had first come to her attention through her book club. They were not the normal book club, Jim told me. They researched each subject to death.

He said he had taken her by car to visit her sister in Florida some months ago, hoping it would get her out of her dark mood. Along the way they passed an old man hiking beside the road with his shillelagh cane and a backpack. It gave her the idea of doing the same, recruiting supporters for campaign finance reform from coast-to-coast.

Jim had managed New Hampshire's institutionalized mentally ill during his career and was an AA sponsor with a great following of people made dear friends. He was not going to tell Doris she was being silly. He instead gave her some mileposts to guide her own decision-making. He told her he would help her make her long walk happen, but on the condition that she first got herself in shape by walking five to ten miles a day and by learning to sleep on the cold ground and hitchhike a hundred miles. He said she must also find volunteers along her planned route. Well, she did all that, and so he had no choice but to fly with her to Los Angeles, meet her first volunteers, including Ken, and wish them luck.

By the time Doris had walked to Twentynine Palms, Ken Hechler was back at his Secretary of State duties in West Virginia but a young man, Doug Vance, was walking with her. Another volunteer, a retired man with a big cigar and a Cadillac, Ralph Langly, had been giving them roadside support but was finished with that as of Twentynine Palms. Jim told me that a support vehicle, while not part of her original plan, had proved essential. I told him one would meet her in Twentynine Palms the next morning. What else could I say?

He knew I would have to figure this out. New Hampshire is the Town Hall state. Its people, politically savvy, are used to having presidential candidates in their living rooms and they can read the political weather. Jim knew someone like me from McCain's own state would have to keep his mother safe or our failure to do so would dominate the news around the reform bill and sink it. He was ticked off at Common Cause in DC for telling his mother to take a hike, but he knew Arizona Common Cause would have to pitch in.

I made some calls for Arizona volunteers to walk with Doris, finding only Herb Weinberg, who would be available in two days. He was a retired rug store owner and contractor from Brooklyn who knew how to keep his word and close a sale. When we were standing in front of Senator Kyl's office around the clock for a week, waving to traffic with our stupid "Ban Soft Money" signs from Common Cause, he had us turn them around and write, with jumbo marker: "Honk if you hate the political bribe system!" Drivers never stopped honking. Kyl's staff came outside to see what was going on. It went on for a week, though Kyle never came around.

After securing Herb's yes, I put on a coat and tie—even more powerful than a hardhat and a clipboard—and drove to a street of car dealers downtown. I spotted a used van that would do— big enough to carry backpacks, food and water, and space enough for Doris to stretch out and rest.

I walked into the dealer's little office like I might be General Eisenhower—a thing I do when useful. A well-fed man in his 50s with too much sun from selling cars in Phoenix sat at his desk like a pink squeeze toy. His desk was piled high with auto trader magazines and sales contracts.

I gave him my Common Cause card and informed him that an 89-year-old woman was walking from California to D.C. to protest the way big money has taken over American politics. I pointed through his dirty window to the van.

"I'd like to borrow that blue van, so she'll have a place to take naps through California's Mojave Desert and then to Phoenix. I will need it for a few weeks."

"You want to borrow it?"

He looked again at my card and asked me what kind of company Common Cause might be—I think he said he'd never heard of it. I explained that it was a nonprofit organization trying to reform government and politics. He said something like *lots of luck with that*, but then he stared out at his van. He might have laughed at me or sneered, but he didn't. It was my Eisenhower.

"Ok. Let me get a snap of your driver's license. Bring it back clean and gassed up."

I am no hypnotist. His assent came automatically from his concern for our country. I would expect such responses in the days ahead.

I don't mean to say that he was worried about democracy in the way we worry today. In January of 1999 Americans took democracy as a given, like firecrackers on the Fourth. But I think he was feeling the anger and helplessness that many Americans, though oblivious to many deep injustices around them, were feeling about losing the leash on their futures, on prosperity, on the front-porch way of life that so many, probably including this man, had fought for at the risk of their lives a few decades earlier.

The next morning, after a long drive chased by the dawn, I parked the borrowed van in the dirt driveway of the venerable Twentynine Palms Inn, well inside that part of the Mojave with the Dr. Seuss Joshua Trees.

From behind the lobby desk a cheerful older woman in a tie-dyed muumuu greeted me: "Doris Haddock? Granny D? She's far out!" She directed me to a meeting room where a brunch was in progress. I hadn't heard far out for a very long time, and it felt good. It was from a more appreciative era, when you only needed to stare at your hands to be amazed.

I was expecting Doris to look crazy and ragged, exhausted by two weeks of walking the littered frontages out of LA and through the sandblasted expanse north of Palm Springs. I hoped to convince her to take a plane home to New Hampshire from Palm Springs, a conversation I had rehearsed on the road.

Far from ragged and beat, Doris looked fresh, sparkling with joy and stylishly dressed in a colorful Japanese print blouse as if her hiking companion might be Anna Wintour. She was short, fit, and decorated with the right wrinkles for her age. Her large, curious eyes were reading the room like a hungry comic or evangelist. Her accent was New England, plus a lilt that would make you think she grew up in the fancier shires of England. That Anglophilic precision of speech, I would learn, was the product of elocution training at Emerson in Boston in the late-1920s.

She was the star of the jolly brunch, surrounded by two dozen people, including the mayor of Twentynine Palms, local artists and high-ranking officers from the nearby Marine Corps air base. Ralph Langly, the man with the Cadillac, had promoted Doris to the Chamber of Commerce just the day before her arrival, setting this event in motion. He had done just as well all along her route, setting a high bar for advance work to follow.

Doris was repeatedly toasted by the room. She made remarks about how large political donations secure special-interest tax breaks and loopholes that enrich the wealthy, impoverish and endanger the rest of us, pollute the planet and destroy representative democracy. She gave examples of egregious loopholes purchased by egregious donations. Everyone applauded everything she said. If some in the room were Republicans and others were Democrats, you couldn't tell the difference, as they all agreed on the problem.

When the event broke up, she hugged Ralph goodbye and came out to the driveway to see her new rig. It was no Cadillac, but she feigned delight.

As we loaded her meager supplies into the van, Doris pointed out her young walker, Doug, chatting up lingering artists across the way.

"Doug's a health nut," she whispered. "He just eats bird seed. He gave Ralph a hard time whenever we had a hamburger, but he gives my legs a good massage each afternoon, which is wonderful because they cramp up terribly."

As it seemed clear I was not going to be taking her to an airport, I told her I would go find a grocery store to get water and camp food. I had brought along serious camping equipment from my garage.

Doris decided to come shopping with me, I think so she could talk more about Doug.

"When we come upon a roadkill, he picks it up with a stick and buries it and wants us to have some words over it. It's strange but rather sweet. I've come to look forward to it."

"You look forward to seeing roadkill?" I asked.

"Well, they're interesting. I'm a fiber artist, I hook rugs and such, and the poor, exploded creatures are fascinating if you look at them that way."

She's so New England, is what I was thinking.

Her routine was already established: Rise before dawn, walk six or seven miles, take a nap, then walk the day's remaining three or four miles. Homeowners along the way had taken her and Doug in as overnight guests. If that wasn't available, Ralph would drive them all the way back to his own home in Upland, then return them the next morning to where they had stopped walking. There would be no such houses in the deserts ahead, so it would be camping in the desert.

This was mid-January and as good as the Mojave gets. Summer would not have worked. Even so, there would be blowing sand and cold nights and speeding semi-trucks inches away.

We headed out. On the edge of town, I let Doris and Doug out of the van to start walking.

I would park a mile ahead and walk back to meet them. We'd walk together to the van where Doris would rest for a moment and have water and maybe a bite of a protein bar. Then we'd do it again for seven or eight miles, one mile at a time. Then a longer nap for Doris, then the last two or three miles of the day.

At night we cooked on a propane camp stove and Doris wrote in her journal by flashlight or the van's dome light. I rigged a solar shower for her from an abandoned political sign.

Herb borrowed my car in Phoenix and met us on the road the next day. He and I would take turns, two or three days and nights at a time, so that I could be in Phoenix when I needed to be. Herb was good at this. If you happened to be passing by Doris and Herb and Doug and you pulled over to see if they needed assistance, it was Herb who gave you a full report on the need for campaign finance reform and who likely got you to sign the clipboard so you could follow Doris's adventure and maybe you would contact your Senator. Doris was good at it, but Herb, silver-haired and well-dressed even in a sandstorm, was as insistent as a Brooklyn rug salesman. I can imagine a husband getting back in a car after talking with Herb. The man's wife asks who those people were and what clipboard did he sign? He would say they are out looking to save the country from something.

Newspeople

Maureen West and I had been together long enough that I did not do any of this without talking it over with her. She initially worried that Doris might be a bit senile and a time trap. Maureen was a Phoenix newspaper reporter and editor.

She was covering, among other things, aging and end-of-life issues. She was one of the nation's top two reporters covering that beat, the other reporter being the New York Times' Gina Kolata, whose name I have always loved. Maureen had recently studied the issues around aging during a fellowship year at Stanford and would later be honored at the Columbia School of Journalism for her stories. She also wrote a syndicated lifestyle and politics column. If you searched the nation for someone best able to think through a problem like Doris Haddock, Maureen would be perfect. But Doris Haddock had a knack for coming across just the right person at just the right moment. Synchronicities happen when you're doing something big and right and holding back nothing.

The time trap thing was a serious concern. I was busy pushing the McCain bill locally and preparing a state ballot initiative to deal with gerrymandering. Maureen liked that I was trying to fix politics, though, as a seasoned reporter, she probably just thought it was cute. A few years earlier, as the editor of the opinions section, she had published my op-eds about the need for affordable housing and the history of homelessness. After four big op-eds, she took me out to lunch at her editor's suggestion, and we learned we were both single and maybe should go on a hike through the South Mountains some Saturday—that Saturday, in fact. We would take many long hikes.

She loved the fact that, years before we met, I invented the "I Voted" sticker that became a national thing and that I had organized the successful passage of Arizona ballot initiatives for public funding of campaigns and for fair redistricting. My most attractive assets, however, were the two interesting teens I was raising. She loved them from the start.

After that first call from DC about Doris, Maureen did remind me that I should not be too long in the desert because I had a high school play to attend in two days, as Austin, my son, had a starring role. I also had to make sure he finished his college applications in the next few days. My daughter, Lauren, was a freshman in the same high school and we were looking forward to sitting together with Maureen at the play, Into the Woods.

Maureen, maybe double-checking my judgment, soon drove out to join us for a day of walking and overnight camping with Doris. They instantly connected.

"She's amazing. She might make it all the way. I think you're doing the right thing to help her."

Maureen had seen many outright PR stunts as a newspaper reporter and didn't like them. This was different; it was PR, but not a stunt. Doris and her sacrifice for her country were real.

The fact that Maureen could see Doris's authenticity as a spokesperson for democracy made me realize that other reporters would see it, too. I figured we needed a serious press operation to get Doris more exposure.

Ralph had rounded up reporters around Los Angeles, but we now needed an operation to make that work everywhere, including in the national press. I called the best PR person I knew.

Cell coverage in the Mojave was thin. I stood on my tiptoes on two-foot sand hills and finally got through to Common Cause's communications guy in DC, John Anthony.

I told him that Doris could be the key to getting the McCain bill unstuck—it had been stuck for several years, despite millions of petition signatures. He half laughed at my suggestion. We argued for a bit. He reminded me that Common Cause didn't want to be accused of elder abuse. I said I understood, but under the circumstances of Doris's physical strength and clarity of mind, that was perhaps an ageist argument. I told him Maureen, a tough newspaper reporter and editor, could see right away that she was not being manipulated to do this. Other reporters would see it too. Doris was clearly her own woman. I told him again that she could make the difference. He finally gave in but said he would help personally and unofficially.

He told me there was a website already set up—her grandson had done it. I should use it to get regular reports out to her followers and to grow an email list, which could be used to get people to contact their members of Congress.

The Internet was a little new for that kind of organizing. The electronics guy at Common Cause, Nicco Mele, would be watching us closely. He would later say that our electronic organizing inspired him to help design "DeanSpace" for the Howard Dean presidential campaign—one of the first national campaigns to use small donors and organizing via the web. DeanSpace, in turn, was the model for the Obama campaign, again including Nicco.

John Anthony said he would try to get Doris some press. I told him we would be into Arizona in a few days, crossing the Colorado River at Parker, and it would be on her 89th birthday.

John said he would see what he could do with that.

When Doris came around the last California bend, after tough days of blowing sand and leg cramps, she saw the bridge over the Colorado River into Arizona. Upon it was a line of red uniforms and shiny brass trumpets, trombones, and tubas flashing in the morning sun. It was the Marine Corps Marching Band, playing Happy Birthday when they spotted her.

They played her across and she hugged each one of them. She loved men, and these were definitely that.

She was met on the Arizona side of the bridge by Ms. Sandy Pierce, mayor of Parker, Arizona, who invited Doris to lead a parade through town that same hour. Covering it were several local papers, plus NPR and a satellite truck and reporter from Good Morning America.

So yes, John Anthony is pretty good. Give him a little more notice and he can do even better.

"If you want to support this brave, 89-year-old birthday girl who just walked here across the Mojave, y'all got to call our Senator Kyl, because he hasn't been voting with McCain on this anti-corruption bill, and we need to let him know it's important for our democracy." This was Mayor Pierce's little speech as she introduced Doris all along the parade route. She continued with an argument that summarizes Gandhian-MLK protest theory: "If Doris can make this sacrifice, we can surely make a damn phone call, can't we?"

John Anthony and I were learning that the good results were not just from us, they were from the aura of remarkable luck that moved with her like a portable rainbow. The Marine Corps Marching Band just happened to be there for the Parker Days Parade. Magical timing like that became a hallmark of her walk—I was beginning to grasp her archetypal power. True, the NPR and Good Morning America cameras and microphones were John's doing, but amazing coincidences became the norm, leveraging her story to the bigger media. That ordinary Americans seemed to be giving her a big parade in support of her walk and the McCain bill played well in the national media and was noticed on The Hill. It was noticed by Frank Bruni of the New York Times, who wondered if her walk was a stunt. After a few more stories in the press, he would wonder enough to go see for himself.

To get politics unstuck, something new and unexpected sometimes needs to come out of the blue. In this case, the something new had just turned 89. Her audacity was giving us hope.

You're Going to Need a Bigger Book

In swaths of the country where volunteers had not signed up to host her, I would just knock on a door ten miles down the road to explain Doris's walk, and always the right person would answer the door. We were never once turned down for a place for her to stay the night, and it usually included a nice dinner and breakfast and then another household to call their senators.

The first town I advanced for her inside Arizona was the little community of Salome. Doug took over driving the support van while I hitched into town. I only gave the citizens there a three-hour notice, but they had that previous day taken delivery of a new and very red firetruck, and they were delighted to fill it with kids and retirees waving American flags in an improvised welcoming parade, siren and all. They paraded her to a meeting room at their tiny airport where she was invited to make remarks. She whispered to me on the way in: "What should I say?" She had already talked to people in homes and little meeting rooms and along a parade route, but this was the first thing that felt like a real speech to her.

Many men in the crowd were retirees wearing Navy, Marine Corps and Army baseball caps and tattoos, I suggested she say what she had said in Twentynine Palms and add something about the sacrifices made by such men and women and our duty to defend and improve the democracy they fought for. She might help them visualize the rows and rows of graves in our military cemeteries and what those spirits might think about that sacred democracy being sold on the cheap to fat-cat political donors.

Her dream as a student at Emerson College, just before the Great Depression, was to become a stage actress. In that little airport room, at age 89, she found the life that had for too many years eluded her. She improvised a great speech, with her arms sweeping before them to let them see, and they did see, the precisely white-dotted memorial fields of Normandy and Arlington. She got a standing, cheering ovation, and more names gathered for her website.

"I think I knocked it out of the park," she bragged as we made our way to the nearby house of a retired couple who offered her lodging. Doug would shuttle her daily toward the next town, Wickenburg; I hitched back to Phoenix to take care of business there.

A few days later she collapsed on a desert trail. An ambulance got her to a hospital in Wickenburg—dehydration, mostly. She rested there for a few days.

I told her that her effort was already a great story. It was being used in the halls of Congress to prove that people do care about the bill. She could go home to New Hampshire and recover fully.

Her voice was weak, but her words were not: "Like hell!" she said.

I agreed to continue organizing for her if she would take a few more days of rest when the hospital released her. I fetched her to our Phoenix home.

There, we invited a few guests to meet her, including Gillian Hamilton, Maureen's favorite gerontology expert, who checked Doris's vitals and her clarity of mind, giving her high marks.

"She is processing grieving in the best way she knows how, by doing something very meaningful to her, which is exercising her patriotism. Besides, walking is good for people, even people with emphysema and arthritis, which she indeed has." The doctor gave us that report as Doris stood by with her arms folded and the look of a kid proven right.

"But you must keep hydrated, Doris. And if ten miles a day is too much, maybe you could cut back, especially in the deserts," Gillian said.

Doris smiled like an old man being told he must quit the cigars.

She enjoyed the few days of recovery in Phoenix. She wanted to know how we had got a public campaign financing program passed on the Arizona ballot the previous year, given our state's conservative image. She wanted to meet McCain, but he wasn't in town for that week. She interviewed my kids, Austin and Lauren, and my neighbors.

Her young California walking partner, Doug, had returned to Los Angeles, so it was time to find some new volunteers. I had returned the borrowed van, washed and gassed-up, so it was time to find another support vehicle—one that wouldn't have to be returned for a year or so.

From New Hampshire her son, Jim, said he had an idea. He called Ken Hechler, who said yes to buying a used van. Jim spotted one for sale beside a road in New Hampshire. He bought it and drove it straight to Phoenix on balding tires, stopping only for naps at roadside rests.

"I think you and Jim are going to become great friends," Maureen correctly told me.

In the new old van, Jim returned Doris to the spot where she collapsed and followed her for seven days and 100 downhill miles back to Phoenix. During those days, I tried to get her an appointment with Senator Jon Kyl at his Phoenix office, but he refused to meet with her.

When she walked into Phoenix we went to Kyl's office anyway. In a garden entrance near his office front door, I set up two podiums: one with her name on it and the other with his, which remained vacant. To a small crowd of Phoenix reformers, plus three television cameras and two newspaper reporters, she made a statement about walking from California to meet him and encourage him to clean up our politics by supporting McCain's bill. Kyl didn't even send out a staffer, which was a mistake. The news story became: Kyl refuses to meet with 89-year-old woman who walked from California to talk with him about political corruption.

From that day forward, members of Congress went out of their way to meet with her. Some walked with her for a few miles or a day.

While she was still in Phoenix, I told Doris she should turn her nightly journal into a book, and it would need to be about much more than what she ate and where she stayed.

"If you make it to D.C., there'll be great interviews and stories, but it will all fade away in a few days. If you have a book good enough for a major publisher, however, you can tour as an author for a year or more, explaining and selling campaign finance reform."

We were fixing dinner during that conversation. Maureen agreed with my assessment. Doris said she would do it if I would help her write the thing.

"I would need your help, because you're quite right. We're going to need a bigger, different kind of book," she said.

I explained that my Arizona gerrymandering campaign was important, and that I didn't have time to help write her book, but we could find someone to help her. I mentioned that Maureen is surrounded by good writers at the paper.

Doris looked disappointed.

"Dennis will help you," Maureen said. She knew I should be writing more. She once told me she fell in love with my writing before she fell in love with me. I had written quite a few op-eds for her paper when she finally took me to lunch as a thank you. That was the second time we met, and the one that took.

I was now drafted for the duration. I would often meet up with Doris on the road, walking with her and interviewing her for the book. I tried to interview her in a way that made sense with the landscape she was currently walking through. The loss of her husband and best friend put her in an emotional desert, and an actual desert was where she began her walk and where we began the book. I enjoyed the deep conversations that taught me to think like her.

> *I am here: that is the sole fact from which, in the desert, all distractions fall away. The desert teases with the idea that spiritual enlightenment, elsewhere requiring a lifetime of discipline, might happen almost effortlessly here. This tease is not malicious, I think, but the natural warp of things in the neighborhood of great truths. Indeed, most of our great spiritual stories begin in the desert, where there is less to misdirect our attention from the fact of our mortality and our immortality.*

The long-term plan of her campaign had taken shape: Her son, Jim, and I would recruit volunteers for walking, driving, and finding places to stay. I would work on the phone with John Anthony to get good press, and I would send her ideas for speeches, almost daily. I would join her regularly on the road to work on the book as we walked. The book would be called, *Granny D; Walking Across America in my 90th Year.* The paperback version was called, *Granny D; You're Never too Old to Raise a Little Hell.*

In D.C., Matt Keller and Claudia Malloy, lobbyists for Common Cause, would use Doris's story to gain cosponsors and votes for the McCain-Feingold Bipartisan Campaign Reform Bill. The incident at Senator Jon Kyl's Phoenix office had electrified Common Cause, though not enough for them to buy new tires for the van when Jim asked. But Matt flew to Phoenix to walk with her after the Kyl moment. He wanted to have his own Granny D stories to use as he worked the Hill. Claudia would come walk, too.

Matt and Herb were with her as she walked through the Sonoran Desert out of Phoenix and toward Tucson. Arizona's Sonoran Desert has saguaro cactus and lush desert trees instead of the Mojave's tiny bushes and, in places, Joshua Trees. I advanced the trail for them, finding a small Native American village, Hashan-Kehk, to host them overnight. After they were served a feast of a dinner in the village's dining hall, a bed was brought in for Doris and the men were excused. A dozen women sat around her in chairs all night as she slept. When the women woke in the morning, Doris was already gone, a mile down the narrow road. They literally ran after her with breakfast and a small leather medicine bag to wear around her neck.

As they arrived in Tucson ten days later, I moved through the town an hour ahead. I got the Sigma Chi fraternity to serenade her on a street corner and make her a Sweetheart. It was a last-minute idea when I saw the

Sigma Chi house near the University of Arizona campus. I found a bunch of the frat boys sunning on their rooftop with their bikinied girlfriends.

"Exactly why would we want to go greet her?" one asked me as he half-lifted his sunglasses. I said because People magazine happened to be walking with her and taking pictures, which was true. The young men ran for their better clothes. They met her on a streetcorner and serenaded her, installing her as a Sweetheart of Sigma Chi. I also got her a nice reception a mile farther at a biker bar, where she received great hugs and a promise that they and other bikers would keep a protective eye out for her on the road. The women bikers cried.

A mile farther, a Tucson-based congressman rolled out the red carpet for her with cookies and lemonade. He promised to co-sponsor McCain's bill. Jon Kyl's mistake would not be repeated.

A few days south of Tucson, Matt walked with her into Tombstone. For the record, it was high noon, and Doris owned the town before sundown. She was toasted in all the best and worst bars, led there by the town's woman mayor, proprietor of the infamous Bird Cage Saloon.

We were learning that it wasn't just the liberals who wanted better representative government. Everyone did, was hungry for it, would enthusiastically raise a toast to someone brave enough to do something about it. Older women cried to meet her. That became a regular thing— women drivers pulling their cars over when they saw her, then greeting and hugging her when she came near. Always crying. If you want to visualize a happy future for democracy in America, remember such scenes, because there's much in them.

"She might as well be Elvis around here," Matt texted from Tombstone. Texting was a new thing.

Early in New Mexico, she was invited to overnight in a nudist commune. She accepted and said it was lovely.

By the time she got to El Paso, Frank Bruni of the New York Times was walking with her. She wore him out on the road. His resulting article, in a way that Good Morning America could not do, established her on the Hill and in national media as the real deal, not just a cute story. His article was long and included:

But she had time on her hands, adventure in her heart, and an issue that she wanted to publicize. She figured, rightly, that reporters and local politicians would be unable to ignore a woman of as many years, her stooped shoulders giving her a forward tilt, marching across the formidable breadth of America... "It just infuriates me!" she said over dinner in a Mexican restaurant here on Saturday night. She balled her hands into fists and struck the table so hard that the tortilla chips jumped a few inches. "I feel we are losing our democracy," she said.

She was already a weekly telephone interview on Jim Hightower's national progressive radio show, conducted as she walked along highways. Her wry New England wit, playing off Hightower's broad Texas humor undressing the sins of political corruption, made the segment a great hit, bringing a flood of new email supporters to her website, which we converted to calls to Congress.

Ken Hechler kept coming regularly to walk with her, and he insisted that I should give her a fresh speech for every town, just as he had written years earlier for Harry Truman's whistlestop reelection campaign. So, I did that.

Doris would call from her cell phone and ask me what I knew about the town of Portal, New Mexico, for example, or Flower Mound, Texas. Before long, the van had a mobile fax to brief her on the interests and issues of the towns ahead, so she might connect local issues to the need for government that represented them, not the billionaires and their corporations.

I walked with her through much of West Texas, finding her a headquarters at the historic Long X Ranch, where we watched bronco busting by starlight and witnessed the dramas of ranch life. From there, she moved on to make a speech in Pecos. I'm going to include it below, because I need to read it from time to time myself, and you may as well have your dose. Of all her speeches, this one seemed to move the most people into action or back into life. It was later taught in a rhetoric class at Penn and has been reproduced widely.

Toyah is a tiny town near Pecos. I went to its town hall and explained that an 89-year-old woman was walking across the nation for better government, and did they please know anyone who might put her up for the night?

They pointed down the road to the home of Berta Begay. Berta said she had a second little house, a yellow cottage by the rail tracks, that she kept for her visiting children. It was ours for as long as we needed it, she said. Doris would stay there a few days as I ferried her back and forth from her daily walk. I slept in the van.

All her effort so far had been "West of the Pecos," an old marker between the frontier West and civilization. As usual, there was an event in the town of Pecos already planned, just when we needed one. It was an all-night walkathon for cancer in the town's rodeo arena. We worked on the speech on an oilcloth-covered kitchen table in Berta's little yellow house. She delivered it by flashlight. Here it is:

Thank you. I am honored to be here in Pecos. On January 1st, I began my walk to Washington D.C. from Los Angeles, some 1,200 miles ago. All those miles so far have been walked in a place that is best described as the land west of the Pecos. On Sunday, I will wade across the Pecos and enter the other half of creation. But tonight, I am here at the center of the world and am proud to meet all of you who live here.

I thank you for having me here on such a beautiful evening. Life is a beautiful experience, and here we all are together, alive at this moment, breathing the same cool air. The issue that brings us here tonight is a terrible disease, of course, and we fight it because we naturally rise to the fight against any evil that threatens those we love.

Deep inside we can be joyful to remember that nobody really dies in this great drama of the soul we live in eternally. Some of us move on faster than others, and we so deeply miss those who have left this stage before us. Tonight, we see that there is something we can do with that loneliness and pain.

When my husband died and then my best friend, Elizabeth, I looked at my life and my lifelong beliefs and said to myself, what shall I do now? What can I do to honor the memory of the people I have loved? How can I turn my pain into something beautiful in the world? Something beautiful? Let me tell you that great Art and great Writing often are the transformation of suffering into beauty. Life is full of suffering, and what we must do when we have more of it than we can bear is to trick it into beauty, through a medium of exchange such as art, or handiwork, or a written story or poem, or good parenting, or good friendship, or the creation of good work in the community, or the pursuit of some unfinished work we may find among our lifelong interests and concerns, some of which we put away in the attic for too long. What work can I do that may be done now as a memorial to those I miss? What can I do to amaze them and fill their angel eyes with tears and laughter as they watch me lovingly from the other side?

And so, if you're here tonight because you are remembering someone lost, you are turning that loss into the Art of this special evening we share together. And if you are here to pursue your own battle with a dangerous disease, or to give emotional support to someone you love who is doing that or who has lost someone, then you are a part of that creative transformation of pain to beauty. What is more beautiful than people warmly sharing an evening together in the glow of candles? What is more healing?

The issue that I decided to do something about as a memorial to the people I loved and still love is political reform of our elections. It is, of course, a fool's errand. It is just an old woman walking across the land, wearing Elizabeth's gardening hat, talking to whomever will listen about the kind of political reforms most people don't believe can really happen. But there is something I would like you to understand about impossible missions: Sometimes, all you can do is put your body in front of a problem and stand there as a witness to it. That is part of healing because it is not denial of the problem, and our individual conscious mind is part of the larger conscious mind of society. What you think and how you think does affect the world, and your actions do matter.

Never be discouraged from being an activist because people tell you that you'll not succeed. You have already succeeded if you're out there representing truth or justice or compassion or fairness or love. You already have your victory because you have changed the world; you have changed the status quo by you; you have changed the chemistry of things, and changes will spread from you, will be easier to happen again in others because of you, because believe it or not, you are the center of the world.

There is a second thing you need to know about impossible causes, and it is this: there are no impossible causes on this earth if they are good causes. We can do anything together, and we really do, in fact, achieve remarkable things together. We will cure cancer most certainly because people like you walk through the night to make it so. We have nearly eradicated polio worldwide, we have cured smallpox, we are curing many of the diseases --the cures for which were thought were impossible dreams a short time ago.

My dream of political reform will come true. I may live to see it from this side of life, or I will smile to see it from the other side. But it will happen. It will happen because people love this country and this democracy and because they have given their sons and daughters and the best years of their own lives to defend it. They will not let it be destroyed before their eyes. I know we will end that outrage, and we will be able to operate our communities and our nation in ways that look after the interests of the common people—for that is what a democracy is all about.

I walk this road for my late dear friend Elizabeth and for my dear, dear, late husband Jim, so that they will be surprised and proud of me and we will have something new to talk about when next we meet. And I do it for myself and for the thousands of people I have met along my path who love this country and who are deeply worried about it. I do it for you.

I wish all of you good health. I wish all of you the courage to live out your emotions and your beliefs in your daily lives, just as you are doing tonight. I admire you all tremendously, and I will always remember this evening at the great center of our beautiful world.

The next morning, she did wade across the Pecos. Yes, there is a bridge, but the river looked refreshing on that hot morning, and she said she would. Also, I wanted the photo to send along to her growing list of supporters and to Matt and Claudia, to remind Congress that she was unstoppable and they might as well pass the bill.

Behind Doris's curiosity and her desire to make a difference was an aloneness and a permanence of grieving. She desperately missed Jim Sr, taken by Alzheimer's. She missed her best woman friend, Elizabeth, taken by stroke.

But her grieving aside, Doris was an adventurer and so wished she were still young. She was always looking for a little more of life's great romance. She looked fit, and not just for her age. She exercised each winter morning back home by cross country skiing on the roads and a snowy trail she cut through her woods. When she was 48 in 1958, she and her husband traveled to Point

Hope, Alaska via Volkswagen bus and small plane to stop the use of hydrogen bombs. Ed Teller, the H-bomb guy, wanted to demonstrate H-bombs for making new seaports, never mind that an Inuit people lived there and wouldn't appreciate the displacement, the radiation, and destruction of their fishing grounds.

The Inuit of Point Hope became her lifelong friends, because she and other early environmentalists did stop that crime. Doris held teas about Teller's plans in uncounted New England living rooms. She wrote and called and visited enough members of Congress to delay it long enough for an atmospheric test ban treaty to come along in 1963 and finally kill it.

Her representatives in Congress met with her and listened to her about Alaska. The fact that she had made the long, difficult trip to Point Hope and could tell the stories of individuals and families there made her worth listening to, as personal stories are politically powerful. She had turned herself from a typical concerned constituent who might not have the necessary background to understand the need for a program into a visiting expert who knew more than any lobbyist.

The experience of being listened to by her political representatives in 1958 set her up for feeling anger when they later wouldn't listen to her about the need for campaign finance reform, even though she and her book club members had read dozens of books and reports and knew every inch of the chronic scandal. She was a woman scorned by Congress, and she was coming for them now. That anger and the muscle memory of trekking through snow her whole life was helping her now as she approached the Appalachian Mountains in storm.

She celebrated her 90th birthday in snowy Cumberland, Maryland, which is a happy porcupine of church steeples near the Eastern Continental Divide—the last hill to climb before Washington.

Jim and I had driven into D.C. two days earlier in a borrowed car to see if the town was ready for her. The roads were snowy and icy, keeping most residents out of their vehicles and into the subways. Jim, who had raced cars on frozen New Hampshire lakes as a young man, was fearless on the empty streets of DC. He would slide the car to the left or right at will, laughing at my concerned grip on my door and seat.

When we returned to Cumberland, I let Jim off at a relative's home where Doris had spent the night. The plan was for the mayor and some others of the town to walk with her later that morning to the old train station. There, she would make a birthday speech from the back of a caboose—something Ken had suggested, probably as a tip of his hat to the old days when he traveled in Harry Truman's campaign train.

Jim and I had barely made it back to Cumberland from DC. The roads were nearly impossible for cars, and certainly impossible for a walker, and the storm wasn't over. Jim and I talked about ways to break it to Doris. So very close she had come. Maybe she could finish the walk a month late, but the preparations in DC would have evaporated by then, possibly with McCain's bill. But we had got used to miracles happening around Doris. Maybe one would come along?

She had been her own miracle so far, and maybe that was enough. Every few days, John Anthony would line up reporters to interview her on the road. Television camera operators and newspaper photographers from all over America and the world would walk backwards for miles.

She met with the opinion editors of the Dallas Morning News, who changed their position to favor the McCain bill. That happened at many smaller papers and radio stations. Emails of support were arriving by the hundreds, and we were asking those people to contact their senators, which they did.

Matt Keller and Claudia Malloy now had ammunition on the Hill. Doris's story and the growing chorus of Americans supporting her was not to be denied.

Doris had made wild new friends through Texas, rested on Bill Clinton's childhood porch in Hope, made a great speech in Little Rock at a church podium once graced by MLK, walked into Memphis holding hands with Dick Gregory and many of the same members of the Sanitation Workers Union who marched with MLK on his last day. She made a great speech from the Lorraine Motel's balcony. Thousands of people who had never heard of campaign finance reform were now enthusiastic advocates.

The miracles around her had changed my notion of reform politics. Logical arguments no longer cut it. For this campaign, madam was the message. Reformers in her wake were catching on to the fact that colorful courage and flint-hard character were the new coins of the realm.

As Doris trudged through the Appalachian snows, nearly thirty layers of coal were underneath her, some several feet thick and some as much as thirty, all gold to the companies who want to burn it for power, come what might. Since the first mines were dug, over 200,000 men have died down there. She was walking through a war zone with the planet's future in the balance. It was inevitable that she would meet some heroes, as Ken was the region's moral center.

Walks in the Woods

Jimmy Weekley got the idea from Larry Gibson, who was walking across West Virginia to save Kayford Mountain and who got the idea from Ken and Doris that a big walk might help save his mountain, too—Blair Mountain. He would walk to memorialize the history of the mountain, and it did have history: In 1921 Blair Mountain was the site of a mine worker uprising that became the largest insurrection since the Civil War. Jimmy would recreate the march taken by armed miners back then. His goal was to have the mountain, or a big part of it, designated a national historic monument, as the battle figures tall in the history of American labor union organizing. That might stop the blasting-away of the mountain.

Jimmy wanted Ken to lead the march. As West Virginia's current Secretary of State, Ken would bring visibility to the event and maybe offer some life insurance. I should remind you that Ken was the only member of Congress to walk with Dr. King over the Edmund Pettus Bridge in 1965. Ken accepted Jimmy's invitation, knowing he was risking his life again by walking for justice, just as he had with Jock Yablonski.

Jimmy's march happened on a morning when Doris was on her way out of Little Rock, still eight hundred miles from her crossing into West Virginia. John Anthony, who was traveling with her at that time, told her that a friend with AP had called to let him know that Ken had got caught up in some violence in West Virginia. Ken had been walking with Doris two days before.

Love and Democracy

Fourteen people had started Jimmy's march that morning in Marmet, south of Charleston. It began with some television coverage. Most marchers were wearing red neckerchiefs and holding flags or helping with a big Blair Mountain banner. It wasn't a big group, but you only ever need eight or so for a good television or newspaper story, as the right camera angle can make eight look like eighty, and reporters and photographers do want their stories to look important.

Narrow Route 94 rises steeply up Blair Mountain from Marmet. The marchers rounded the first curve, where an overloaded coal truck had recently killed a walking mother and her daughter, smashing them like garlic cloves against a guard rail. Speeding coal trucks kill far more people in these mountains than you will ever hear about. The news crews that day only went as far as that first curve, then the marchers continued.

Carol Jackson, an artist in her early fifties with a big laugh, was marching inside a giant papier-mâché head of Mother Jones featuring a black cap and granny glasses.

At the second curve, forty big-bellied men approached, shouting.

Through the screened hole in her costume's neck, Carol watched as the men poured from the side of a church onto the road. She wanted to feel safe inside her shell, like Scout Finch, but she knew she wasn't. She was at the front of the group, walking with excitable Jimmy, who was wearing his hunter's camouflage t-shirt and pants. Carol had calmed him down moments before, when a man yelled obscenities from a passing pickup truck.

Jimmy saw the approaching men just when Carol did. He pointed them out to Ken, who wore a collared white shirt and sunglasses, looking like the Secretary of State that he was.

There was a half moment when some of the marchers thought the men were coming to join the march as supporters. Not so. Their shouting could now be understood, and they began spitting and hurling eggs and tomatoes that had been ripened for the occasion.

"Where do you motherf--ers think you're going?" their leader shouted.

Ken turned around, quietly giving his own orders: "Just keep walking straight, and don't argue with them. Don't fight. Walk straight ahead," he said. The word was passed back to the marchers, who were inclined to obey Ken, as he knew about this sort of thing.

Ken, Carol Jackson and her husband Andrew Maier, Laura Forman, Jimmy and Sibby Weekly, Shireen Parsons, Judy Bonds, Cindy Rank, Doris McGan, Janice Nease, Harvard Ayers, Gillian Aldrich, and Peter Senedella marched straight ahead as the big men sliced into their ranks, surrounding each of them. I include their names because heroes don't get their names in books unless you put them there.

"You motherf--ers better go right back where you came from. Turn around or somebody's going to die today."

Carol felt something swing against her costume, and she stumbled and spun around, almost falling.

"Who's in there?" someone shouted. "Why don't you just come on out of there."

She regained her balance and tried to see out. A great commotion of shouting and screaming was all around her. She could see that Ken was hemmed in and in trouble. Two big men were walking backwards right in front of him and two men close behind, shoving and kicking his legs from behind as he walked. Tall and dignified, Ken was unmistakable in the middle of the throng of pushing, shouting, kicking men. She thought Ken was a kick or two away from falling. Then he did.

My God, Carol thought, *Ken is the most respected man in West Virginia. How can this be happening?* He was their insurance policy.

The men were shouting ever more furiously. "You ain't goin' no farther, you mother--er. Turn around and go back to Charleston where you belong."

Ken got back on his feet and sidestepped the enclosure of men and strode ahead. Someone on a walkie-talkie barked a command, "He's gettin' away. Get him. Go get him." The men ran ahead to resume kicking and butting him and beating on the others.

Laura Forman, 37, struggled ahead and called out, "Leave him alone. He's in his eighties! He's your Secretary of State, for God's sake!"

Someone yelled back, "I don't give a f--k how old he is. He ain't gettin past!"

In denim shorts and white t-shirt, Laura did not have the protection of a costume. Her long red hair, which would soon be grabbed, swung from her baseball cap. She turned to order the marchers to close ranks.

"We have more company coming. Stick together!" she shouted.

The bullies butted their big stomachs against the walkers. Some threw eggs and tomatoes. Men in white pickup trucks arrived to convey orders received through walkie-talkies.

Some of the men had brought their kids and wives to watch, to see how it's done. They were not going to be of any help, but Carol was able to flag down a passing motorist who called 911. A twelve-year-old girl watching from the window of a nearby home made another call. At 10:41 the SOS was routed to the sheriff's station.

As the marchers approached the Hernshaw Post Office, which shared a wide spot in the road with an abandoned schoolhouse, the thugs hauled their stomachs ahead to form a line. It was clear that some decision had been made that no marchers were to get past that point.

The marchers closed ranks tighter and headed for the line.

As the worst seemed about to happen, state troopers and a county sheriff's deputy arrived, along with two ambulances and a fire truck. They refused to arrest the attackers, but they did arrest one of Jimmy's marchers and they took away the banner and the signs. The walkers limped on. The men who had driven from the coal town of Logan to stop them finally drove away, each truck swerving across the middle line to come as close to the marchers as possible, with the police watching.

"You'll never get to the top alive, Jimmy," someone shouted from a truck. Jimmy, his skinny frame steel with anger, glared but kept walking.

By the time they got to the top of Blair Mountain, five days later, the paid bullies had got their cowardly nerve back: 250 men would be waiting for the marchers in the woods. But Jimmy had his own spies, including one of his grown sons, and Jimmy's marchers slipped past the thugs by night via a forest road.

Photos of the attackers were later submitted with a complaint, but the county prosecutor refused to pursue the case. Within days of his decision, he was given a job with a coal company.

Laura Forman had warned Jimmy that the march would be violent. She knew the pulse of the mountain and its people. She knew. When Jimmy's lawsuit to save the mountain was being prepared, a retired miner named Carlos Gore, who lived in a hollow behind the Blair Post

Love and Democracy

Office, bravely added his name. That was partly the good work of the lawyer, as Carlos and Jimmy were not best friends, but mostly it was Laura Forman.

When I later met him, Carlos told me Laura was Mother Nature herself. "The real deal."

"She come to my door. Never seen or heard anyone like her—not up here. That long red hair of hers—like the Irish who settled these mountains. Anyway, I had to say yes to her," he told me.

She had knocked on every door on the mountain to get people to join the suit. It was hard and dangerous work, but she got some of the old guys to sign. Sometimes organizing is just a matter of showing up and looking your best.

When Jimmy's march was attacked, I was in New York City, meeting with NYU's Brennan Center for Justice to make our Arizona anti-gerrymandering ballot initiative as Supreme-Court-proof as possible. Doris called to say that, on my way back to find her, I should drive down to Charleston to see how Ken was doing.

Ken had a serious limp as he came up from his basement apartment to the street, but you never quite knew if Ken was putting you on. He was. He waved and did a few steps of an Irish jig to show he was fine. We picked up Larry Gibson and Larry's new girlfriend at her place. The four of us had breakfast at a place near the University of Charleston campus, probably so Ken and Larry could look at the girls while Ken told us what had happened up on Blair Mountain.

Ken asked me when I needed to get back to Doris. I was set to take over for John Anthony in Memphis, and Maureen was going to fly into there from Phoenix to walk with us for a few days, so I had a week and a half to spare.

Ken suggested I therefore take Larry back to his home on Kayford after breakfast, as his truck was stuck up there. He had hitched into town for a fuel pump, which he now had in his little backpack, probably alongside the gun he toted since being driven off the road one too many times. He didn't want his girlfriend to take him up there, as she'd have to drive down the mountain alone, and the thugs knew she was Larry's girl.

"After you take Larry up to Kayford and look around up there, why don't you take a loop south through Matewan and get to know that part of coal country, maybe get up to Blair and see how Jimmy is doing," Ken suggested. He liked the writing I was doing for Doris and wanted me to do some writing about mountaintop removal coal mining next, so that's what this suggestion was all about. Ken wanted me to get hooked on the danger and beauty.

"This here is Cabin Creek. My family's been miners here forever," Larry told me as we took a turn off the main highway at that town. "This is Mother Jones country," he continued. "She was up in here raising hell like Doris does, supporting the miners and promoting the union. She once led a walk of starving coalfield children all the way to President Teddy Roosevelt's house on Long Island in New York. That's right where Ken's family lived, too. Did you know that?" Larry asked.

"Anyway, old Teddy did not receive them, though they walked all that way. He eventually got behind child labor laws that kept little kids out of the mines and he got some laws passed to stop corporations from giving political donations, so he done some good things and Mother Jones might have put those bugs in his ear."

Love and Democracy

A few miles and a hundred curves later, he was still thinking about Mother Jones.

"So, she was a walker, like Doris. She hated those mine company thugs. She started holding rallies. She was arrested after one of them, just for reading the Declaration of Independence. They gave her twenty years, but we got a new governor who was a Hatfield and a doctor, and he saved her life from pneumonia in a terrible jail cell and pardoned her, just in the nick of time."

A year or so later, I would be up on Kayford with Larry again and get to tell him that Doris had recently been arrested for reading the Declaration of Independence. He was driving at the time and nearly went off the road. He said he believed in reincarnation, at least in the instance of Mother Jones and Doris. "I guess we knowed who she was from the start," he said on that occasion.

But on this first occasion, I was driving, and he told me to slow down for an old bridge under repair.

"They're reinforcing all these older bridges so the coal companies can run their overweight trucks on 'em. They steal our state tax dollars for it instead of enforcing truck weights. That's why we need election reform like Granny says."

The steel railings on the tighter bends were smashed all the way to the ground by *fly rock*—boulders coming out of the sky from the dynamiting of the mountain.

His cabin up top had been set afire more than once. His tires had been slashed in the absolute darkness of the mountaintop a few times. His dog had been killed—lynched from a porch timber when Larry was away making a speech to some green group at a university.

"They hung my dog, Dennis, honest to God!" he said.

We walked through his family cemetery of several hundred graves so I could see the big cracks in the earth from the blasting and his kin starting to come out, then we got on our stomachs to peer over a cliff into the carnage of the mine operation that was scooping steep the sides of his mountain like Richard Dreyfuss carved that mountain of potato salad and then dirt in Close Encounters. The view in three directions was of total devastation as far as we could see.

The way they flatten a once-beautiful mountain is this: They drill hundreds of holes along a mountain ridge, fill them with the kind of nitrate and fuel that Tim McVeigh used in Oklahoma City, then ignite them in a sequence. Hundreds of acres rise in a great wave and rolling quakes move through the region, shaking sludge dams perched above schools and towns. The explosives used are equivalent to a couple Hiroshima-size bombs a week, Larry said as we watched machines bigger that Godzilla with claws as big as houses eat away at the broken rubble.

They dump anything that doesn't look like coal into the hollows, covering thousands of miles of once-pristine streams. Long-term, of course, the water supply is more important than coal, but that is not a concern to the coal companies or the corrupt politicians who let them do it. The corruption has gone right up to Republican presidents like Bush and Trump, who appointed coal company officials to dismember the agencies that are supposed to be watchdogging.

It was coal money, after all, that swung both Bush and Trump into the White House.

Once the overburden of fractured rock is hauled away, the revealed layers of coal are shoveled into other trucks and sped like locomotives through towns, sometimes killing as they go. From there, it's onto barges to the power stations along the Ohio.

Larry's two-room cabin atop Kayford was lit by lantern, though I didn't stay into the evening.

"You met Laura Forman yet? Larry asked me as he made me a coffee over a camp stove. I had not.

"She cried like a baby when she first come up here. She just sat down right about there, covered her face and bawled. Her red hair come around her so you couldn't see her cry, but she was sobbing."

It seemed to me that all the men of these mountains were a little in love with Laura.

Two of his remaining kin dropped in as we talked. They had seen my car on a ridge.

"Him and me played baseball down by the coal tipple at Number 9 Holler when we was kids," Larry said of one of them. A coal tipple is where a conveyor belt finds the trucks or rail cars that will carry it farther down the mountain. Usually, a tipple has piles of coal about, and corrugated tin towers, usually painted green forever ago. Sometimes the coal is washed near the tipple, creating ponds of toxic sludge behind earthen dams that have a history of washing away towns and people in something like a cold lava flow. Buffalo Creek was the worst: 125 people swept away in 1972, some standing on the roofs of their moving homes and waving goodbye to each other.

I've been up there. The methane still leaks out cracks in the earth and ignites in a low blue flame when it gets to the oxygen at the surface. You can light your cigar with it, and I have.

Excuse me. Larry continued: "We used a stick for a bat. I didn't ever see a real bat until I was grown up. We didn't have no ball, either, so we would borra the head off my sister's doll. But one day it was so bashed up from hitting homers that I couldn't fix it back on the doll's neck, and my sister told on me, and Dad whupped me bad. I was five."

Larry's kin Brian and Red were at the table. Red, of rosy round face, suspenders and striped railroad cap, had worked a lifetime in the mines, most recently in "low coal," 26-inch coal. Hold up a yardstick from the floor and mark it at 26 inches. A tunnel only 26-inches high, going a mile or so in, is where Red had been working. You ride in fast on a conveyor belt, laying on your back with the timbers and ceiling pins and everything you need going in with you on the same belt. There is a 240-volt wire and ragged coal about an inch above your nose, all the bouncing way.

Just the same, he had been glad for the job. There were fewer jobs available as the big machines took more of the mountains apart from the top.

There used to be eleven schools and 35,000 jobs and people in this hollow, 4,000 in Kayford alone, Larry explained. Now there was a handful. The mines were using every trick in the book to push people out so the mountains could come down, even pushing their way onto school boards and then shutting down schools. They paid local fire departments to burn down vacant houses so nobody would move back. With the loss of the thick forestation, every time it rained it now flooded chest-high mud into the remaining homes and towns.

So Red was happy for any mine job at all, even if it meant going from a real tunnel to working low coal, and even though he had to lose 20 years of seniority. One day a rockfall from the tunnel sent the conveyor and Red into the ceiling and into the power wire. That pretty much retired him out and completed his lifetime collection of broken bones with a broken neck. But he now didn't have to worry about his weight as much, so he didn't.

Larry wasn't through with the doll's head story:

"I was so mad about that wuppin that I pissed in Dad's work boots that night and I pissed in my sister's bed to get her in trouble," he said.

"Next morning, Dad put his foot in his boot and then smelled his sock and started cussing and I was trying not to laugh under the covers, but I couldn't help it. He whipped the covers off me and got me good. But my sister got whopped for pissing her bed, so that was worth it. Next night after he whooped me like that I shit in his boots and got it even worse!"

"Dad come home from the Korean War in '51. I had worked all summer making a B-52 bomber out of balsawood. When my 7-year-old brother and two other kids got killed by a drunk driver over in Wealthy Acres—the name don't mean nothin'—Dad come home and knocked my airplane off the ceiling with a broom handle. That's how he handled losing a son."

"He got fired from the mine because we kids were playing on the conveyor belt and jumping off the chute at Number 9. But kids don't know nothing."

"My Uncle Vern had 42 years in the mines. Another uncle had his leg ripped off working in there. After Reagan, it was harder to get black lung benefits that Ken got for everybody. Dad couldn't get it. He worked in the mine right underneath us. He was scared every damn day he went in the mines. Broke both his legs in a cave-in and, many a month, couldn't earn a penny. I can tell you what it was like to go to bed with nothing to eat; it was a hard way of life."

"Granddad raised twenty-two kids in a smaller house than this. I was given away seven times before I was 11, because they couldn't feed me. That was called being farmed out because they would likely use you in the fields. I was sowing corn in Putnam County when I was 9 or 10."

Larry noticed Red sneaking a hit from an inhaler buried in his calloused fist.

"Look, hell, Red shouldn't have to spray that thing to get a breath of air on a clear day. Red gets a little money each month from black lung after a lifetime of work so everybody else can have their electric toothbrushes."

There was a bit of silence. Unlike most wooded mountains, there's not too much to hear on Kayford, as the forest wildlife has been mostly killed. I asked about it.

"There's not too many critters out there," Larry said. "Red, here, goes coon huntin' with his coon dogs all the time. He don't catch much except from his wife."

Another silence until Larry had another thought.

"And these valley fills, you know, where they dump everything in the hollers—such beautiful places when we was kids—and they don't just dump rocks. Them trucks that should be coming back from the tipples empty are coming back full sometimes, with old car tires and any other kind of illegal dumping. The coal companies, or somebody, is making a lot of money using our hollers as dumps and putting the rocks on top so you don't know, but the water will know."

Red agreed. He said he had seen the trucks coming in full of junk.

Larry took a grip on an imaginary bat: "I would like to knock those coal companies right out of here. Part for the way they treated Dad and part for what they are doing to all these people and this land." He took a few swings and watched imaginary doll heads fly out of the park.

Larry went on to say that his grandmother was full-blooded Cherokee, "forever from this mountain." She told stories of her great-grandmother trading with the settlers. Native remains and pottery are found on the mountain, he said. She married a settler from Virginia. It was a time when soldiers of the French and Indian War and the Revolution were being paid with land grants in the region.

Larry wanted me off the mountain before dark. "Zombies, that's what they are, Dennis," he said. "They come out of the dark at you, fat and stupid as anything."

In fact, they were McDonalds-fed family men worried about providing for their families. They had been set against Larry because that's what the rich do to us. Larry's walk across West Virginia had put him in the crosshairs of the rich, so they set some of his own neighbors against him. The coal operators had cut the number of good jobs in the region ninety-five percent by shifting to mountaintop removal mining, but nobody blamed them for that. They blamed Larry for trying to save the beauty of their own homes.

It was getting dark and overgrown as I headed on backroads toward Matewan. I saw only one motel along the way and kept going when I saw Anthony Perkins in its window. I decided to camp near a stream.

Love Served Rough

I drove into Matewan after finding a creek for a cold splash and a shave. Matewan presented itself that morning under black and blue clouds that made the red-brick town of covered sidewalks look like a movie poster of itself. *Matewan* is in fact an essential John Sayles movie starring David Strathairn, Chris Cooper, James Earl Jones and others.

The town is an origin story for much of the American Labor Movement, for Hatfield-McCoy mythology and for what happened on Blair Mountain in 1921—a battle Jimmy started up again.

I found a small restaurant open as the rising sun trained its moving beam along Matewan's main sidewalk. A woman eating her breakfast at the counter and everybody in there, I soon learned, was born and raised locally, and all from mining families. I turned it into a sort of focus group. I was able to do that because, when the waitress behind the counter asked if I was some kind of tourist, I said, no, I was a friend of Ken Hechler's, and he told me this was a great town I should learn about. I said that loud enough to make the room my own.

The Sayles film got it mostly right, they all agreed. I asked if it missed anything important. They looked at each other and seemed to want to change the subject.

"Did you see the museum, two doors down?" someone asked. Yes, I said, but it wasn't open yet. A woman in a booth said she would open it special for me, as I was Ken's friend, when she finished her breakfast.

Love and Democracy

"Did you mean about the mayor's wife?" she asked when taking me inside the museum, a pancake later.

I didn't have anything in mind when I asked the question. It was just the kind of open-ended thing you ask when you want to learn—a pincushion question that people use for any pins that need sticking.

In the 1920 shootout between the good sheriff and the bad mine detectives, as I then learned from her, bullets were flying everywhere. Sid Hatfield and Mayor Testerman were on the same side, but Testerman was killed, and nobody could know if it was friendly fire or not. You can put your fingers in the bullet chips in the town's bricks, which I later did.

The thing is, she explained, Sid married the mayor's widow two weeks later. Solace can be important for a widow, but that was pretty quick solace. In any case, it was a short marriage, as Sid, too, was shot dead soon after, which started the Blair Mountain War.

"Personally," she told me, "I think it was on the up-and-up between them. But times was different. This was sort of a war zone, so people didn't have long engagements, at least in some cases. Even now, maybe on account of the changes in coal mining and all that, and what it does to families and towns and all, it hits your marriages and would-be-marriages. Love goes down hard around here."

Sayles ends the movie with the shootout. What happened in the months following was the bigger story—the Blair uprising.

Jimmy Weekley wanted to turn that history into his walk to save the mountain.

After the museum, I walked into McCoy Insurance and introduced myself to Bob McCoy. We visited a long time about his family.

Everyone knows about the Hatfields and McCoys, which story has a comic patina thanks to television comedies like *The Real McCoys, The Beverly Hillbillies*, animated cartoons with long beards and shotguns, and the more recent hill country pornography of J.D. Vance. These stories turn real people and their families into *the other*. People who are *othered* are made to seem less worth our time and their mountains less worth defending. I figured Bob McCoy would help me see the human beings under the story, and he did.

"If you want to really feel those times, you go up here," he said as he drew me a map to the grave of a child. It was on a hill above the Tug Fork River that runs through Matewan and is the dividing line in the Hatfield-McCoy disagreement and between West Virginia and Kentucky.

Bob explained that the McCoy's were mostly free-range farmers on the land, while the Hatfield's were more the industrialists. The Hatfield's had generally volunteered for the South in the Civil War, while the McCoys mostly fought for the North. When coal mining came in, it was often Hatfield's owning and McCoy's down below dying.

"But the child's grave is the soul of the thing," Bob told me.

I want to be clear that the feud is ancient history to these families today. They now have annual joint picnics and tug-of-wars over the muddy Tug Fork River. They have monetized the whole feud thing with t-shirts, as we Americans do. You can't even knock down our skyscrapers without creating whole industries, from *Never Forget* t-shirts to airport x-ray machines. Anyway, the McCoys and Hatfields happily marry each other, and have for generations. But their friendship did have a tough start.

Love and Democracy

I read everything in that museum and had other things to do around Matewan, so it was spooky evening by the time I climbed up to see the baby's grave. It's on the Kentucky side of the Tug and looks down on its dark waters. I used the flashlight on my phone to find the grave. There are a dozen or so little stones up there. One is for Sarah Elizabeth, 1881 – 1881. It doesn't have her last name, because that's really the story. It does say, *Daughter of Roseanne McCoy and Johnse Hatfield.*

It is a quiet and forlorn place. All you can do is say a prayer for the dead in the loving breasts of life that these mountains are.

Johnse Hatfield was in love with Roseanna McCoy, or enough to get her pregnant, but the Hatfield's would not have her. She rode one night through the dark rainy forest to warn Johnse of a McCoy trap set for his next visit to her. She delivered the warning to the old man himself, Devil Anse Hatfield, the man who would not have her or his own son's child in his family.

She saved Johnse's life by making that ride, but Johnse, obeying his parents, forever abandoned Roseanna and the baby. The baby died before its first year. Roseanne buried her atop the hill, and every day, the story goes, lay weeping on the little grave until she died herself.

Not long after that tragedy, and after a county fair knife fight that killed a Hatfield boy, Devil Anse ordered the kidnapping of three young McCoy boys, had them tied them to slender pawpaw trees along the Tug, and shot them in cold blood, even though their mothers had come to beg for their sons' lives. The worst of the disagreement then commenced.

I've met some Hatfields more recently who tell it differently. To start with, they say Johnse was after every woman in the region and his parents knew that and didn't want him ruining the life of a nice McCoy girl that Johnse's mother had come to like. The mother knew that her son was getting the girl's brothers murderously upset, so that's another reason she might have told her son to break it off, baby notwithstanding. Johnse Hatfield did later marry a McCoy girl, so that lends some credence to the theory that it wasn't just a McCoy v. Hatfield situation. It's complicated.

All I know for sure is that little grave in the dark of a hill overlooking the Tug is a miserable place and you can feel all the heartbreak that seeps out of these hills as the coal ledges are chipped away.

Bob McCoy figured the baby's grave might not get me sad enough by itself, so he also suggested I honor another love story by stopping at a particular McDonalds restaurant on my way to Blair Mountain.

Princess Aracoma, he told me, was the beautiful daughter of the remarkable Shawnee Chief Cornstalk. She fell in love with a captured British soldier and begged her father to spare him from execution. The princess and the soldier were married and sent away with her entourage to start a new village on an island of the Guyandotte River, now next to the McDonalds in Logan. When illness struck the village, the British husband, Boling Baker, went eastward over Blair Mountain to secure food and medicine from the white settlers. Maybe because they didn't like his story of marrying an Indian, they followed his tracks back and massacred his family and the entire native community. That was in 1780, when the United States was doing that sort of thing under its new name. If the killers let Baker escape, which is unknown, I expect he is still up in those mountains.

I tried to have a late dinner at that McDonalds but just kept looking at that little island next to the parking lot and tossed my food into a trash barrel, though you shouldn't need that much of an excuse to do so.

I spent the night in a little Logan hotel room overlooking the town's main street, mostly boarded up because you don't need many coal miners if you're just blowing up mountains. This town was one of the main objectives of the Battle of Blair Mountain and hasn't changed much, except for the McDonalds and the empty buildings. Logan is named after an important war leader and a son of an Oneida chief. His unlikely first name is John. You might think the town would be named for Cornstalk, owing to his daughter's village, but maybe Logan sounded better. I am fine with honoring an Oneida instead, because I happen to know the current chief of the Oneida. He has used income from Oneida casinos and golf courses to buy back the land of his people. He told me the story of how the Oneida saved George Washington's rebel army over the hard winter in Valley Forge, when Oneida warriors literally ran food and supplies to the new American army, saving the Revolution.

But Cornstalk deserves remembering, too. He was the principal warrior of the Battle of Point Pleasant, which I didn't know much about at the time, but a schoolteacher from Point Pleasant, who later became a birdwatcher in Huntington and friend of Laura Forman and Ken Hechler, would tell me the story as she took me through the fresh Eden of Greenbottom, a miracle preserve along the Ohio River.

The television in my Logan hotel room only got I Love Lucy reruns, so I read a book Ken loaned me about 1921. As I read, the old hotel occasionally rumbled, as everything does in coal country. It does so from long coal trains that stop and start, even a mountain away. It rumbles from the collapse of old tunnels or newer longwall coal mines under the mountain that, when they pinch close behind withdrawing machinery that holds everything up, slump the mountain down a notch, which tends to wreck the flow of wells and crack walls and chimneys. Often the rumble, if early morning, is from the simple blasting-away of nearby mountaintops.

The old windows of my hotel room rattled as I read about 1921.

The coal miners of that year thought Sid Hatfield was their hero for standing up against the Baldwin-Felts mine guards in Matewan. Those mine guards were killers. To try to break a miners' strike, they had come through with an armored train, spraying the family tents of the striking miners with machine guns. That's the sort of thing that made union organizer Mother Jones hold up the bloody jacket of one of the dead mine guards and tell a crowd, "Bring me more like this, boys."

As revenge for Matewan, the Baldwin-Felts men assassinated Sheriff Hatfield on the steps of the Mingo County Courthouse. That was a last straw for the miners, many of whom had served in the First World War and knew how to use a Springfield rifles, which you could buy war surplus for two dollars in Charleston. They rifled up. Some 2,000 miners had shown up for Sid's funeral, and 10,000 showed up for war.

After provisioning themselves and holding a big rally across the river from Charleston, the miners marched south to the coalfields, intent on pushing out the corruption from Logan and Mingo counties. They couldn't afford uniforms, so they just wore red bandanas around their necks. That's where we get the term *rednecks*. They are not hillbillies; they are American Labor on the march, and they were showing solidarity with a worker uprising called the Russian Revolution. As I mentioned, the Battle of Blair Mountain remains the largest labor uprising in American history and the largest armed uprising since the Civil War.

They lowered their guns only when President Harding sent U.S. soldiers to put down the rebellion. As many of the miners had been U.S. soldiers, they were unwilling to take aim at their fellow grunts. The insurrection ended. Not too many men were killed, as Blair Mountain was more of a standoff than a running battle, and everyone had the advantage of a tree or a dugout. No one was stupid enough to do a Pickett's Charge, as the Baldwin-Felts men had machine guns, and the First World War had taught everyone about such things.

A young Army flier named Billy Mitchell dropped bombs on the miners, but all the bombs missed, though two of his planes crashed while swooping low and maybe taking fire. It remains the only instance of the American military intentionally bombing its own citizens on American soil.

The uprising launched an era of successful labor organizing throughout American industry and spurred improvements in labor law and mining conditions. Blair Mountain stands for that.

The rebel leaders were put on trial in the same West Virginia courthouse where John Brown, who also wanted people to be treated fairly, was sentenced to hang. I've stood in that courtroom and it's the same now as it was then, as is the lawn across the street where Brown was hung in 1859.

But in 1921, the jury felt differently. They let everyone go home. The nation had changed since the time of John Brown. Corporations had risen as the new owners of human beings and a threat to fairness, democracy and the personal form of democracy which is freedom. The jury believed it was only fair for the miners to have resisted violent abuse.

So, yes: Jimmy's march would commemorate the Battle of Blair Mountain, which was otherwise nearly lost to history. If the mountain could get status as a national monument, that might save it from the approaching mountaintop removal bombs and machines.

Jimmy put out the word that he was going to do it. Anybody who signed up knew they would be in for trouble, because some people love coal livelihoods more than their mountain and some people love their mountain more than their lives.

It's not enough for me to say Jimmy wanted to save his mountain. That sounds like a mountain is one thing when it's a trillion things. I have been up there many times in every season and will give you a short tour before I take you along on my first visit.

In the buzzing spring, layers of green and flowers of white, yellow and orange are everywhere. Pigeon Roost Creek, as it runs in front of Jimmy's house, is only a few feet wide but brims in spring and summer with salamanders, crayfish, blacknose minnows an inch or two long, silvery little creek chubs a few inches bigger than the minnows, and every now and then a slimy sculpin, scooting among the mussels on the bottom rocks. The fish will dart up to catch insects on the surface, which presents a good show on a quiet afternoon. A fish will jump to catch a big stone fly now and then. The stone fly looks more like a winged termite with horns on its head. It has been living on the mountain for fifty million years. It requires a lot of oxygen in the water and cool water temperatures, so if you see them, you know the stream is still good. The minute the mines start putting toxic sludge around, or damming up an area, or denuding the hills or putting too many roads through, all of which raise the water temperature, the stone flies die, and the fish will have to look for something else to eat, if they can. Pigeon Roost is a headwater, so its critters provide the nutrients that keep the rivers below healthy. It keeps the people healthy, too, especially the still-developing children, like Jimmy's grandchildren.

One of Jimmy and Sibby's grandchildren, Alicia Dawn, took me around with Jimmy once and I took notes. They knew every bird and beast and rock of Pigeon Roost. They regularly traipsed its trails up to the Witch's Rock, where Alicia Dawn and her cousins would find mysterious things left for them by a mountain spirit or maybe—he winked—by Jimmy. We hiked up to the ridge where you can still find brass cartridge shells from 1921 and arrowheads from more ancient times.

Alicia Dawn's great-great-grandmother was a full Cherokee. Her great-grandfather fought in 1921 with Bill Blizzard, a red kerchief around his neck, same as Jimmy would sometimes wear.

They showed me rows of beehives, producing 300 quarts of honey in a good year, each drop hand squeezed through cloth. There were ginseng plants here and there, if you know where to look for them and you should, as you can make a living from ginseng.

They showed me an old, thick chain hanging from a tree near the creek, where hogs were hoisted to drain them out, turning the creek red. There's a grave across the creek. There's the sweetheart tree where Jimmy courted a girl named Sibby who lived farther up the hollow.

In spring the creek has a special garnish of flowering dogwood, dashes of goldenseal, resurrection and woodsia ferns, Virginia snake root, and yellow lady's slipper orchids.

The dogwood is easy to spot because it has four big heart-shaped petals. The goldenseal is a big, floppy affair of five tongue-shaped leaves that, together, look like a splash. The thing in the middle is like the royal seal of a document. Resurrection ferns are the long ladders like you see in ancient fossils. The woodsia ferns come more quickly to a point, like ferns in a floral arrangement. Snakeroot has a waist-high stem with alternating little leaves all the way to the top of tiny pale flowers.

Above the creek are steep hillsides overgrown with a million years of everything. The north-facing hillsides have sweet cicely, waterleaf and goldenseal down low, and yellow poplars, sugar maples, sassafras, princess trees, umbrella magnolias, and white ash overhead, shuffling their leaves in the wind. South facing hillsides, drier, have red maple, black birch, beech, white oak, black locust, black oak, chestnut oak, scarlet oak, white oak, butternut, mockernut hickory, sourwood, to name some of them. The great providers of critter food are the flowering dogwood, wild grape, serviceberry, beech, gum, cherry, ash, hickory, and oak.

Regulars at the feast are the white-tailed deer, wild boar, wild turkey, gray squirrel, the white-footed mouse, beaver, opossum, mole, shrew, an occasional black bear and bobcat, chipmunk, and the red and gray fox. Flying in are the short-eared owl, northern harrier, meadowlark, chipping sparrow, field sparrow, grasshopper sparrow, ruffed grouse wood thrush, cerulean warbler, black and white warbler, Acadian flycatcher, and worm-eating warbler and the little brown bat and the scarce Indiana bat. There are many more creatures, of course, including the aggressive cardinals and robins and the polite towhees.

What would it cost to build such a sanctuary, such a zoo, if you had to? Well, here they all are taking care of themselves if we will let them.

This is the richness of any Appalachian hollow, upon which the mine companies dump enough broken rock, used tires and other crud up past the tops of the trees. Over a thousand miles of such streams have been buried already. You and I and our families are the life forms living downstream.

Sediment from mountaintop removal mining is filling up the streams farther down the mountains, sometimes to a depth of six feet. That makes the water run warm. Streams like Coal River used to be home to cold water trout. Many streams are now so hot they can't even support warm water fish like bass and sunfish.

The water is poisoned locally, but it also pollutes the Ohio Valley to the west and the Eastern Seaboard to the east, because the Eastern Continental Divide runs through these mountains.

Alicia Dawn, then 11, explained all this to me. She understood that the mines were trying to take down Blair Mountain and leave her grandparent's house at the foot of a huge slurry dam. She told me her dream was to have a family and raise her kids in a house across the creek from her grandparents, in the present fairyland of flowers and critters.

Governor Cecil Underwood visited her school—it has since been closed by coal mine politics. She stood up in front of her fellow sixth graders to address the Governor, who had just told them how hard the state was working for all of them, though she knew better. She had asked her teacher if it would be all right to say hi to the governor, and the teacher said that would be fine, so long as she was respectful. So, she stood and said hi to the governor and added that, respectfully, she didn't much like him.

"And why is that, young lady?" the governor said.

"Because you're trying to take my Poppy's house away."

He looked at her intently.

"You wouldn't be Jimmy Weekley's child, would you?"

"I am Jimmy Weekley's granddaughter, and if you have a problem with it, you can kiss my butt."

The old governor dropped his head and said he'd talk to her later, which of course he didn't.

Love and Democracy

The Exploited

At dawn I drove from Logan toward Pigeon Roost Hollow on Blair Mountain. The road was layered in a turquoise mist that smelled sweetly of rotten eggs and pie. Often the coal smoke is from potbelly stoves that heat the cabins and trailers of the hollows—stoves stoked with wood or chunks of coal pulled from the mountainsides or swiped from coal tipples, which are where coal trucks are loaded from roadside piles and conical silos. Sometimes it is smoke from the burning of family homes bought by the coal company and destroyed to prevent anyone from moving back. Often it is the fire department that burns them down, paid by the coal company. I guess I didn't know all this, driving in for the first time.

Old schoolhouses stood empty and broken, forced closed, as I would learn, by a corrupt alliance between coal companies and government officials. Any families remaining had to send their children far away to school. It became easier to just sell out like everyone else, so the mountains could be blown up in peace and the hollows filled in, leaving a rounded moonscape where nothing much grows, and rainwater flows in great floods to encourage the families in the next towns to move along or die.

You won't see many private cars on the two-lane at early hours, but you will see coal trucks and pickup trucks with drivers who don't smile back, because just who are you and what are you doing around here? If they are coming from the other direction and you raise a couple fingers from your steering wheel as they approach, they will at least do the same and give you a reflexive nod.

There is soon a Methodist church, a post office and that's about it. From the tiny community of Delbarton, overgrown Pigeon Roost Road goes off to one side and chases up a hollow of the same name. Because a parade of storms has been coming up from the tropics, everything is humid and the coal seams along the road cuts are dripping.

The little road opens into a meadow where Jimmy's old horse is grazing. Then Jimmy and Sibby's yellow house shows through the half-autumn trees. Jimmy is smoking on the porch, waiting for me with his granddaughter. The smoke from his cigarette combines with the fog from his breath in the cold. He waves and then looks at his watch to let me know I should have started earlier or driven like everybody else up there, trusting the Lord's plan for you when passing trucks on curves and such. Having seen that the Lord's plan also includes little roadside memorials and wrecked, kudzu-draped vehicles in the steep woods below curves, I had taken it more carefully.

In their tiny living room and sometimes in their kitchen for more coffee, mostly Sibby told me how the thing started with Jimmy trying to save the mountain. She said Jimmy was outside, standing in their overgrown vegetable garden, and she was watching him from behind bedroom curtains. She had not been outside herself in the months since the killing of their son Jackie.

She said Jimmy was just looking up toward the top of the mountain for the longest time, and she watched him watch. She thought she could see the anger and depression draining out of him. She could see him loosen into a peaceful slouch. He looked good, like she remembered he could.

When she got to this next part, I glanced from the kitchen into the living room and saw Jimmy put his face in his hands, an unlit cigarette sticking out from his fingers. He didn't want to hear it. Their granddaughter, Alecia Dawn, was swinging on the porch and reading.

Sibby said Jackie's death was still with them. She said there was always, even sometimes today, a movie playing in her head of Jackie's last moments: She described how the thin-set young logger sets a silver quarter on the edge of a pool table in a roadside bar to reserve the next game. He hops out the door and descends the stairs down the hill behind the little bar.

The bar is an old, gray-shingled frame house within sight of the Spruce River Market in Jeffrey, not far away from Pigeon Roost. Jackie clearly isn't planning to be gone long, according to the quarter. He heads to a single-wide mobile home in the little valley behind the bar. It's still there.

He is on his way to visit Kay, his ex, who lives in the trailer when she and her kids aren't hiding from him in up in Number Three Hollow with her folks.

According to some, Kay called him three times to get him to drop by the trailer to visit his kids, and he finally agreed to make an appearance. According to others, he was not at all welcome there, especially after the knife fight that had sent him, Kay, and two others to the hospital ten days earlier. According to this view, he was just going down to hit her or otherwise have a piece of her between pool games, because he knew she was down there cleaning up the blood. His reason for going down there was something he never had a chance to say.

Sibby's mental movie has the boys look up from their pool game when the boom of a shotgun rattles the little bar.

That was it for Jackie. He stumbled off the porch of the yellow trailer and fell dead into the muddy furrows of a vegetable garden.

Sibby had always been proud of her Jackie. He did a man's work, logging for Buck Harless of Gilbert Creek, southwest of Blair Mountain.

Harless, Sibby knew, took care of his own in Mingo County, near Matewan. He built a recreation center for his town. He was a man of the world who had clearcut logged the rainforests of Brazil in the 1970's. He was one of the pioneers of strip mining in Appalachia. In 1999 he worried that Al Gore, if he won, would end the practice of mountaintop removal strip mining and would move national energy policy away from coal. So Harless turned the historically Democratic state of West Virginia over to George Bush by raising all the money in the world from coal interests and supporting Bush, not only in West Virginia, but all over the country. The West Virginia electoral vote made the difference. It was a source of pride for Sibby that Jackie worked for a man as influential as Buck, though she said she didn't know much about the politics.

The police, who had a thick file of domestic abuse complaints against Jackie, including photos in black and blue, just winked at Kay, declaring it a righteous shoot. But Jimmy and Sibby brought up enough evidence to suggest that maybe Kay and her brothers lured him there to settle scores and that Jackie was the victim of a drug-dealing bunch of murderers, and that he had only been trying to save his kids from them.

Love and Democracy

There was a trial. Kay was sentenced 15-to-life, and Jimmy and Sibby went into dark times up in Pigeon Roost, fearing they would never see Jackie and Kay's darling kids again.

On a subsequent trip to Blair Mountain, I did meet Kay. I will lay it in here, just so I don't have to keep bringing up this awful episode. But it makes a point about how reform politics can come out of the blue, and often out of great violence and pain. I wanted to know the truth of what happened, because it had moved a mountain.

As I had been visiting Jimmy from time to time by then, and because word gets around best in places with the least means of communication, I was concerned that I might not be too welcome up where Kay was living with her kids and parents, now that she was out of prison. She got out early because a new governor, Caperton, looked at the situation and could see that Jackie had it coming, regardless of who pulled the trigger. Also, the concept of Battered Woman Syndrome was just becoming understood.

But if her family was, as Jimmy described it, drug-dealing killers, it might not be a good place for me to visit after being friendly with Jackie's family. But your best approach is always to be honest and clear, so I called her and said I had been talking to her former in-laws about everything and thought I should get it from her, too. There was a long pause and then she said, sure, come on up.

Driving slowly up the hollow where her family had long lived, I passed the kind of houses you might expect, and there were people on the porches looking hard at me.

After a few hours with Kay, her mother, Christine, and her preacher father, Chester, I felt ridiculous for worrying about my safety. They had me stay for lunch. Chester and

I talked religion and all about how growing up in the hollow was so different for kids today than it was for him.

The difference? The reverend said that, in his youth, there was no television. When you had no television and no money, you get pretty good at outdoor games, fishing, hunting and other adventures. When TV came, kids played indoors and drugs became the thing, then selling drugs got them the money to buy all the crud they saw on the television. "Drugs get them in trouble and ruins their lives," he summarized. I could see just by looking that his daughter and her brothers were not part of that scene. They were the Waltons.

Their memories of Jackie were rough: Jackie and his brother and a few friends roared up to Chester's church one Sunday to get Jackie's kids away from Kay. They arrived in two trucks from two directions to block off the little bridges over Spruce Fork. Jackie went into church and grabbed the kids from the back row where they always sat. He tossed the kids in the cab of his truck. One of the men with him, standing in a truck bed, fired a machine gun into the air to chase the churchgoers back inside—they had started streaming out to help Kay. Jackie stabbed Chester, the minister, a couple of times and pistol-whipped Christine when they tried to save the kids.

On another occasion Jackie and some friends with guns blocked the road into Number Three Hollow, waylaying Chester and Christine in their car to complain about the way they were keeping Kay and the kids away from him. Chester somehow got himself and his wife through with only a shattered windshield. During that time Chester had to keep looking under the house because Jackie had bragged to Kay that he had some dynamite for her father and mother's place. It was well known that Jackie could get the stuff, as he and his friends and brothers sometimes would take sticks of it up the mountain on the Fourth of July to blow up trees.

On the other side of it, there was testimony to the fact that Kay had once shot up Jackie's car with him in it, maced his face, and that she woke him one morning with a frying pan to his skull. But all that happened after the police had refused to protect her and her kids, telling her that Jackie's kicking her through the house and calling her a pig because she looked fat when she was pregnant was just a marital squabble.

When I visited back with Jimmy about all this, he sighed and admitted he believed all of it, but he still thought Jackie was ambushed and murdered when he didn't have to be.

"I don't think Kay pulled that trigger," Jimmy said. He wanted to love the mother of his grandkids. He blamed Kay's brothers.

"Families is the thing up here, you see. They was waitin' for him when he come down to Kay's trailer. Kay told the sheriff she pulled the trigger because you can get away with it if you've filed reports that say you've been beaten, and you say you're defending yourself. She maybe didn't even know her brothers were in the bushes."

On another occasion he told me that he was trying to settle things with Kay, as he had always loved her and didn't want to think she had killed Jackie herself, and he knew his son had it coming. He still had not seen his grandchildren since the killing and wanted to fix that. He said he wanted to hold them again. He wanted the people on his mountain to be happy again.

I didn't write about Jackie and Kay until now because I didn't want to reinforce false stereotypes of mountain people, but I can't do any worse than Vance did with his book. And I will attest that Jackie's story was a wild exception, as were the Hatfield and McCoy stories. The Waltons, if you remember them, are the truer stereotype of mountain families: hard-working, God-fearing, and very kind, unless you threaten their coal jobs or let them snack too long under the gaslight of Fox News.

I'm telling this story because it's the necessary factual background for understanding the moment when Sibby is looking out through the curtains as Jimmy looks up at the mountain. He looks up at one of the ridges of Blair Mountain and spots a smoothed-over area that mine bulldozers recently made—the start of a big push of debris into the hollow. Mountaintop removal mining machines are the largest siege weapons short of nuclear bombs.

Jimmy had worked in the mines until an accident took him out, but climbing up and down the steep hills of the hollows had kept him strong. Since losing Jackie, however, his cheeks had hollowed and his eyes darkened. He had not come to terms with his son's death until that moment.

He stared at the new scar on the mountain for a long while. Then he walked inside.

"Sibby, we've got to save the mountain."

It was the first thing anyone had said in a long time that made sense to her. She was very much alone lately. Her neighbor friends had sold their land to the mines or been otherwise pushed out, some on account of school closings. And Jimmy had been miserable company. But he had come back alive in that moment.

The mountain had been their family's source of health and stability for generations. Protecting it might somehow put things back in order. Maybe Jackie wouldn't have been as crazy as he was if the mountain had been a peaceful place, a place of balance. That was Jimmy's thinking. Exploitation makes everyone crazy angry.

Soon after that epiphany, Jimmy found a lawyer, Joe Lovett, who soon arrived in Pigeon Roost and went up to the meditating rock with Jimmy. From there, you could see the approach of the mine operation.

The lawyer was encouraging. He said the whole mountaintop mining thing was illegal, top to bottom. You can't bury streams, not according to the Clean Water Act. The battle was on.

Jimmy's suit was the opening salvo in a battle for Blair and all the mountains. Despite the political pressure that usually twists justice in coalfield courts, Judge Charles Hayden did the right thing. The explosions and big shovels were stopped. Four hundred angry men were laid off.

The lawsuit and mine activity would go back and forth, so Jimmy opened another front: He planned a march up the mountain to shine a light on the historic role of Blair Mountain in American Labor history. The manager of the approaching massive mountaintop removal mine would organize a violent reception committee for the marchers.

When Alecia Dawn heard about the violence on the first day of the march, she found her way down the road to walk with her grandfather the rest of the days.

That march was just the fourteen people. A dozen years later, after Jimmy and Sibby had passed away, 600 people did it again. There was some progress with the historic landmark fight. Less than a month in the Gold House, Donald Trump published a Statement of Administrative Policy to again allow the burying of streams with coal mine wastes, something Jimmy and others had stopped for a time. The big wars go on and on, one battle at a time, greed versus beauty, greed versus people. Some of Blair and Pigeon Roost is still there, still being fought for.

Larry Gibson is gone now too, as is most of Kayford Mountain. But he started a foundation that keeps fighting for the rest of all that beauty, sometimes one email, sometimes one protest pilgrimage at a time.

So much of their energy has been from Doris's simple dedication. The memory of her example has coursed through the region like a vagus nerve of creative resistance. Interesting term, vagus. It comes from wanderer, vagabond. We get *wave* from it. We get *vague* from it. It is here and there, like the inspirations that invisibly move us to action through the generations, long after the names of heroes have been forgotten.

Birds

Why do people like us flock to protests? Is it that we still believe in a better world and a better nation and get angry, while others have given up? In any case, we always seem so joyful, despite the serious concerns that bring us to the street. For some it is the joy of finally having a say, even if just on a cardboard sign. For some it is the joy of friendship, new or old.

On one of my first trips into coal country, Ken took me to lunch with Laura and another organizer, Janet Fout of OVEC, the Ohio Valley Environmental Coalition, based in Huntington. The three of us, plus Vivian Stockman and Dianne Bady of that same organization, would talk from time to time as I got deeper into the coal issue. Ken had asked them to keep me in the loop.

Janet grew up in Huntington, the daughter of a glassblower who ran a bait shop on the side. He would take her fishing but would have to bait her hooks, as she couldn't kill the worms. She would park her young self in a closet under the stairs to read books about people living lives that counted for something.

She grew up to teach school in Point Pleasant, marrying a man whose family company still makes the heavy equipment used to bolt-up the ceilings of coalmines. That is done by driving long threaded rods up into the coal formations on tunnel ceilings. The company had made a fortune, especially since the passage of Ken's coal mine bill, which mandated more roof bolting. Janet went to the Coal Association meetings on her husband's arm, hearing about the whining coal miners who would strike over the number of bars of soap in the washrooms. She would mix with the politicians pocketed by the coal men. Her father-in-law was on first name terms with Jay Rockefeller. They had yachts and summered in the Caribbean. Janet became an ace sailor. It was a dream life for a girl from a modest neighborhood.

When the coal sludge dam at Buffalo Creek broke and washed away a whole community. Janet was horrified like everyone else. One of her friends, Terry, was down there recovering bodies with the National Guard. But the opposing realities around coal mining would not collide in her heart until some years later.

Like many marriages, theirs wasn't forever. Janet found solace in watching the birds feeding outside the window of her house in Huntington. The previous owner had left a birdbath and a wooden feeder, thereby changing the history of many lives, as little loving things do.

Despite a cold and snowy winter, one bird was trying to make the best of it. Janet could relate. She bought some seed for it. She painted watercolors by night and, with the enthusiastic help of her little girl, Julia, kept an eye on the bird by day.

The bird was an Eastern Towhee, slender black and orange, with a white belly, a small beak and a tail as long as a Cardinal's. She bought a Golden Guide to identify it, and she soon could identify all the visitors that came after the snow: a Barred Owl, a Coocoo, Grosbeaks, Cardinals, Chickadees, and the bird that truly seemed to speak to her with its brave song, a Carolina Wren. By spring, the Thrushes were pulling her out of her cold house into a warming world.

Her first volunteer bird count was in Greenbottom, a wetland upriver from Huntington. A great flock of Rusty

Blackbirds greeted her. She started learning their sounds so she could talk back to them. She became active with the Audubon Society, soon taking her turn as its president. With the Society, she became active in protecting Greenbottom, and she went back to school at Marshall to beef up her biology credentials. Annual bird counts led her up the hollows and into the coalfields, where she was appalled to see the destruction of habitat. She learned that hardwood seedlings—always the future of Appalachia—just won't grow on the land "reclaimed" after mountaintop removal mining.

"The birds showed me the truth of what I needed to be doing," she told me. Her Audubon chapter became a tough legal player under her leadership.

Also in Huntington was Dianne Bady, mother of much of the environmental efforts on both sides of the Ohio River. She offered Janet a job as an organizer. Had Janet's marriage still been in place, that would have been an impossible conflict for her. But she could now accept Dianne's offer to become the third employee of the Ohio Valley Environmental Coalition, where she organized the fight to stop a proposed pulp mill that would have further polluted the Ohio River and the air of the Ohio Valley.

Janet's daughter fought at her side and was interviewed on Nick's News, the Nickelodeon channel's national news show for kids. A representative from the proposed pulp mill explained how the mill certainly would not pollute very much at all. Cut to little Julia: "That's a lie," she explained.

The pulp mill was stopped. Activists always get the blame for the loss of jobs, but never the credit for the drinkability of the water or the breathability of the air.

Their Coalition's victory came to the attention of Larry Gibson of Kayford Mountain. He had another thankless and impossible fight for them: Stop mountaintop removal mining. He was traveling in the credible company of Ken Hechler and was soon on the Coalition's board.

A second marriage put Janet in the company of back-to-the-land newcomers from the peace and justice movement of the 60s and 70s—young people from big cities seeking to create cooperative, sustainable enclaves in green places. One such group had a forest parcel they just called The Farm, and Janet's second husband was a member.

Janet said I should come up to The Farm some weekend and meet their friends. It was not a commune, she said, though that had been the original dream. It had become a weekend commune, like summer cabins, as people got jobs and kids and more regular lives. It remained a place for friendship and music. They had regular events to celebrate the change of seasons, sometimes playing particular parts. I asked Janet what her part might be. "I'm a mud fairy," she said.

When she was still president of the Audubon chapter, Laura Forman walked into a meeting one evening. She was the young wife of an air traffic controller just transferred to Huntington from Long Island. They had been volunteers in the animal preserves near Teddy Roosevelt's Long Island estate and were looking for ways to get involved in their new community.

Laura and her husband, Mike, were avid birders. They had just bought a home in Kenova, near Huntington.

After the meeting, Janet took her aside with a warning: The refinery in Kenova was a problem, she said. Hydrogen fluoride hung over the town in a cloud. Laura listened, but she and Mike loved the house and the ten green acres around it.

Love and Democracy

Laura had grown up in Upstate New York, famous in her family for walking ahead of her dad when he was mowing the lawn, getting any tiny critters out of the way. She had kept a forested place near their home free of litter, and she sent petitions to Japan and Russia with strong letters about saving the whales. Her mother, who received and shared nature magazines from Sierra Club and other groups, was her inspiration. She told me that when we were hiking Route 94 so she could give me details about Jimmy's Blair Mountain march and its violence. She talked about the Roosevelt nature sanctuary at Oyster Bay, where her Mike was the better volunteer, she said.

"He was willing to cut rats in half and all the nasty, foul stuff—and clean out the turkey vulture cages. I did the much less messy stuff. But I always felt that, you know, I just wanted to be involved."

On a cold 10th of December, three months and a day after the 9-11 attacks, Laura, Janet, Larry Gibson, Jimmy Weekley and several other activists visited the sidewalk outside the Corps of Engineers office in Huntington for a protest. It was no time to become distracted by that attack, as the trouble in the Middle East would only increase the demand for coal. The Corps of Engineers was one of the federal agencies that had been instructed by the Bush White House to turn a blind eye to the many violations of law involved in mountaintop removal coal mining. The activists were there to ask the Corps, please for Christmas, to enforce the laws like they would certainly do for any other community.

Monroe Cassidy was there from Inez, Kentucky, just across the Tug Fork from Matewan. Monroe, a lifelong miner, had crossed the line into activism when a sludge impoundment above his hollow sprang a leak on account of an abandoned mine below it, sending more toxic sludge down upon them than all the oil been spilled by the Exxon-Valdez. The goo went all the way into the Ohio River, spoiling countless homes and farms on its way. There was very little notice of it and very little cleanup, as Senator Mitch McConnell, who had been Granny D's biggest enemy on campaign finance reform, put the clamp on a local judge.

Monroe, a month or so before the protest in Huntington, had taken me though the whole messy land that had once been his Eden.

At the sidewalk protest in Huntington, Vivian Stockman, an important part of the Ohio Valley Environmental Coalition, dressed the part of King Coal. Julian Martin, one of the leading lights of the movement, was there. Dianne Bady was there. Marshall students were on hand as well.

FBI agents were there to watch them all, as the Bush government was coming to the position that environmental activists were just one file folder away from terrorists. True homeland security, of course, is in protecting the mountains, the air, water and people from poisons and destruction.

Jimmy Weekley met up with Laura on the sidewalk. He thought she looked a little wore out. He told her she should slow down. She said she couldn't slow down any more than he could. He asked her if she knew where he could get a cheap computer. He had always used his old computer for spreading the word, but Sibby had thought he was corresponding a little too much with someone in particular, and she took a hammer to it. Laura laughed and said she would look around for a cheap one.

Larry Gibson rolled up. "How ya doing, you sexy thing?" he greeted Laura. Larry could say that sort of thing without offending. They talked about his upcoming speech at Kent State and about their next lobbying trip to D.C.

Laura made her pitch to the reporters. She touched her head several times. Then she whipped around as if some invisible fist had punched her from the left. She was on the sidewalk, unconscious. People did what they could, but there was no sign of life. By the time the ambulance arrived, Janet, her friend of nine years, was in a heap next to a planter box. She managed to stand and get into the back of the ambulance with Laura's body.

The autopsy said her heart tissue was scarred, and she had two or three kinds of cancer. She hadn't had a clue about any of it. But the snowflakes of toxin that had fallen on her for her last few years took their toll.

There were a hundred people at Beech Fork Park for her funeral, despite the rain. Her favorite music was played: the Second Movement of Mozart's Clarinet Concerto, which, she liked because it soars birdlike.

Her husband described her likes. I'm going to repeat what he said, because a person's heart is as rich a treasure as any mountain creek or hollow. He said she liked motherhood, animals, her work, chocolate, authors Denise Giardina, Barbara Kingsolver, Rachael Carson, and Wendell Berry. She loved Ken Hechler, the Simpsons, Cleveland Amory, Cherry Garcia, Cabernet Sauvignon, Mahalia Jackson, picking out clothes for her son, Donald, to wear in the morning, *To Kill a Mockingbird*, rollercoasters, Alice Walker, Walt Whitman, Jimmy Carter, a night out with the girls, the City of Boston, Bob Dylan, Christmas, the Guggenheim, Blackwater Falls, Dolly Sods, Canaan Valley, Cranberry Glades, the New River, snuggling, John Lennon, Granny D, California, big bowls of cereal.

Some months after that, when Carlos Gore had taken his name off the lawsuit in Blair, I visited him on his porch. After Laura died, he said, he "kinda lost heart for the fight."

For others, her memory became a motivation. Doris Haddock would later speak of Laura in speeches around the country. "Be Like Laura" was a speech she delivered on Earth Day at George Washington University.

What has come of all this love? Blair Mountain received its historic status, so part of it is protected now. Most of it is still under attack. It shouldn't be that hard. It shouldn't take that many skinny heroes and redheaded heroines for governments to just do the right thing. The Fourteenth Amendment says we are all due equal protection under the law, but would the EPA allow toxic ash to fall on DC or Beverly Hills? It's unconstitutional, what they do.

Hell Freezes Over

A few thousand words ago I left poor Doris stuck in the snow on her 90th birthday, stopped cold from her goal of Washington DC by the worst blizzard in 40 years, as I've mentioned maybe three times.

I loitered at the Cumberland train station where she would make her birthday speech. Doris was an hour late, which gave me time to explore the area. To the west of the station, you can see the well-preserved cabin that George Washington used for his headquarters during the Whiskey Rebellion—when the citizens of the new nation took serious exception to taxes on the essentials. Washington was the president, but he insisted on putting down the rebellion himself, probably because he was the best general in the nation and because he knew the area well. As a young man, he had surveyed a line for a canal to open the Eastern Seaboard to the Ohio Valley. The resulting Cumberland & Ohio (C&O) Canal and its adjacent tow path where horses and oxen would pull barges, are preserved by the National Park Service. The canal and the tow path run 184 miles from Cumberland right into Georgetown in DC.

I knew that much history and took an icy walk to find something remaining of it. I found nearby a National Park Service office the size of a guardhouse and what was clearly the start of the towpath. It presented a wide snowy clearing through the woods that headed gently downhill beside the frozen canal, invisible now under thick snow. The path was chained closed due to the snowstorm.

I went back to the train station to wait for Doris. Soon, the whole town came up the snowy road, brass band playing and children singing—the mayor, Rotarians, everybody marching and singing like a Hollywood musical. They brought along a big birthday cake, hefted little Doris onto the back of a red caboose and she made a great speech.

After all that I pulled Jim over to see the snowy path. A few weeks earlier, I had asked him to send us Doris's cross-country skis, as I thought they might help her in the blizzards she had already weathered. They didn't work for that, but they were still in the van.

Jim and I loitered there long enough for a park ranger to come out of his office. We explained the situation. He insisted that the path was closed, and the chain was not coming down. Jim asked if someone ducked under the chain anyway, might the ranger be looking the other way? The ranger paused, then said he might be busy with paperwork or something and not see it. He returned to his hut.

When Jim and I showed the path to Doris, she laughed with joy. Things had always worked out for her on this adventure. Grail Castle drawbridges always opened. This might be the last miracle she needed.

On the tow path, starting at zero degrees Fahrenheit, she would cross country ski the remaining 184 miles into Washington. The only reporter sturdy enough to accompany her was a woman from the London Sunday Times.

Nick Palumbo would meet them with the van for some rest and sustenance wherever a back road intersected with the snowy path. Nick and another volunteer, Jason, would also take turns on used skis they purchased at a town along the way to break trail through the deep snow.

Mitch McConnell had said McCain's reform bill would pass "when Hell freezes over," so we sent him a photo of Doris getting close to Washington on skis. She had previously burned him by making a speech in front of his Louisville office about his opposition to reform, and that speech was reported all over the Kentucky newspapers.

After two weeks of strenuous effort, Doris skied right into Georgetown, almost in the shadow of the Washington Monument.

On the final morning of her long walk, February 29, 2000, she walked across the Key Bridge in DC. Reporters from Good Morning America and the Today Show were with us, rather yelling at me because I had accidentally promised exclusives to both morning shows. They settled down and stayed to cover the story.

We stopped at the entrance to Arlington Cemetery and waited there for volunteers who had pledged to join her last miles to the Capitol Building. California was now 9 million steps ago.

Only a dozen or so people were present at first, so I was worried. But a Metro subway station is located right there, and each arriving train delivered more people to walk with her—and then a flood of them, cheering, carrying signs, hugging and congratulating her.

When approximately 2,300 people were on hand and the new arrivals were trickling down, we began the final miles, led by Jim Hightower with his white cowboy hat and a megaphone. He stood on every statue pedestal along the way, getting the crowd chanting and cheering. As we detoured along K Street to wake up the lobbyists, two young women who couldn't get off work draped a *Go Granny Go!* banner from a high window and shouted their cheers.

Wellstone, Boxer, Feingold, Levin—more members of Congress than I could recognize, joined us along the way. Our goal was the Capitol's East Steps, where Wellstone and several other members of Congress planned to speak alongside Doris.

When Doris's 2,300 supporters—the size of Trump's mob 21 years later—approached the Capitol grounds, the Capitol Police stopped us. I told them we had a permit. I rather wished I had it in my pocket, but Common Cause assured me that one was in place. A police captain said, yes, Common Cause had taken out a permit. It was for two hundred people, max.

I told the police we were accompanying a 90-year-old woman who had walked 3,200 miles from California for this moment, and that several senators and representatives were walking with her to speak on the East Steps. They looked over the heads of the stalled crowd, and I expect they recognized John Lewis, Marty Meehan, Russ Feingold, singer David Crosby and others. "Is that Granny D herself?" a Black officer asked me. "She doesn't look any the worse for wear."

"That's her. Do you want to meet her? You'll brag about it someday," I offered.

They got on a walkie-talkie with their chief, then waved us onto the grounds on the condition that, when we rounded the building and formed up below the East Steps, we would please divide the crowd into clusters of no more than two hundred people each, with aisles between them, which we sort of did. It worked out. We didn't break anything. We certainly didn't go inside. We didn't wave Confederate flags or defecate in the halls, threaten to lynch anyone or cause the death of Capitol Police officers. So, there is perhaps a better way to press your demands. After all, we could later say, just as in Henry V and unlike anything Trump's mob could say, that the day was ours.

Doris gave a stemwinder on the steps of the U.S. Senate. An excerpt:

The people I met along my way have given me messages to deliver here. The messages are many, written with old and young hands of every color, and yet the messages are the same. They are this: Shame on you Mitch McConnell and those who raise untold millions of dollars in exchange for public policy. Shame on you, Senators and Congressmen, who have turned this headquarters of a great and self-governing people into a bawdy house...

While we are here to speak frankly to our representatives, let us also speak frankly to ourselves: Along my walk I have seen an America that is losing the time and the energy for self-governance. The problems we see in Washington are problems that have been sucked into a vacuum of our own making. It is not enough for us to elect someone, give them a slim list of ideas and send them off to represent us. If we do not keep these boys and girls busy, they will always get into trouble. We must energize our communities to better see our problems, better plan their happy futures, and these plans must form the basis of our instructions to our elected representatives. This is the responsibility of every adult American, from native to newcomer, and from young worker to the long-retired. If we are hypnotized by television and overwrought by life on a corporate-consumer treadmill, let us snap out of it and regain our lives as a free, calm, fearlessly outspoken people who have time for each other and our communities. Let us pass election reforms and anti-corruption measures in our towns and cities and states, winning the reform wars where they are winnable, changing the national weather on this subject until the winds blow even through these old columns.

Now, Senators, back to you. If I have offended you, speaking this way on your front steps, that is quite as it should be. You have offended America, and you have dishonored the best things it stands for. Take your wounded pride, get off your backs and onto your feet, and go across the street to clean your rooms. You have somewhere on your desks, under the love letters from your greedy friends and co-conspirators against representative democracy, a modest bill against soft money. Pass it. Then show that you are clever lads by devising new ways for a great people to talk to one another without the necessity of great wealth. If you cannot do that, then get out of the way—go home to some other corruption less harmful to a great nation. We have millions of people more worthy of these fine offices...

The People of our nation do care. They have told me. They laugh with disgust about you on the beaches of California. They shake their heads about you in the native village of Hashan Kehk in Arizona. In Toyah, Texas, they pray for deliverance from your corruption. In Little Rock, they understand in anger how you undermine their best dreams for our society. And in Memphis and in Louisville and in Chillicothe and Clarksburg, through Pennsylvania and Maryland and into this city today, the people see you for what you have become, and they are prepared to see you another way: boarding the trains at the great train station down the street. They are ready for real leaders, unselfish and principled leaders who will prove their worth by voting for meaningful campaign finance reform this year.

In the name of the people who have sent me along to you, and in the name of the generations before who have sacrificed so much for the sanctity of our free institutions and who stand with us in spirit today, I make this demand.

After several welcoming parties in DC, including one that got us an introduction to the town's biggest book agent, I let Doris know she had offers to speak all over the US and in some other countries. What did she want to do next, after walking 3,200 miles through blistering deserts and blinding blizzards and making nearly 200 speeches?

"Go home and take a long, hot bath," she said. So, Jim drove her back to New Hampshire, and I flew home to Arizona to finish her book.

Enemies of the McCain bill followed me to Phoenix. The U.S. House Administration Committee, led by Rep. Bob Ney of Ohio, borrowed the Phoenix City Council Chambers to hold an official U.S. Congressional hearing on the House version of the McCain bill. C-SPAN arrived to cover it. Ney's clear objective was to embarrass McCain in his own state, mostly with a parade of conservative witnesses who would speak against the bill, and with a few of the bill's supporters revealed as the commies they are.

I complained to the mayor about our City Council chambers being used for the freak show. If the City couldn't renege, I asked him to personally insist that I be included as a witness. The mayor was Skip Rimsza, a Republican and an old friend from realtor days—someone I had encouraged into leadership.

Ney—the perfect if backwards name for a horse's ass—agreed to call me as a witness, but probably to use me as a whipping boy for that "liberal commie" organization, Common Cause. Ney didn't know I had already left that organization because they were not cool with Arizonans taking the redistricting power away from the Legislature and giving it to a politically balanced citizen commission. Organizations make mistakes. Common Cause opposing the idea of redistricting commissions was in the same file folder with the ACLU later supporting the Citizens United decision.

Ney's chief of staff was outside the Phoenix City Council chambers just before all that began. We visited. He looked at Phoenix's cute mountains on the horizon and asked if there were snakes up there. "Not all of them," I said. He had a confused look.

During the hearing, March 17, 2001, Ney and his crew brutally grilled Ann Eschinger for her leadership of that suspicious organization, the League of Women Voters. Her treatment was despicable. I was next for the firing squad. Ney asked how much I was being paid to promote the McCain bill. I answered that I was not being paid. I was a volunteer. The bull's horns passed harmlessly through my red cape. While they struggled for a relevant next question, I interrupted to say that the McCain bill, because it would limit political contributions from big industries, ought to be something each one of them should personally welcome.

How so, Mr. Burke? It was a strategic error for him to ask a question with an unknown answer.

I spread out five file folders in front of me, each with one of their names printed large enough for them to see. I opened the Ney folder.

My reply, from the C-SPAN transcript:

"Well, Representative Ney, you are Congress's highest recipient of donations from coal companies. It must make the many coal miners in your district worry unnecessarily about whose interests you represent when it comes to the mine health and safety issues that their lives depend upon."

My exchange with Ney was enough. No more questions for Mr. Burke. But C-SPAN ran and reran that moment all throughout the coming U.S. Senate debate.

Bob "Freedom Fries" Ney would later resign in the wake of bribery allegations during the Abramoff lobbying scandal.

When the McCain bill finally came up for Senate debate, I returned to DC, as did Doris. We had finished the book, and Random House had rushed it to press.

Doris made speeches on the Capitol grounds to various youth activist groups, but we didn't seem to be making a difference. She decided to up the sacrifice.

The new plan was for her to walk continuously around the Capitol, day and night, in freezing cold rain while fasting. All this would be done to secure personal appointments for her with senators. Matt, Claudia, and I informed Senate staffers that such meetings were the only times she would agree to come out of the cold.

It worked. Doris met with nearly half the Senate, sharing the heartfelt emotions of the people she met along her walk—citizens who wanted their democracy back. As she had an open door to NPR, The New York Times, The Washington Post, Good Morning America, and the Today Show, her threats were taken seriously, as were her stories about how people were discouraged by the corruption of the system. She turned a few votes.

It helped in those Senate visits that the book was finished and that Random House had sent us a few cases to pass around the Hill. She signed them, sometimes with tough love: "I hope you will support the McCain bill. If not, be assured I will walk across your state about it. Love, Doris."

Bill Moyers wrote the book's introduction. Pete Seeger promoted it widely. He bought cases of them and passed them out to influential friends, He wrote a great long letter to Doris and me about the book, telling us it stood next to Silent Spring on his bookshelf.

The book was warmly reviewed:

From the Library Journal: "a multilayered memoir, populist reform treatise, roadside nature field book, Whitmanesque treatment of America, and philosophical summation of a life well spent. It is chock–full of portraits of the countless citizens who welcomed, joined, cared for, and walked with Haddock. Her graceful descriptions of the manifold kindness routinely shown her are collectively a stunning portrait of the American soul."

And from the Keene Sentinel, one of her hometown New Hampshire papers: "Huck is present in this book, as are Thoreau and Whitman, and Jack Kerouac, too."

As Maureen had foreseen, it led to another book for me and then a dozen more, ghostwritten or cowritten with people of interest to Random House or to agent Gail. Writing would later take me into the horrors of African genocides and to joyful communities of Nepal and India. I would work with a shipwrecked family, a Medal of Honor winner, a bank robber, the president of the World Bank and many others. Every book was an education for me.

But to the moment at hand: How does a 90-year-old person fast and walk around the clock in deadly weather? Mostly it was courage, but there were tricks. I had discouraged the part about fasting, but she was unmoved by my argument.

"Call Dick Gregory. He knows about fasting," she told me. "I'm sure there's a trick to it," she said. He had famously fasted as a Civil Rights activist.

Dick Gregory had held her hand as they walked across a bridge into Memphis, and so we now had his home phone number. I called, pulling him away from his family dinner table. I could hear the clatter and laughter of the dinner behind him.

"She has to have water," he began. Then he gave me a long list of clear fruit juices and other clear and healthy things that should be in the water.

"Is that cheating?" I asked.

"No, man, it's show business!" he laughed.

He told me that Gandhi sometimes fasted on water alone, but sometimes there was a bit of fruit juice.

"If you value life and you're out there representing life, then you must value your own life, too," Gregory told me.

So, that was part of it. And we also needed a second bit of magic. John Moyers, son of Bill Moyers, would provide the extra bit, but I should first tell you how John came into the story.

We met in jail.

Love and Democracy

American Valentine

A few weeks before the Senate debate on the McCain-Feingold bill, I got a call from John Passacantando, head of Greenpeace. They were planning a protest at the Capitol in support of the McCain bill, and they wanted to know if Doris and a few of us with her would be willing to be arrested. He said the environmental groups wanted to make the point that we can't save the environment if corporate interests continue to rule Congress through their huge political donations.

The plan was for forty of us, representing a number of environmental and government reform organizations, to go into the Capitol Rotunda with the rest of the tourists, but then we would step out of the rope line to unfurl a banner promoting campaign finance reform while Doris read the Declaration of Independence to make the point that we needed independence from the shackles of the corrupt campaign finance system.

Passacantando would be in the group, and many others including John Moyers. I have our group photo somewhere, which looks awfully respectable.

It started the evening before with a meeting at the venerable United Methodist Building, which is wedged between the Supreme Court and the Dirksen Senate Office Building and always something of a surprise to see sitting there, like a reminder for public officials to say their prayers. The forty of us reviewed and discussed the rules of peaceful resistance. The next morning, we assembled on the Capitol grounds and prepared to get in line with the other tourists. We first had a preliminary meeting with the Capitol Police, describing our plans and telling them our intentions were not to be disruptive or dangerous or to resist arrest. "We will certainly be violating your rules, at which point you arrest us." I remember hearing those words—this gang was all Harvard and no Hee-Haw.

The Capitol Police lieutenant made a head count and called ahead for zip ties and a bus.

Once inside the Rotunda, we unfurled our campaign finance reform banner and Doris began her recitation of the Declaration of Independence. It came off very nicely and the tourists present applauded and seemed shocked when Doris and the rest of us were zip-tied and led away.

Outside, history professor Lou Hammond from Gettysburg College was pushed a bit and fell, cutting his nose badly on a curb because his hands were zipped behind and he couldn't break his fall. He bled in jail without medical help. Otherwise, it was fine.

I made my one phone call from jail to Maureen in Phoenix. I didn't need to call a lawyer, as a crew of lawyers had volunteered in advance to represent the forty of us. I just called her to say, "Honey, I'm in jail," because I thought it would be a way to spark up what could sometimes be a dull day in her newsroom.

She knew it was all planned. "Remember everything," she said. "It's content."

Around midnight we were released one by one from the D.C. jail as our assigned lawyers posted bail. We trickled into a rented church hall where each new-arriving criminal was cheered. The party ran late.

Days later, the D.C. trial judge gave Doris a hug after finding her guilty but beautiful. From Judge Hamilton's sentence:

"As you know, the strength of our great country lies in its constitution and her laws and in her courts, but more fundamentally, the strength of our great country lies in the resolve of her citizens to stand up for what is right when the masses are silent. And, unfortunately, sometimes it becomes the lot of the few, sometimes like yourselves, to stand up for what's right when the masses are silent."

He gave us all time served. Anyway, that's how we met John Moyers. And as it happened, he and his father owned a brownstone directly behind the Supreme Court. John was living there at the time with a student friend or two. The house was always full of interesting people. At one gathering, I had a visit with Tucker Carlson. He approached me with a request to interview Doris for an article in New York Magazine. John Moyers told him he must deal with me to interview Doris, which wasn't true, but I welcomed the role of gatekeeper as far as Carlson was concerned. I knew his writing well enough to suspect he would make fun of her and trash campaign finance reform, right on the eve of the Senate debate.

I told him he could interview her, but only if he would do it over the dinner table in his own home, with his wife and kids at the table. It worked well—Doris sold his kids on campaign reform, and the article came out kindly and respectfully to Doris, at least for him.

Now, as to Doris's around-the-clock circling the Capitol while fasting: Every third or fourth trip in her circle around the Capitol, she would make a detour behind the Supreme Court, often at the insistence of the volunteer walking with her, watching her strength and breathing. Behind the Court, she could disappear as if by trap door into John's house for a brief rest—even a catnap during late night hours. She could warm up and get a leg massage. That's how she did it. It was a real 24-hour, four-day walk, and a real fast, but she did it with the support any athlete would need for a swim across the Channel. You don't do heavy stuff like that without a team and a plan to stay alive. This was happening as the Senate was now debating the bill.

By the fourth day she was wearing down, and I was asking her to call it off. Then I received a call from McCain's staffer in charge of getting the bill passed. The staffer said there might be a deal for passage, and it could happen fast. He said McCain and Feingold wanted Doris to be in the gallery above the Senate floor for the big moment of passage.

"What kind of a deal?" I asked.

"Do you think you folks are going to hold out for the perfect bill, or could you go along with a pretty good bill?" he asked.

"What kind of a deal?" I repeated.

He described what sounded like a big loophole—state parties would be exempt from the restrictions affecting national parties, which meant the baffles on the maze would just be slightly rearranged, and the rats would still find their way to the cheese. There would be no control of independent expenditure groups, which could act, raise and spend just like parties or candidates.

The bill would put a thumb in the leaky dam over here but open a floodgate over there.

The original intent of the reform, and the thing Doris had gathered petitions for and walked 3,200 miles for, was to eliminate "soft money." That was defined as unregulated donations. If you gave $1,000 to a candidate, that's hard money, and there was a strict limit. If you gave $1,000 to a political party for "party building," that was soft money, even if everyone knew it was going to be used to elect a particular candidate or slate, and there was no limit on money coming to the candidate from the party. But yes, the bill would regulate soft money at the federal level. So, if you were desperate for a win, you could call it that. McCain wanted to call it that, I gathered.

His staffer on the phone said it was the best they could get and maybe it could be strengthened in the House or in conference. We both knew that was unlikely, but I could sense that McCain's people, who had fought hard for years on this, were finished. They wanted something that looked like a win so they could move on to other issues.

It was an opportunity to get Doris out of the cold. I told the McCain guy that we understood the situation, but I should have bluffed and said we would carry on with our protests. It wouldn't have changed anything, but I should have anyway. We needed millions of people who would call and march, but we only had a few thousand. We would need McCain and Feingold, but they were spent. McCain didn't want Doris out there saying it was a shitty deal, but she—we—should have because it was.

Anyway, it passed the Senate. Doris walked with McCain and Feingold across the Capitol grounds to deliver the bill to the House. Those two guys knocked her famous hat off with a group hug. Doris understood that the victory was slight, but she was not afraid of gradual progress, nor should any of us be.

New York Times, April 3, 2001: The Senate voted today to approve the most wide-ranging overhaul of the nation's campaign finance law since the aftermath of the Watergate scandal, shifting the struggle over the influence of money and politics into a divided House.

Yes, the bill now had to get through the House, and again through the Senate if the House changed it. We would come back to D.C. for that, and to see if they would eliminate the loopholes—unlikely in the extreme—but you must be an optimist in this world if you're going to have enough joy to keep going.

It was now time for Doris to go home and recharge, as it would be months before the bill was up for debate in the House. We disbanded our happy few. The collection of people who regularly showed up to support our efforts in D.C. included history professor George Peabody, who was at the time helping to plan the World War II Memorial on the Mall. We also had the beforementioned and still nose-bandaged Professor Lou Hammond and his wife, Patricia, and author Mathew Lesko, who wore an outrageous suit of question marks. Ken Hechler came often, as did Doris's grandchildren and a few mountaintop removal activists from West Virginia, led by Janet Fout.

George Ripley, who converted the basement of his D.C. brownstone into a factory for ten-foot-high protest signs for us, would come and would always be the first person I called when we needed big vertical signs on tall poles. He could deliver giant messages within the hour.

Strange people also came, including a woman who lived in her car with plastic sheets taped over the air conditioning vents to foil the CIA from taking over her brain. I never got the full details on how all that worked, but she was there, night and day, nice as pie, sometimes in an oversize orange hazmat suit.

Also always on hand were John Anthony, Matt Keller, Nick Palumbo and of course Doris's son, Jim.

Love and Democracy

When debate finally started on the House side in February of 2002, we returned to Washington. The big news of those weeks was still the emotional aftermath of the 9/11 attacks and now also the Enron scandal, in which many members of Congress had taken Enron money in exchange for protecting Enron from investigation. I asked George Ripley to make a good number of 10-foot-high pole banners that said *"Enron Congress! Redeem Your Sorry Selves! Pass Campaign Finance Reform Now!"* We occupied the sidewalks between the Capitol and the House office buildings.

On the day before Valentine's Day, our volunteers perched on the Capitol steps making pretty, *"Don't break our Hearts!"* valentines for hand delivery to each House member. When Doris and I tried to leave a valentine with John Lewis's staff, we heard him from inside his office:

"Is that Granny D I hear?" He came roaring out for a hug. We visited quite a while in the hall as he pressed the message into us that, whatever happened with the bill, we must never give up. He gave me his card and said to call for any inside advice or contacts we might need. I still have his card—a magic thing on my desk.

It was freezing weather. At one point, the wife of Republican Chris Shays came along with hot tea for all of us on the sidewalk. Her husband had partnered with Democrat Marty Meehan to put the bill forward in the House. At another point that day, Doris invaded Congressman Bill Ney's office and started reading off his unsavory campaign donations for a TV reporter. Chris Shays ran from his office to prevent her arrest and inform her that Ney had suddenly come aboard the bill, thanks to the CSPAN hammering he was getting from the Phoenix hearing.

Toward the end of that day, a courier came down from the office of Dick Gephardt, asking Doris and a few of us to come up to his leadership office. He said he had the votes for passage, and we should please be in the gallery that evening. We were. It passed at 2 a.m.

Gephardt, Shays, Meehan and others looked up from the House floor and saluted Doris. I told her to stand up and she did. In the dawn's early light, Doris and a few of us walked down the House side of the Capitol's East Steps with Shays, Meehan and their wives. It was Valentine's Day.

It had to go back to the Senate one more time to iron-out differences in the two bills, which would be easy. President Bush would then reluctantly sign it into law. The measure's four main sponsors, to a man, said for the Congressional Record that the bill would not have passed without Doris.

"John McCain and Bill Bradley were looking over her shoulder, reading her speeches and watching how she succeeded in making campaign finance reform an emotional and patriotic issue with many Americans. When presidential candidate Al Gore finally signed on to campaign finance reform, his speech cited McCain, Bradley and Doris Haddock." —Bill Moyers

"Granny D, you exceed any small, modest contributions those of us who have labored in the vineyards of reform have made to this Earth." —Sen. John McCain, from Senate floor

Love and Democracy

It's important to understand why Doris was successful while so many reform efforts fail. Doris was consciously following Gandhi's five steps. With her "Tuesday Academy" book club friends in New Hampshire, she had made sure of the facts around big money's corruption of democracy. Making sure of your facts before spouting off is Gandhi's first step. The second step is respectfully asking those in power to fix a problem. For that, she spent two years gathering petitions, often in freezing parking lots, and making phone calls and writing letters to her members of Congress. That didn't work. The third step is to engage the conscience of the community. She did that with the publicity around her walk.

That was Gandhi's third step but also his fourth, which is to demonstrate the seriousness of the issue by engaging in personal sacrifice, and then to increase that sacrifice as needed. Her effort at her age and infirmity was indeed a creative sacrifice. She was doing it the right way: make it very difficult but not self-destructive. If you are signing up as an agent of love, you can't also be an agent of destruction, even self-destruction.

Down the road, Doris and I would meet Julia "Butterfly" Hill, who perched in an old-growth tree south of Eureka, California to prevent the clearcutting of its grove. She came down from that tree just as healthy as she went up—after two years and eight days aloft. Volunteers sent her food and supplies by rope. The grove stands today, protected by an agreement finally made with the lumber company. Her sacrifice was Gandhian in that it didn't involve self-harm, just incredible fortitude and deprivation of personal comfort. Julia's daily messages from her high perch, just like Doris's emails from the road, were joyful celebrations of beauty.

Protests are far more effective when they are joyful, because joy gives activists the energy to carry on. We all have experienced the joy of participating in marches, even when the issues are grave. Joy also makes it more likely that humor will be used, and very few villains can survive that, because humor shows confidence in victory. ICE thugs are no match for people dancing in inflatable animal costumes—not in the long run, which is how we must think of things.

If you wonder why today's protests often don't achieve enough, it's often because the element of sacrifice is missing. Showing up somewhere convenient on a Saturday with a sign and a water bottle won't usually do the trick, though everything helps.

Gandhi's fifth step is to take your victory with grace, letting your opponent save face, but that would be a long way down the road for Doris. The fifth rule is necessary because the first four, done correctly, usually succeed, so long as the villain is even a little sensitive to public opinion. So, you take your victory with a graceful bow to your opponent because you will likely meet them in combat again, and you'll be more successful if you have been treating them like people all along and maintaining a respectful line of communication. When World War II gave India the perfect opportunity to split from the very distracted British Empire, Gandhi said, no, we'll not take advantage of them at such a time. We'll wait until after the War so that we can part as friends.

All this history may seem from another world, given our current crisis. But Gandhi still works, and we will still want friends in our neighborhoods after our victory for democracy.

Book II

Coexistence

After the passage of the McCain bill, Doris asked what I thought she might do next. She was afraid of becoming bored, she said. I asked what other issues she might want to get more involved with, though I'm sure I didn't end the question with a preposition, as her grammar was as exquisite as her elocution. Climate change, she said immediately. I asked her what she thought she could do, physically or in other ways.

She loved cross country skiing. The 184-mile slug into DC on skis hadn't worn her out at all, as she had always cross-country skied around her woods whenever the snow allowed.

"It might be nice to go up to the North Pole," she said. "I could see it while there's still some ice up there. It's going fast, you know. Maybe we could do that to promote a good environmental bill, if there's one in Congress. You might call Al Gore and see what he thinks. It might cheer him up."

I let Maureen know about the conversation.

"I have no response to that," she said, using a favorite Meg Ryan line from a John Patrick Shanley film. John Passacantando of Greenpeace provided me with the very long-distance phone number of a Norwegian boat captain who had been taking activists close to the Pole from a port in Murmansk, Russia. My conversation with the captain was memorable. He first thought this old woman I was talking about wanted to go out on the ice to die. "People don't do that anymore," he said. I explained that she wanted to go there to bring attention to the thinning ice, not to die.

"Thinning ice isn't the problem. The *leads* are the problem," he said.

We were yelling into our phones, as he was talking over his ship's engine and the crash of the sea and we were no doubt connected through ten countries, Moscow and the NSA.

I asked him what *leads* are.

"They are the blue water channels between the ice. They are getting too wide," he said. "They are all over the place. Your friend could not ski there. It's too dangerous. It's all breaking apart. Tell her she is beautiful but there is no way to do this. I can show her things at the Pole or very near the Pole from my ship, but she cannot ski."

Doris was not interested in a sightseeing cruise. She asked me to get his address so she could send him a thank you note for his advice. She would instead go state-to-state, where invited, to promote campaign reform bills in legislatures. Groups were asking her to do that. She said she would write to the environmental groups in case they wanted her "to get arrested or an anything."

Mostly she worked with campaign and election reform organizations over the following two years to push through state measures. She made the difference in many efforts, drawing in the news cameras and the wider public. Those efforts kept her busy, but she was missing the road, and as it happened she was not finished with the road.

At Ken Hechler's insistence I had been making trips into the Appalachian coalfields to learn enough about coal to someday write about it. You know all about that. But the

Love and Democracy

first of those trips had been between the Senate and House passages of McCain—the time of the 9/11 attacks.

I was doing research in West Virginia in the first moments of it, staying in an old log cabin above Huntington. I woke from a bad dream that morning. In the dream, Maureen was in a gaggle of reporters outside the Arizona Supreme Court building when a terrorist bomb exploded, wounding her in the chest. Upon waking, I felt ill until I could convince myself it was just a dream and not a meaningful one. But I couldn't remember ever having a dream that heavy. I had been learning about the explosive destruction of countless mountaintops by coal companies. Mountains are feminine. It must just be that, with coal companies as terrorists. That was my interpretation for an hour.

It happened to be her birthday, and I didn't want to wake her in Phoenix with that dream. I went down the road to a little restaurant for an orange juice. Sipping it and watching their ceiling-mounted television, I started to pay attention as other customers began to stand and gather to watch closer. It was September 11, 2001, and we were watching in horror as terrorists attacked the World Trade Center—our own airplanes filled with our own people.

Like most people, I feared that there would be attacks all over the nation. I don't usually think of my dreams as predictive, but I did in that moment. I woke her up with a call to Phoenix and told her what was happening in New York. I asked her to please stay home. She said she could not do that on a big news day like the one clearly unfolding.

I told her about my nightmare. She was quiet.

"Stay away from any gaggle of reporters," I pleaded.

"Ok. Sure. I'll try."

Did she believe dreams? She was open minded. Before we met, she had attended a retreat in the San Juan Islands that was pretty New Age for her, and I think it changed her a bit.

I said I would fly back to Phoenix immediately, but of course that would not be possible for at least a week, as all US air travel was cancelled. I drove home instead.

Lauren was in her first week at college, and some of the students in her dorm were from New York City, waiting for news from their Wall Street parents. Austin was at home, still on summer break from college. Maureen woke him with the news.

He went to work that morning in the Phoenix coffee shop of his summer job. People from neighboring office buildings stayed watching television, not wanting to risk returning to their midrise towers, because fear had infected every city. That evening, Austin and Maureen forced themselves to go out for her birthday. They went to a Cheesecake Factory, which Austin remembers as surreal—like the restaurant scene from the film *Brazil* where a bomb goes off, but a divider panel is set up and the dining goes on.

Shortly after I arrived home, Maureen had scheduled a mammogram. I insisted on going with her, which I had never done before. I was still worried about my dream.

Something was found. She was sanguine about the diagnosis.

Her doctors of choice were in North Scottsdale, a long drive for us downtowners. On our first trip for a consultation there, I took a favorite route—I knew we would be making the trip many times.

We talked about the big decisions ahead for her, and then we were quiet for a few minutes.

"You know, it's not a bad way to go," she said, smiling bravely, I thought.

"Honey," I replied, "you caught this early; you're going to be fine. We're going to be fine."

"I meant Shea Boulevard," she said.

She told her editors about the diagnosis and said she wanted to cover her experience as any other medical story, because many women and families go through the experience, all facing the same hard decisions. A first-person account could be helpful, she argued. It turned out to be a great series, and she survived the cancer after surgery.

The story was in line with her coverage of aging Baby Boomers and end-of-life issues—I am slipping a few years back in time here, closer to when Maureen and I first met. She created that beat after her 1997 Stanford fellowship, where she studied those issues in depth. In her reporting she met doctors and experts who would come back to advise her own health decisions. Elisabeth Kubler-Ross was one of them. Maureen's reporting on the hard subject of aging and death was honored later by a ceremony at the Columbia School of Journalism.

One of her other expert sources was Dr. Gillian Hamilton, an MD and psychology PhD, and the chief medical officer at The Beatitudes, a well-regarded retirement and care center in Phoenix. Gillian was the friend Maureen called for advice when Doris was walking through Phoenix and a guest in our home. Over the years, Gillian introduced Maureen to several stories, including the story of twin 100-year-old women facing the fact that one of them would soon be alone for the first time in a century.

Gillian called late one evening to tell Maureen that the chief medical officer for the Lake Powell Recreation Area in Northern Arizona and Utah had told her that there were many drownings of young people at the lake, but he suspected they were carbon-monoxide deaths from kids playing behind and under houseboats. He said the operators of the recreation facilities didn't want to hear about it—the deaths were simple drowning deaths, as far as they were concerned. A big flap could scare away business. The doctor resigned.

Maureen instantly recognized this. In her years editing the Daytona paper, she often had to deal with city tourism officials and beachfront businesspeople who wanted to downplay shark attacks. She reported them anyway. This was the same story, as houseboat rentals are the whole economy at Lake Powell.

She and another reporter, Judd Slivka, went to the lake. Then Maureen found a Utah family who had lost their two boys. It would be a very difficult interview in their home, but she got them to agree to it. The story broke the issue wide open; hearings were held in Congress, a national recall of houseboats was ordered, many of which vented their engines in airspaces under the boats or behind them where children played. High smokestacks solved the problem. Houseboats worldwide were made safer. I was immensely proud of her, of course. How many children, how many families, had she saved? That's why you become a journalist, isn't it?

Interviewing Barry Goldwater's wife, Susan, one day in her Hospice of the Valley office, Maureen noticed a newspaper clipping on her desk. It was an op-ed about the centennial of the Spanish-American War and that war's role in Arizona statehood. Maureen stared at it for a moment, and Susan noticed her interest.

Love and Democracy

"I clipped it for Barry. He loves Arizona history, and this is a great piece," Susan said. She handed it to Maureen and asked if she had seen it.

"I have. I love that writer. Literally. He's my significant other," Maureen replied.

After that, Susan called me several times for help with her speeches. She was a national leader in the growing hospice movement and needed a collection of speeches for her travels.

About a year into this, in 1998, the year before I met Doris but when I was already involved in supporting McCain-Feingold and local election reforms, her husband, Barry, died. Susan asked me up to their house.

The Senator's signature dark-framed glasses were folded atop his personal desk on a raised area of the living room.

"I haven't moved them," Susan said quietly. She saw me looking at the glasses when she brought me a coffee.

The Goldwater home on Scorpion Hill overlooked central Phoenix. A fine telescope, a foot from his desk, was trained on the still-new downtown arena for the Cardinals.

"He watched its construction through that scope. He thought it was too massive for the Phoenix skyline," she said.

Susan had not spoken at Barry's recent funeral, but she had been asked to do so for an upcoming event in Scottsdale.

"There's too much to say about him, so I don't know where or how to begin," she said.

"I'm a serious Democrat, you know," I advised her. "I might not be the right person to write your eulogy for him."

"It's okay," she said. "I am, too. And I don't want a speech about politics; I want people to know who he was outside of politics."

I had only met him twice, both times at a private Phoenix dinner club and both times when he was quite sauced. But there were things I admired—his opinion about gays in the military, for example: He said if they could shoot straight, that was straight enough for him. Also, he didn't want men in Congress inserting themselves between women and their doctors—he was, in fact, one of the founders of the Phoenix chapter of Planned Parenthood. He desegregated the Arizona Air National Guard and then pushed the Pentagon for nationwide military desegregation, which happened.

People are complicated and never the caricature you think they are. He had supported the Civil Rights Acts of 1957 and 1960, supported the 24th Amendment to the Constitution, which prohibited poll taxes, but he voted against the Civil Rights Act of 1964, disagreeing with Title II and Title VII, which prohibit discrimination on both sides of the lunch counter.

In the middle of our conversation, Susan received an emergency call from her hospice organization.

"I'll be back in an hour or two. Just make yourself at home. Look around. Nothing's off limits. Get a sense of him," and she left, driving out past the Senator's ham radio shack I had seen coming in, where Barry and volunteers had helped American soldiers talk to their families during the pre-Internet Vietnam War—a 24-hour operation during all those years.

There was a portrait of Barry in the hallway—an original oil by Norman Rockwell. Near the living room was a pie-shaped storage closet where the Senator built model airplanes—the plastic kind that kids build. Dozens were on shelves, and the last plane was unfinished on his worktable. The painted details were the work of a shaking hand. The chairman of the Senate Armed Services Committee liked model airplanes.

When he was still healthy, he would fly a small plane up to the Navajo and Hopi reservations where he took photo portraits of the people, expressing the dignity of these Americans. When he was a little boy, his mother, a nurse who had jumped a train to come to Arizona, would drive him to the Phoenix Indian School to see the flag raised and meet students and teachers. His respect for Native Americans was, I believe, a way of honoring and communicating with his late mother. He had lifelong friends in Native communities. Susan loved flying with him over Arizona to take his photos and see the beauty, and he told her the history of every feature below.

He seemed to live in the present moment, which is what confident, comfortable people do. Flying is very much about the moment. Model building, too, is all about the building, not about the finished thing. Photography is the containment of a present moment. A soldier finally getting time on the radiotelephone with a sweetheart or family is a present moment.

We talked about that when Susan returned. I suggested a speech that became "Seven Things About Barry." His centeredness in the present moment was one of the seven.

So, yes, a liberal can write a warm speech about an arch-conservative—maybe not in some countries, but here, because America is a state of grace where that sort of thing is possible—if not right now, then again and soon.

Goldwater's respect for Native Americans was, for me, the main connection I had with his otherwise very different mind. When there was a Goldwater's Department Store in Phoenix, built on land that had been my grandfather's dairy farm, there was a two-story wall you would look at as the escalators took you up or down. The wall was filled with his collection of Kachina dolls. Collecting them now may be frowned upon as religious appropriation, but I am rather sure that Goldwater collected them with great respect for Native religion and certainly not for profit, and probably mostly as gifts from the artists. The collection—now in the Heard Museum—is stunning.

My own connection with Arizona's tribal nations is complex. My great-grandfather came to Arizona as an Army sergeant during the Indian Wars. The comforts of my life are the spoils of a genocide, and I am conscious of that and let it adjust my politics, donating to Native candidates for office and in other ways.

During my years at an ad agency, I had an opportunity to do something respectful if not remedial: One of my clients was the secure communications division of Motorola, makers of the encrypted telephones that generals use to talk to the Pentagon and that the Pentagon uses to talk to the White House. Motorola was coming out with a new model, and my assignment was to make sure everyone in the Pentagon knew about the new, improved model. Since Native American Code Talkers had sent their coded messages on Motorola walkie-talkies during World War II, I asked surviving Code Talkers if they would send one more message, this time on Motorola's new phone, communicating directly to the top brass. It would be a commemoration of their 50th anniversary as a unit, and it would be the most secure message ever sent, anywhere.

They asked around the community of fellow Code Talkers, then said yes. One of them, too ill to travel, would stay in Arizona to initiate the call, and the rest of them—

Love and Democracy

35—would go to Washington with their wives to receive and decode the official last Code Talker message.

It was a great event. The men wore bright yellow shirts, sharp caps and Marine Corps emblems. Their wives wore full traditional native dress—big skirts and gorgeous turquoise necklaces.

I asked their leader to pen the message but was asked to do it for them.

"We sent a million messages in the War, Dennis but we didn't write them, so you write it."

The message was one of peace and its responsibilities. Peaceniks like me don't get many opportunities to pen a note to the Pentagon brass that they will have to sit and hear with rapt attention, so I took the shot.

The message was indeed sent and received on the new Motorola phone at a standing-room-only event at the National Press Club in Washington, with the New York Times and the Washington Post in the front row. It was followed by a reception in the D Ring—the inner sanctum—of the Pentagon for all the gray, long-haired Code Talkers and their wives, Joint Chiefs Chairman Colin Powell, several senators including McCain, Navajo Nation president Peterson Zah, and Motorola's CEO. It was a perfect event for Motorola, but it was also the beginning of a wider disclosure of the heroism of the Code Talkers, whose very existence had been unnecessarily kept secret for decades after the War. At the time of this event, 1992, they were still unknown to most Americans. The first Hollywood movie about them was still years away, as were their overdue honors at the White House.

Maureen discovered my involvement in the event—I hadn't bragged about it, and it was getting to be my ancient history—when a Christmas card arrived one year from one of the Code Talkers.

"How do you happen to know a Code Talker?" she asked.

"Just a PR event," I replied, or something like that. But she thought it was cool, and I was relieved she didn't see it as a cheap stunt. It certainly wasn't.

I rarely talked about advertising or PR stories with her, unless they were funny, like how I put the owner of a new Danish furniture store on radio ads when you could barely understand his English through his excited Danish accent. It was a hugely successful campaign, as the only message of these otherwise incomprehensible ads was that this man is truly Arizona's Danish furniture guy.

It taught me a lesson about the power of authenticity, which is usually a more powerful message than anything said. That, believe it or not, was Donald Trump's early magic with so many voters. He was authentically a bull in a china shop, and that's all many supporters wanted of him. If you want to reach such voters, you must first knock down a considerable shelf of champagne glassware yourself.

The year of Goldwater's death was also the year I chaired the local Common Cause chapter and helped pass the *Clean Elections* Arizona ballot initiative. The program makes it possible to run and win a political campaign without the use of the big donations that usually come with strings attached. Under the program, if you can get a certain number of $5 donations to demonstrate that you are a serious candidate with a following—which generally means that you have done some good in the community—the state will fund your campaign with a grant. It is simply the public funding of campaigns, using dollars collected from criminal and civil fines, not tax dollars.

It's hardly a perfect idea, but the alternative at the time was to let the rich buy our candidates out from under us, which is not democracy. As a part of that reform effort, I audited every campaign contribution made to Arizona's legislative candidates. Seventy-seven percent of the dollars were connected to lobbyists representing special interests. I did the audit because the first rule is to have your facts straight.

Too much backstory, I know. Almost finished. I want to mention a lesson for reformers.

We pushed the "Clean Elections" ballot initiative at the moment we did because Arizona had just experienced a major campaign money scandal. It was called AzScam, which name was taken from the earlier federal scandal, AbScam. In each, someone connected with a prosecutor's office posed as a rich person wanting to buy votes or political protection. Both scandals sent elected officials to jail. When the political moment comes when a reform can work, you want to have a ready-to-wear reform available. We looked at Maine's public financing victory and refashioned it for Arizona.

Our ballot initiative was approved by Arizona voters in 1998 and has survived U.S. Supreme Court challenges in the years since. It's still up and running today, providing resources, enforcement, and voter education on candidates and issues. It funds fewer campaigns than it did in its first years, mostly because the US Supreme Court whittled down one of its provisions. But there is now another option for funding campaigns without fatcat donations—something not imagined when we wrote the law in 1998: small, legal, political donations via social media.

The first major national campaign that was funded with small donations was DeanSpace, the Drupal-powered electronic organizing side of Howard Dean's presidential campaign. It was created by a core of young progressives, including Zack Rosen, Kieran Lal, and the electronics wiz of Common Cause, Nicco Mele.

Nicco told me on several occasions that, to him, the proof that social media could drive a political campaign was Doris's walk across America and our organizing around her to get McCain-Feingold passed.

After the Dean campaign, Nicco and his tech friends improved the platform as CivicSpace, the technology that got the Obama campaign "all fired up." DeanSpace and its improvements not only made fundraising easier, but helped people organize all over the country with a common strategy, common talking points, walking lists and action reports.

I still hear from Nicco now and then. His central piece of political advice then and now is, Things Will Get Crazier. So far, he has been right.

Because of these social media young wizards, the Democrats were far ahead of the Republicans in social media outreach and small-dollar fundraising—at least until Trump came along with fiction-based politics to exploit grievance storylines, which are sold like torrid romance novels to grievance-addicted donors.

Another interesting thing about the Dean campaign was that my son, Austin, was a part of it. He had just graduated from college and landed on our couch. When asked what was interesting to him, he mentioned the Dean campaign. Maureen reminded him of the fact that he had a pickup truck parked in the driveway, and I pointed in the general direction of Burlington, Vermont, Dean's headquarters. He was gone the next day.

Austin learned skills and met people in that campaign that grew into his career in political research and strategy. In another campaign after the Dean scream, Austin met his wife, Elanna. They have two brilliant kids and live in occupied D.C. All kinds of bad political outcomes had to happen for that happy family result.

I need to connect a few dots here. The Dean Campaign was in 2004, but I want to back up just for a moment to the year of Goldwater's death, 1998. During that year, in addition to pushing the Clean Elections reform for Arizona, I was one of many people pushing for passage of the McCain-Feingold Bipartisan Campaign Reform Act, as I have described. I had our Common Cause members camp around the clock in front of the Phoenix office of John Kyl, Arizona's other US senator, trying to get him to cosign McCain's bill. It wasn't happening, but we kept our protest going.

Because his campaign finance reform bill was the big fight in Congress, McCain was the reigning voice in Arizona and elsewhere for campaign reform. We knew, from some of his comments, that he was not in favor of the public funding of campaigns, and we knew that he could scuttle our Clean Elections ballot initiative with one comment to one reporter. So, we kept the campaign a bit under the radar and hoped for the best.

"You should just go talk to him," Maureen told me. "People have a harder time saying no, face to face, and you can be very convincing. He's usually in Phoenix on the weekends. He knows what you've been doing for his bill. Besides, you've talked to him before."

I had gone to him when I had the idea of sending a mailing to all of Jon Kyl's donors, arguing for them to contact Kyl to endorse McCain's bill. I didn't know if it was kosher or legal to do that.

"Whatever it takes," was McCain's reply and sort of his life motto.

So, I made an appointment to ask him to not kill a reform that I knew he would rather see killed. I sat down across from him in his Phoenix office. White-shirted aides were buzzing through his office. I told him we understood that the public financing of campaigns was not his preferred method of campaign reform, but, on account of our working hard for his bill, maybe he would consider waving off the questions he would surely get from the press with a response like "ballot measures are local issues, so I'll leave it to Arizona voters."

He just stared at me for a moment. I thought I might have offended him or shocked him with my political naivety. But then he pushed a newspaper clipping across his desk and turned it toward me.

It was the article I wrote a few months earlier about the Spanish-American War's key role in Arizona's quest for statehood—the same article Susan Goldwater had clipped for Barry.

I didn't know at the time that McCain's hero was Theodore Roosevelt, a central character in the long article. His affection for TR is probably why McCain had a ranch in the Verde Valley, north of Phoenix. If you know someone's hero, you can deal with them more successfully, because you can frame your issue accordingly. Mine was by accident.

Near the end of the article, I wrote that I had visited the cluster of graves of the Roosevelt Rough Riders, including many Arizonans, in Arlington Cemetery. That visit was on a very rainy Washington D.C. day on my way to some Common Cause meeting. The rain came up as a surprise, so I didn't have an umbrella. This was before we all had weather radar in our pockets. I took refuge on the porch of the Custis-Lee Mansion on a hill in the cemetery. The place was built by slave labor and is now called the

Arlington House, withdrawing honor from Robert E. Lee. My business suit was soaked.

I then fell through something of a time tunnel.

Three women in antebellum hoop skirts leaned out the front door. "Come in here, young man, or you'll catch your death of cold!" one or all of them said.

They were costumed volunteers for that museum house, and they had no visitors except me on account of the rain.

They took my coat to dry it somewhere and probably to keep me there. They sat me in front of a fire and brought me tea. I explained my mission, and they helped me figure out my rain-soaked map of the cemetery. When my coat was dry and the rain had turned to a drizzle, I bid them farewell without encouraging their rebel cause.

They stood on the porch and waved, one of them calling after me, "We do hope you find your people!"

I didn't put all that in the article, but I did include the fact that, when I finally found the graves hidden by overgrown shrubs, I could barely read the names through the corrosion.

"Listen," McCain said as he punched the article on his desk, "I want you to know that, after reading this, I had those graves cleaned and polished. I want you to know that."

I sat back in a moment of silence.

"Does that mean we have a deal?" I asked.

"Yes," he said. I shook his hand and got out of there before anything could change.

But things change. Deals can go awry. Ellen Miller, then the head of the D.C.-based organization Public Campaign, had offered to raise most of the money we would need for our ballot initiative. It came with a string: She would send, and we would hire, a campaign manager from D.C. People in D.C. don't think people outside the Beltway can win reforms without them, even though we nearly always win and they nearly always lose.

But Josh, the young man Ellen sent, was a good manager—a good organizer who made only one mistake. Against my advice, he agreed to have coffee with a particular woman reporter from the town's alternative newspaper. I told Josh to be very careful.

I told Maureen about the coming meeting, and she made the sign of the cross.

The reporter asked Josh why our campaign didn't have an endorsement from Mr. Campaign Finance Reform himself, John McCain.

Josh told her it was a local issue, so we weren't expecting it.

Have you even asked for it?

He said we wanted to keep it local.

The conversation was along those lines. They ordered food. When some of the walls came down after personal stories—and Josh has remarkable ones, including a swimming escape from attacking natives along the Amazon River that killed his friend—the reporter said something like, between you and me, why is McCain staying out of it? I imagine her leaning in and implying that it will be off the record.

Josh offered after relentless prodding that, yes, McCain associated himself with campaign reforms after getting caught red-handed in the Keating Five scandal, where he had taken large donations from Charlie Keating in exchange for protection from prosecution. Josh offered that McCain probably didn't really care about reform. But they were talking as friends, now, right?

Her article reported Josh's remarks.

Love and Democracy

I had just picked up Austin from his high school and was letting him drive us home—he was in the first months of his learner's permit. I got a cell phone call. Shouts were coming out of the little speaker so violently that I held the phone at a distance. I had been expecting the call because the weekly tabloid had just hit the racks.

"Who is that?" Austin whispered as he drove.

"It's your senator," I whispered back.

All I said to McCain in that moment was that I understood the problem, that I considered it a disaster, and would he please take a call from me in about thirty minutes? He paused but then said he would and abruptly hung up.

The deal was surely off, but I made a flurry of calls to my board members and to Ellen in D.C.

I called McCain back within the thirty minutes and he took the call.

After my apology for the interview. I told him, accurately, that Josh would be on a plane back to D.C. before high noon the next day, and we would manage the campaign locally. I also told him that Arizona Common Cause would that evening be naming the senator as our public official of the year for his leadership on campaign reform.

Pause on the phone. Long pause.

"Okay, Dennis," he said and hung up. The deal stayed on, and we went on to narrowly win the ballot campaign.

If there is a political lesson in this, I'm not sure what it is, other than you should keep your board members on speed dial if that's even a thing now. Otherwise, Arizona would not have the Clean Elections system it now has. A thumb's down from him would have done us in. It was not my finest Truth to Power moment, but it worked to serve the greater good.

When I remember McCain, I remember my father's admiration of him.

Dad often volunteered for McCain. They became friends because Dad just did that with everyone. For example, when he was in pharmacy school in Denver, Mel Tormé was singing in a club. Dad and his pharmacy school friends met him over several evenings. Being Dad, the friendship took and was lifelong. One Christmas, Dad brought home some chestnuts and asked our house guest, composer Buddy Pepper—composer of "Vaya Con Dios" and many movie themes and a friend from Dad's high school days—if he knew how they could roast chestnuts by the open fire of the fireplace.

"Call Mel, it's his song," Buddy said to Dad, who also went by Bud or Buddy because his given name was Beverly.

So, they called Mel, who said, "Hell, I just sing the songs, guys. I have no idea."

Dad overcooked the chestnuts.

It wasn't unusual, then, that McCain called Dad one day, looking for help. He had a big rally planned in Tempe for his reelection launch. The senator wanted Native Americans represented among the speakers, but Republican Native Americans were hard to find, just as they are today. McCain knew that our family goes way back in Arizona, while McCain himself was a carpetbagger.

Dad's best friend in the years near the end of his life was an Akimel O'odham man named Jose Ramon. Dad asked Jose if he would speak at a McCain rally. He reminded Dad that he was a Democrat but said he would do it out of friendship.

Love and Democracy

At the rally, Jose took his turn at the microphone and looked over the large crowd. He stared quizzically at a big banner that stretched across the third-floor windows of one of the buildings surrounding the plaza. It read, "This Land is Your Land."

Jose shook his head and said, "Huh, I thought it was my land." The crowd roared. I think he made a few remarks about McCain being an honorable man.

And he was, at least when it didn't conflict with "whatever it takes."

Not long after that McCain event, Jose's family performed traditional hoop dances at the annual Indian Fair at the Heard Museum. After the dance, Jose called my mother and father up to the stage to receive some handmade gifts. Jose said they were family. Dad was his brother. I had never seen my father so moved. Dad's grandfather, the first Dennis Burke in our line, had come to Arizona with the U.S. Army to hunt down Geronimo, and here were the descendants of both sides of the Indian Wars now standing there as best friends. That seemed very American to me, at least the America of our aspirations.

In New Hampshire at that same time, an 89-year-old woman was preparing to do something to support her own aspirations for America, but in a quite different way. And because everything connects, I should mention that Doris had for years been hooking rugs and selling them for cash that she then sent to Arizona tribes in need.

Bishop's Gambit

Austin and Lauren were now away in college. The anti-gerrymandering ballot measure had passed in Arizona. McCain-Feingold was signed into law. Maureen and I thought it might be time to live for a few years in a bigger city, such as New York, Boston, Chicago, or San Francisco. She thought she would enjoy working for a bigger newspaper and I thought a big city might be good for my writing. We loved museums and shows. My agent was sending me books to co-write that could be co-written from anywhere.

During Maureen's Knight Fellowship at Stanford, a journalism thing, she made several good friends at the Boston Globe who had ever since been encouraging her to work for their paper. She started that process and I began looking for opportunities in Boston for myself—as new writers need day jobs. I got an immediate offer from a venerable peace and justice organization there, but I would have to start immediately. I took it. At that same moment, newspapers nationally went into a financial funk and stopped hiring—Craigslist and the Internet had been pulling the advertising rug out from under them. Maureen was stuck in Phoenix, and I was alone in Boston.

I would remain in Boston long enough to handle the group's organizing against the imminent U.S. invasion of Iraq—a country that had no role in 9/11 but was being targeted by the Bush-Halliburton Administration for its oil and because Suni-dominant Saudia Arabia wanted our military bases out of its country and moved to a nice place like Iraq, where we could keep the Shia-dominant government under our thumb and out of their way.

I rented a bedroom on Beacon Hill from a good guy, Joe Davis, who had posted the room on a neighborhood grocer's bulletin board. Joe had barely escaped with his life from the World Trade Center on 9/11 and was still recovering emotionally from that. His building on Beacon Hill had a roof deck where I could see the whole town as I talked with Maureen each evening. The view was of the purple-lit cables of the big bridge over the Charles and the gold breast of the state capitol.

One morning, soon after starting the job, I was in the home of a Rockefeller—the husband of a Rockefeller, anyway. I was there to pick up a donation he had promised, and he wanted to meet the new guy.

"People like me keep writing these checks, you know, but nothing ever seems to change," he said as he signed the check and handed it to me. "Why is that?" he added.

"Because you don't give nearly enough," I said, setting the check down in case he wanted to snatch it back.

"Is that what you think?" he asked.

"I do think we are like toy trains to some donors," I said. "They only give us enough to keep us going 'round and 'round but not enough to make a dent in the status quo, which happens to serve them pretty nicely."

He gave me a cold stare for the longest time and then laughed.

"Well, you may have something there." He pushed the check back toward me and told me to have a good day. I took the check, as our little train needed fuel.

Boston is a cold place for an Arizonan, and I missed Maureen terribly, but it was a rich experience. I got to see how Eastern and Western progressives are very different: Easterners are very proud of their stern positions, and they take their defeats as honorable scars. Westerners are proud of their compromises, alliances, and victories.

The difference in friendliness between Phoenix and Boston was also a hard adjustment. I was walking to the Massachusetts State Capitol building one morning with our chief organizer. I figured that, as a people person, he could tell me why the folks we passed on sidewalks never returned my smile or a Hi. Was it the cold? The hurry of the city?

"Why do you smile at them? You don't even know them," he replied.

I did appreciate the town's political seriousness. I was amazed the first time I rode the Red Line train between Cambridge and my Boston Commons office. Every passenger on the train was reading Foreign Affairs, The Economist, or a literary or science publication—not a tabloid in sight.

It was thrilling to be embedded in historic Boston. From my fire escape I looked down to Park Street Church, where William Lloyd Garrison had preached an end to slavery. His words of non-violent change made their way to Ruskin in England, then from Ruskin to Tolstoy in Russia, and then from Russia to Gandhi in South Africa and India, and from Gandhi to America via MLK, and from him to people like all of us, right back on the doorstep of that very church.

As my father's mother was a Warren and had often bragged of being a descendant of Joseph Warren, a founding father, I had an interest in exploring Boston's "Freedom Trail." My research said our guy was only a brother of Joseph, but I took that as close enough.

I found the window where the townspeople passed Uncle Joseph bodily into the crowded Old South Meeting House so he could make one of the great speeches leading to the Revolution. I had a drink or two in the Green Dragon, named for the original North End pub where much of that Revolution was hatched. I held my hand against the door of Paul Revere's house—which still stands in the North End—and imagined the evening when Dr. Warren knocked on it to send Revere on his ride to Concord. I felt the beauty and emotion of standing in Faneuil Hall, where so many, from Sam Adams to John Kennedy, delivered great speeches. I could not at the time imagine that Doris would be speaking there in less than a year, via the strangest turn of our story.

In Boston, my group was involved in substantial work against the Iraq invasion. We managed large protests locally and sent 100 busloads of protesters to the big protest march in New York City. Lauren came to that one with some of her college friends, so we marched together like old times—like the MLK Holiday marches in Phoenix when she was little.

I did some lobbying on Capitol Hill on the issue, sometimes crossing paths with the chief weapons inspector, an American, who was telling members of Congress that there was no point in invading Iraq, as his team had full access to wherever they wanted to go in Iraq—they had never been turned down by the Iraqi government any time they wanted to immediately inspect any area. They had found no weapons of mass destruction or anything close, and if anyone in the U.S. Government or its military had a better idea as to where they should search, he said they would and could go search there right now, which would be easier than sending in Marines to blow up people and things.

Every member of Congress who voted for that war knew there were no weapons of mass destruction in Iraq. Morally, it was the worst vote many of them would ever make, costing hundreds of thousands of lives and costing Kerry and Hillary the White House, as enough Eastern progressives stayed home on election day or went with Nader or some other spoiled spoiler.

I met Nader a couple of times. Didn't like his attitude. We were in a meeting room at the Carnegie Endowment once, planning an arrest or something, when he popped in. Someone asked him if he would be willing to get arrested for whatever it was—peace or campaign reform.

"No. That's not what I do," he replied. "I file lawsuits."

It sounded like admirable frankness, but it was not the truth. He had not stuck to lawsuits when he ran for president as a spoiler, sending Bush into the White House.

I also lunched a time or two with Jill Stein. Very nice person. Hate what she did in several elections.

Back to the Iraq War: Because Senator John Kerry represented Massachusetts, we were trying to get his attention and get him to oppose the coming Iraq Invasion. He would not meet, so we were having people stand in his Boston office until arrested. At one point, I had a bishop willing to get arrested.

I called the Boston Police Department and talked to the officer in charge of dealing with protests. I told him that the only time we could get the bishop was, unfortunately, during rush hour, and we needed to do it on a public street to assure arrest, but we could do it on a side street, as Cambridge Street would have high traffic at that time.

He was silent for a moment. These are his exact next words, because how could I forget them?

"You got a bishop?"

"Yes. *The* bishop."

Love and Democracy

"Listen... the bishop, you say? You don't want to do something like that on a side street. I mean, that's what we're here for. We can handle the traffic. Do it right."

On a Friday evening in May of 2003, two months after the start of the Iraq Invasion and the failure of our protests, I was working on and off with Frances Moore Lappé in Cambridge. Frances was a former board member of Common Cause and is the author of the famous environmental book, *Diet for a Small Planet*. Richard Rowe, her boyfriend, dropped in one day with some interesting data from the very reputable pollster Celinda Lake, whom I had relied upon for both our successful Arizona ballot initiatives. The data showed that there were huge numbers of working women who would vote Democratic if they could just get time off to register.

I made a copy of the data and went over to the Charles Hotel to rent a car. I ran into the Dalai Lama in the lobby, which I took as a good sign—you really must take it as a good sign when you run into the Dalai Lama. The car rental clerk who had been helping me at a lobby desk sort of melted into a standing yoga pose when an elevator door opened behind me. I turned and there he was. I was close enough to shake the Dalai Lama's hand, if one did that. One doesn't. I watched the holy man move through the lobby as everyone, I think without even meaning to, stopped in silence and bowed their heads.

Thus blessed, plus and I had also seen Robert Reich in the hotel restaurant, I made the quick drive to New Hampshire to show the report to Doris and Jim and to a gathering of friends who were due there.

"Very interesting," Doris said as she looked at the numbers. "I suppose we should do something about it?"

On Doris's back porch that evening—a wooden bridge that extended into her woods—were Texans Molly Ivins, Betsy Moon, Jim Hightower, Ronnie Dugger and a few others.

Ronnie, a Texas Observer founding journalist and biographer of LBJ, was saying, as we looked over Doris's woods and creek, that the coming election would be a turning point, and that if Bush got reelected, we would be cooked as a country.

The American Republic turned out to be more durable than that, maybe, but Ronnie was right that we needed to do everything possible to elect someone decent.

Molly was a California-born grad of Smith and the Colombia School of Journalism who, after a news career in Texas that included syndication by the New York Times, had become so Texan that she remained its best voice for the rest of her too-short life. She was in New England for some tests that didn't come out well. But she was funny on that porch, and she agreed with Ronnie that another Bush term would a Bush too far.

Wine was involved. Everyone agreed that they would do whatever it might take to help the Democratic candidate win the White House. Lots of Democrats were running, John Kerry, John Edwards, Howard Dean, Wesley Clark, Dennis Kucinich, Al Sharpton, Carol Moseley Braun, Dick Gephardt, and even Joe Lieberman—any of them better than W. The main project would be to get out the vote.

I drove Hightower to his book event in Vermont the next day. We were in a little black VW Cabrio with the top down. He held his cowboy hat on the whole way. I took that as symbolic of the wild ride coming: Doris, Jim, and I were considering another adventure. We were calling it Working Women Vote.

Love and Democracy

I did call Maureen about it first. She liked the part about the Dalai Lama. She was not crazy about a new road adventure that would keep me away, but she knew the coming election was vital and that all this was part of my new writing life.

She was still reporting and editing for the Arizona Republic and managing the remodeling of our house. She was emailing me color schemes, hardwood floor images, and a few ideas for rooms to be opened up. The separation of a few thousand miles during home remodeling is not a bad way to do it, as you get to be excited by a big reveal every time you fly home, and the rest of it is emails of encouragement.

Maureen looked for ways to make my new project work for us.

"How about two or three weeks on the road, then a week home, back and forth like that until the election?" she said. "We have a ton of frequent flier miles."

With that modified green light, I raised some money for Working Women Vote. So did Doris's son. In the three years since Jim and I met we had become good friends and were always seeing political moments and opportunities the same way. He knew his mother's limits, that she wanted to stay relevant and engaged, and that she didn't mind if a worthwhile adventure might use her up. Her opinion was that she just might register the one voter who turns the tide.

What did we have to work with? Doris's supporters around the country were a resource. Her story and her remarkable energies were also resources. But what might she do? She certainly couldn't walk across all the critical swing states.

We had her old support van. I suggested that we could drive into a city where she would do some local walking with voter registration volunteers. She could take over the jobs of working women long enough for them to register to vote. We would push that story to newspapers, radio, and television to put pressure on voter registration officials to make registration easier for working people, and to encourage women to register. We could focus on big media markets. We could spend time in states that were truly in play—it was clear that the election would be decided in the margins.

At the age of 92, could Doris still command media attention, and would her message to working women be persuasive? The message would be, "If I can do this for my country at my age, you can surely figure out how to get registered to vote."

We could meet with voter registration friends and volunteers along the way to get everyone fired up.

As it turned out, no news editor could, or would, turn us down, as the stories we offered were visual, zany, and easy to explain. Write those three things down for the next time you need press.

We would tour the critical swing states east of the Mississippi, then give Doris a rest back in New Hampshire for a couple of weeks, then hit the swing states of the West. That was the general plan, though it got interrupted.

The support vehicle Ken Hechler donated for her long walk had been moldering under leaves next to Doris's house—Ken had not wanted it back. Jim cleaned it up and had some repairs made, though it tended to overheat.

"The van might or might not make it," he said. "Like Ma."

The vehicle was a small, older class C motorhome, meaning just a bit larger than a camper on a pickup truck. Inside, it had a bed loft over the cab, a dinette that folded into a bed, a tiny kitchen, a tinier bathroom, and a larger bed in the back. Outside, it was a stained beige blob after too many sandstorms and blizzards and those several winters in the snowy woods. As a political visual, it would not do at all. But my plan was to make an early stop in Asheville, North Carolina, where I thought we could recruit artists to make the vehicle special.

To honor Don Quixote's trusty steed and John Steinbeck's hardy camper truck of the same name, we rechristened the van Rocinante, which we soon shortened to Rosie. The nickname stuck, especially after a self-described Ashevillain painted Rosie the Riveter on the port side.

On the first day of the project, the ugly van pulled up to my Boston apartment. Jim was driving and Doris waved from a window. I jumped in—my stuff now reduced to one duffle bag, a laminated map of the nation, and felt markers to plan our routes.

To formally launch *Working Women Vote!* Doris was invited to make an atrium speech at Harvard's Kennedy School of Government. She had worked at Harvard as a young girl, checking lunch tickets in the dining hall, and had come back now as the center of attention.

The previous atrium speaker had been Lech Walesa, the president of Poland and a hero of democracy. In describing the critical days of the Solidarity Movement at the Gdansk Shipyards, he had said, "There are special places where you can feel the future." That's how we felt. Everyone we knew was organizing to make the coming election mean something. The Harvard students, layered on balconies around her, gave Doris a cheering ovation to send her on her way. After the speech, we walked over to the Charles Hotel for a drink with Betsy Moon, who was in town with Molly, and we ran into ice cream magnate

Ben Cohen, right where I had seen the Dali Lama a few weeks earlier. Ben was a Doris fan, though we never got any ice cream out of him.

A young reporter from the Harvard Crimson interviewed Doris. He asked if her political involvement was new. She described her work to stop the use of H-bombs in Alaska in 1960. He asked about her new project, and how it would compare to her long walk of 1999-2000.

"I find that if you make a real effort, people give you the time of day and will listen to your message. Political leadership, even at my modest level, is about sacrifice. That's what Gandhi taught us, and King."

He asked if she identified with Forrest Gump. She reminded him that while she shared a love of chocolate with the character, her work was not comic—that she had flipped the position of major newspapers, that thousands of people had walked with her, and that a bill had passed Congress.

In the few years since we met, she had blossomed into a seasoned political leader and one of the preeminent spokespeople for democracy. She understood that the preservation of democracy must always be a seduction of sorts—requiring honesty, humor, and selfless dedication.

After her Harvard speech, we drove out of Boston as if leaving its harbor for a year's sail. We were heading into the wild winds of the 2003-2004 election, with peace, democracy, and nature in the wind.

We stopped in New Haven to dine and spend a night with my daughter, a junior already. Lauren had recently returned from a close call in Guatemala, where she had spent her summer helping villagers get an economic foothold and to resist the so-called free trade agreements that was impoverishing local farmers. Three gunmen rushed through her front door of their little office and forced her and another young woman to lay down on the basement floor, a blanket covering their heads. The men with guns were rifling the files of the group's little office. The girls got through a basement window and over splintery fences to safety. Remarkably, I first heard of it from an Amnesty International alert. She was now planning a trip to Miami, where protests would oppose the same free trade agreements. All this was Bush's doing.

I had insisted that she visit the school's counseling office, as she had suffered a traumatic experience.

"I did, Dad, but, you know, I was sitting there, looking at this lady who was expecting me to complain about my boyfriend or my class load or my dorm mates, and, I don't know, I just don't think what I said made any sense to her."

Watching my daughter at dinner and thinking about the seriousness of the times stirred me. A few months earlier, my son had graduated and was now in Vermont with the Dean campaign, as I mentioned. He was up there working twenty-hour days and nights.

I knew we were not alone as a politicized American family. My daughter had been in college only a few days when the 9/11 attack occurred. It colored all her years there and changed many students from art majors to political science. The CIA had a busy recruitment desk in the careers department.

I gave her a goodbye hug in the morning and told her to be careful in Miami. She correctly predicted that the Miami Police would overreact. Indeed, they would fire on students with eye-gouging rubber bullets, even as the students were trying to peacefully follow police instructions. Hundreds were rounded up and bused to jail, with their personal gear and ID's left in the street to be run over by paddy wagons and regular traffic. The right to peaceably petition our government was being shredded.

The Power of Story

I should pause here to tell you how the kids got into great colleges. If you have young kids or grandkids or nieces and nephews, you will want to hear this. It offers a lesson in politics, too, and that lesson is this: stories are power. Story is one of the great political powers. Others include authenticity, sacrifice, communication—but this is about story.

Maureen had been concerned—this was before we married—that my small income working for nonprofits wouldn't go far toward two college tuitions. She explained that the most expensive colleges happen to have the best financial aid packages and so I should encourage the kids to aim high. She encouraged them, too. Even before our fourth or fifth date, she took Lauren to see a film version of *Pride and Prejudice* to help her write a better paper on the book.

She was our in-house advisor on so many things, and I was a big believer in bringing in the experts. I had brought in Celina Lake for our ballot battles, and the Brennan Center, and Joe Trippi. When Austin was a struggling early teen, I remembered that, when I was his kid, there used to be a book called *How to Pick Up Girls* advertised in the back of hot rod magazines. I had never ordered it but always wished I had. I did some research for Austin. The book was long out of print, but I located the author, and older retired man in New York somewhere. I bought an hour on the phone with him for Austin. They had a great conversation about how to actively listen and care and show respect and mean it. It helped Austin get started on the right foot when he was maybe a year from starting high school.

A few years later, for his senior high school project, Austin researched Steinbeck's *Tortilla Flat*. In that book, the characters believe that buried pirate treasure will glow brightly from under the forest soil on certain moonlit nights. The characters think they find something, but it turns out to be brass, not gold—a geological survey marker, stamped: *"United States Geodetic Survey—1915—Elevation 600 Feet."*

Austin's paper asked a question: As Steinbeck often wrote from his own experience and because he was known to take daily hikes, and because there was a large hill near his home in Monterrey, might that marker be a real thing that he often saw and that might still be there?

He corresponded with the U.S. Geological Survey Office, and they sent him some old maps. They told him that recordkeeping of the older markers was poor, and they had no record of the marker in question. He also corresponded with the most respected Steinbeck expert he could find, Martha Heasley Cox, at San Jose State, who thought his question was a very good one and wrote him a nice letter telling him so.

After seeing Professor Cox's letter, Maureen said that Austin and I should get on an airplane and go find the marker. I believe she was thinking ahead to his college application essays as a secondary thing, the first being that this would be a good father-son moment. She was always looking for those because she was an agent of love in the world.

Austin and I did get on a plane. We found the house where Steinbeck wrote and the hill where he hiked. Equipped with topo maps and an altimeter, we found where the marker would have been, had the Army not carved off that part of the hill for a commissary. So, no marker. But his senior paper was nevertheless stellar.

A year later, as a new student in a literature course at Stanford, his professor, when he heard Austin's name for the first time, said, "Oh, the Steinbeck guy." His paper had made the rounds, even beyond the admissions staff.

We got a useful glimpse of the whole admission process when we were with Austin at his admit-day event at Stanford. We were in an auditorium full of accepted new students and their parents. The moderator introduced himself and said, in essence, you don't know us, but, boy, do we know you. Your applications and essays are dogeared and full of our margin notes. We have passed them back and forth over our office partitions with comments like, "You have got to see this kid."

In that moment I understood how Austin's application had charmed them. I knew that Lauren, coming up next in the sweepstakes, needed to understand the work culture of the admissions people—they can't help but compete to find the most interesting kids, and you must support them with good material for their quest. Like politics, it's show business. Story is everything.

Two years later she was a freshman at Yale and working in a New Haven coffee shop. She overheard some college staffers at one of the tables talking enough about their department for Lauren to know they were in Admissions. She interrupted them to promote one of her younger friends who had recently sent in an application. The women complimented her for her respectful approach and her compelling pitch on behalf of her friend. One of the women asked Lauren's name.

"Ah, Lauren Burke. Gun-shaped cookies," the woman said. It was a reference to the fact that, a year after Columbine when Lauren was a junior in Phoenix's North

High, a member of the Arizona Legislature introduced a bill that would have required all teachers to tote guns. Lauren and her school chums from the Drama Club set up a table and banner on the Arizona State Capitol grounds to sell gun-shaped cookies, supposedly to buy a gun for their teacher. They staged the satire on February 14th, the anniversary of Arizona's statehood, when the governor and press cameras would be all over the grounds for the annual celebration. The cameras zoomed away from the governor and toward the kids. The sponsor of the gun bill, pursued by reporters, escaped into her office and withdrew the bill the next morning.

I thought we had learned enough from Austin's own success to know how she should write her college essays, but she pushed away angrily my offer of writing assistance. She did mention the cookies in her essay, of course.

Did the kids belong in those colleges? They did. Austin took his junior year at Oxford because he's who he is. Lauren graduated Yale with a double major and highest honors. They both are in the middle of careers serving our nation's highest aspirations.

Lauren's effect on the Arizona Legislature taught me an important thing about politics beyond story: When you make someone smile or laugh, you can get right past the anger that guards their opinions. Joy is a valuable commodity in politics, though it is remarkably unappreciated and unused. Joy's energy is more durable than the energy of anger, as it doesn't burn out in those who are giving it, and it is devastating to the opponents. The person with the dignified sense of humor is always considered the reasonable party. Dignified or zany. Inflatable is fine.

Love and Democracy

Joy was the thing that got Austin and Lauren into their colleges. People want to be around joyful people. That's politics, which at its best is about positive leadership. Getting into college is politics, and not too distant from the elective kind. If you're a voter or a college admissions staffer, you're looking for people to travel with for four years or longer. You want serious but seriously fun people who have an open curiosity about life and the future.

Doris's walk across the U.S. never got old for Good Morning America or the other shows and papers covering her because the story was essentially joyful, even zany. She was fun to report.

So, zany would be our plan for Working Women Vote. Mermaids, even. Real ones.

Who the Holy F is That?

We crossed out of New England after the stay with Lauren in New Haven. There is a spot near the west end of the Tappan Zee Bridge where you used to be able to glimpse the World Trade Center's twin towers in distant Manhattan. There was nothing on that southern horizon now but the rolling banks of the Hudson, red with the autumn of a changed world.

Traveling south in our nondescript van, we dropped Jim off at the New Jersey home of one of his sons, a Wall Street trader who was one of many who left Manhattan after 9/11. His basement was now a Starfleet captain's bridge of day-trading computers with wrap-around screens. I looked at his setup and understood how naïve the terrorists had been to think they could slow down Wall Street with a couple of airplanes; they had only increased investments in new businesses, from "Never Forget" t-shirts to trillion-dollar airport security systems and smart new carry-on luggage and slip-off shoes. The genius of American enterprise is such that any brick you throw at it will be caught, patented and resold at a profit—we are still remembering even the Alamo and selling tours and mementos.

The other thing 9/11 did was to bring Americans closer together, at least for a time. Whenever people are killed wholesale like ants under a shoe, there is an opposite reaction in favor of rehumanizing daily life. Friends got together and drank longer. There was more romance, as happens in the pink sunset after slaughter. Even head waiters were nice.

Love and Democracy

From New Jersey, Doris and I continued to Easton, Pennsylvania for the 100th Anniversary of Crayola Crayons. The streets were filled with hoop-skirted young women representing each Crayola color. Ms. Lavender walked with us after we registered her to vote, covered by television. We then did a good registration business at a booth in the town square and left stacks of voter forms with local volunteers.

In Bethlehem, a man working in a coffee house told us about the great job he once held at the famous steel mill down the hill.

"It was shuttered in '95, when Clinton refused to stop China from dumping cheap steel on us," he said. The man turned down a voter registration form, saying he didn't much get involved in voting anymore, "You know, it's all just special interests."

I asked him what kind of special interest groups bothered him the most. I expected him to say developers who need cheap steel for their high-rise buildings or something like that. He went wider: "Special interests? You know, Republicans and Democrats," he said. What he meant by that, I think, was that the parties didn't seem to represent the people anymore, only the candidates and their reelection, with very poor trickle-down political representation for the rest of us.

We moved through Philadelphia for a few days of organizing and media, including a downtown voter registration walk-along with a BBC reporter. We were accustomed to foreign news services sometimes having more interest in Doris than the domestic press. For example, Japan, Britain and Germany covered her long walk and sent reporters and film crews. Their attention was useful, as it helped prove the seriousness of the story to American news editors and television producers.

Doris spoke at Independence Hall at the day's conclusion. That night, at an organizing meeting in the White Dog Cafe, a woman and her daughter invited us to stay overnight at their farm in New Hope. As usual, I slept in the van and Doris was provided a bed in the house. I woke early the next morning, shivering but listening to the layered birdsong along the Delaware River. I had the remarkable sensation that I had been there many times before.

Was it reincarnation? No, it finally occurred to me that I once had an environmental tape recording of birds in a meadow. I used that tape to help my kids get to sleep, and I often fell asleep, too. The tape was called Dawn at New Hope—this exact place. It was satisfying to think that, despite the global changes afoot, this place sounded the same, bird by bird, even after almost twenty years, and it might sound the same after all of us leave.

We then headed to Gettysburg College for campus organizing, including a speech to students and an overnight stay with Professor Hammond and Patricia. They had created a family commune of sorts and a Christmas tree farm to keep it going.

The Hammonds, as you will remember, had been arrested and jailed with us when we did the Greenpeace action at the Capitol. Lou, who is gone now, had silver locks and a big, serious face that made him look like a signer of the Declaration. His scarred nose only added to it.

Lou and Patricia's kitchen, above the frosty battlefields of Gettysburg, was a good place to talk politics and get advice. As we left, they packed us up with apples and cashews for the road.

We drove west across Pennsylvania, making stops in small towns and then on the Penn campus to meet with student organizers. We were having coffee with people we had only met before by email—getting everyone on the project of voter registration.

Pennsylvania seemed like an endless state, which told me I had been too long away from Arizona, which is more than twice that size but seemed intimate by comparison. But this was lovely; we had caught up with the fall colors and were counting the horse carts of the Amish.

Feeling a bit drowsy as I drove through one afternoon, I called behind me:

"Doris, I think I would like a cashew."

She was happily rearranging her contact notes back in the cabin, but came up, sat sideways on the passenger seat and faced me with a serious expression:

"Oh, Dennis; you might think so now, but someday you might really regret it."

I pinched my waistline, which wasn't too bad.

"Really Doris, one cashew?"

"Oh, I thought you said tattoo."

She went to find the stash. It would not be the first time that Doris's poor hearing somehow tapped into her ability to predict the future: I would have a small tattoo—a bluebird on my shoulder from an artist named Blue—by the end of the adventure.

We were flying by the seats of our pants, as usual, but we were flying, finding enough volunteers along the way to avoid high expenses. When we ran out of friends here and there, we sprang for a cheap motel room for Doris.

Pittsburgh was filled with students and elder activists—including a riotous chapter of peace and justice groups like the Raging Grannies and Code Pink—all anxious to make a difference in the coming election. As we moved between meetings and events, I took names and got a sense of their leaders. It was our job to add energy and encouragement, to connect them to new volunteers and each other, and to get news coverage about the importance of registering to vote. Then we would move on.

From Pittsburgh we drove south into West Virginia, stopping in Morgantown. College towns are always full of minimum-wage-working young people who are more interested than their parents in racial and gender justice and more committed to peace and the environment. But many of them need encouragement to take time away from their busy days and party nights to register to vote. We had volunteers in Morgantown, gained when Doris walked through, three years earlier in heavy snow, and where she had made a good speech at the University about the efficacy of sacrifice in politics. In the several years since, she had kept up with everyone with little handwritten notes, as always. We knew they would turn out to help and they did.

In Morgantown, a twenty-something friend of the Haddock family named Charles, who had very long dark hair and a demeanor common to descendants of old New England families, arrived in Doris's old silver Toyota. The extra person and vehicle would allow me to do advance work in one or two towns ahead.

The three of us used the fast little car to make an unscheduled overnight side trip into D.C. We did so because I had received a call from Ann Eschinger, president of the League of Women Voters of Arizona and one of the several of us who pushed through two successful ballot reforms there.

"I'm in D.C. for our national meeting. I tried to get them to endorse your trek, as you asked, but they turned me down," she said. "They say you're too partisan—all about defeating Bush."

Love and Democracy

Our mission was to encourage voting, and we had already registered some new Republicans along with the Democrats, but they were right about our deeper intention.

But I still wanted the League's endorsement, as it would generate more volunteers at every stop.

We got into D.C. about dawn, well before the League's big meeting. The city had tightened in the two years since 9/11, with roadblocks and checkpoints still up, here and there.

We parked in front of John Moyer's townhouse, behind the Supreme Court, hoping John would be at home and open for coffee. He wasn't, but we waited there on his iron porch for the League's meeting to start across town.

A few steps up the street, the rear columns of the U.S. Supreme Court were turning gold in the sunrise. A few doors the other way was the former home of Frederick Douglass, now a small museum. Across the street from that was Attorney General John Ashcroft's townhouse. Gray men were sitting in black cars to watch over it, taking up valuable neighborhood parking, and obviously calling in our New Hampshire license plate.

On any morning, you could watch the limos of the Supreme Court justices slide into the parking garage under the Court. On any evening, they slid out. Sometimes Sandra O'Connor drove herself. I know that because I saw her once and waved, but she didn't wave back. She certainly didn't recognize me from the old days in Phoenix. I was older now and wouldn't have known what to say to her other than, what were you thinking?

The whole Bush tragedy belonged in a basket at her door. What are you to say when your mother's friend is responsible for such damage to the country and the world? Jeepers, Mrs. O'Connor!

But my mother did respect her. As new Junior Leaguers together, they toured all the charity needs of Phoenix—part of the education to make socialites well-informed for better volunteerism and philanthropy. Mom was very impressed with Sandra for taking notes of every fact and asking penetrating questions everywhere they went. Mom wasn't the least surprised when Reagan nominated her for the Supreme Court. We would see them at parties, Sandra and John, even when she was on the Court.

There is a quaint place between Phoenix and Scottsdale—it used to be way out in the desert—called the Valley Field Riding and Polo Club. No one has played polo there since 1930, but there is a great BYO bar and that's where we would run into them and other Phoenix old-timers. I never saw her drink too much, unlike Barry Goldwater, whom I never saw sober.

When Austin was admitted to Stanford, the first thing Mom said was, "Oh, that's where Sandra and John O'Connor met, and they were married in the school chapel." That was the significant thing about the school.

John O'Connor was a member of the Rotary Club that Dad, my grandfather and I belonged to. John's philosophy of life, told in a fake Irish brogue one day when the birthday boys at the head table were asked to share their philosophy of life in ten seconds, was: "You don't need to be taking a drink to have a good time, but why take the chance?"

Small, small, very human world. That is what you think when you're far from home and you see a familiar face. I watched a few limos slip down under the Supreme Court but didn't spot Mrs. O'Connor that morning.

I took a last look around before we headed off to the League meeting, where Doris commenced a chocolate-only fast right there in the hotel lobby, talking to many League members who stopped by to chat and partake of chocolate, but the League would not relent.

We headed back to West Virginia, though Doris wanted us to stop so Charles could get a haircut. "We are, you know, a public relations campaign," she explained. But, no, he liked his hair Fabio long, and so did some of the ladies along our way.

We did stop by the home of Doris' daughter—Jim's sister of course—in Chevy Chase, who was reaching a final stage of Alzheimer's. Doris decided we should overnight there so they could have more time together. After so many years caring for her late husband with that disease, Doris knew the territory. Her daughter had been a brilliant psychologist and knew what was happening to her own mind. Her husband, a D.C. physician, cared for her in their home until her last breath, which was now but months away.

Their neighbor was Richard Perle, one of the architects of the Bush horribles. I waved to him the next dawn as I was bringing in the morning paper and he was fetching his. He did not wave back. In fact, when Doris's van was parked on the street for a day after Doris's long walk, he called the police to have it towed. The police would not do it.

Our drive out of D.C. was through morning fog and mist. West of Frederick the velvet Maryland farms and battlefields fold up into the eastern fringe of the Appalachians. The northbound Shenandoah and southbound Potomac flow through the troughs of long mountains, coming up on both sides of Harpers Ferry where the rivers join and break through between Maryland Heights and Louden Heights, bluffs made bloody in the Civil War. The conjoined rivers then flow beyond the last rib of the Appalachians as the Potomac. sixty miles more into Washington.

From these mountains and westward, all the way to the Mississippi, America receives its water and power, many of its birds and fish, much of its music and stubbornness. As to America eastward of these mountains, this is the coal-fired source of the great blue haze that invites itself up the Hudson River Valley and into the far reaches of New England. The mothers' milk of New England's women is laced with its poisons.

The highway stitches in and out of Maryland as you come into West Virginia. Civilized Maryland makes a last stand at Cumberland.

We stopped to stretch our legs at the old railroad station—the red caboose of Doris's 90th birthday party was still there. Leaving town, I spotted on a corner the homeless woman whom, those three years earlier, Jim had helped with some food and cash and a new blanket. I believe her name was Sarah. The town must have been taking care of her, at least to the extent that she looked well-fed. I gave her some cash and said hello from Jim. She pretended to know whom I meant.

We saw homeless people in nearly every town—always a few more with each year.

Every person you see on the street is a story. When I was raising money for the shelter system in Phoenix, I was standing outside the shelter in Phoenix one hot but rainy night, waiting for a TV reporter to come do one of the annually predictable hot weather stories at the shelter. There was a protective alcove at the door, and that's where I waited, visiting with a shelter resident who had volunteered to be the doorman for the evening. We were joined by a man with a Slavic accent, trying to make himself understood into the intercom box near at the door of the upstairs women's shelter. He was spelling his wife's last name slowly into the box, helping the difficult English letters through his mustache with gestures from his thumb and forefinger.

He waited for the woman to go find his wife so he could talk to her.

"I get my driver's license here tomorrow," he told me. "That helps me get a job."

He stamped around a bit, brushing the rain from his worn jeans. "This is not a good place," he said. "It was better in Colorado for jobs."

He said how he had found a job in Denver and had been doing well, staying in the apartment of some Romanian friends. But he couldn't get ahead, and there were too many people in the apartment. He heard that things were better in Phoenix. When they arrived, they stayed in a cheap motel on Grand Avenue, then a cheaper one. Then they were locked out of their room for nonpayment, and their clothes and papers and family pictures were locked away from them somewhere. They walked to the shelter with the help of a hand-drawn map given to them by the motel manager. That was a week ago.

"This is no place for people," he said to me. He was in his fifties with thick, black and gray hair and a strong, pockmarked face. When we shook hands, I could feel the calluses of a life's work. "It's terrible for my wife. She would rather be home in Romania. We are twenty-three years married this week," he said.

"She checked out," the intercom finally said. "She checked out at 5:30 this evening and said she would not be returning."

I could see him becoming heavier and shorter, his breath like a tired horse.

"OK," he said. "Maybe she will come back later. Maybe she went that way," he said, pointing to the higher buildings farther downtown.

"Which direction is Romania?" He asked me. I pointed eastward to those buildings.

I think of him every time I think of homelessness and what we might yet do. The man's experience was the way too many American journeys end. Not everyone gets a hot dog cart and then a restaurant and sends their kids to college, no matter how hard they try, no matter how much they love each other and want to make a good life for each other. For him, the gold that the streets were paved with was just evening rain in puddles.

That was a long time ago. It's possible that he found her, and they started over again and did well. America keeps folding things around with new chances. But we are a harder place than we need to be, pursuit of happiness-wise.

Doris and Charles and I were soon back in Morgantown, where we had left the van at a repair shop, hoping to stop its overheating. No luck for that, but we were soon talking to members of a progressive student group in a coffee shop. They were hosting an event later that evening in a popular club, featuring several local rock groups and rappers. They had an idea:

Would Doris like to do a rap routine to encourage voter registration?

She looked at me.

"When will you ever get another offer like that?" I said.

"Well, alright. I'll need my dark glasses."

I later sat her down with my headphones to listen to Dead Prez, Eminem, and other rappers. At first, she seemed confused and frozen, but then her body started to move. She asked me for some ideas for lines, but she ended up mostly freestyling.

That night the college students, packed in tight, grew silent when, after three earlier acts, she appeared onstage in her dark glasses. I heard someone say, "Ok, shit, what's this?"

Scraps I remember of her rap: *You have so many dreams—they run the gamut / But it's not just a game for your matrix mind / There's a culture war—you're on the front line! Vote, dammit!*

Mouths fell open as she built up steam. Cheers rose and the band behind her found her groove: *Yeah, you better register and you better vote / If you don't take your part—if you take a pass / Let me tell you my children / It's SO your ass!*

The crowd started going wild for her. There were maybe four verses—war and peace, the fate of the environment—with lots of Vote Dammit punchlines. A few hundred waving fists were in the air as the young crowd responded with *Yes! and Tell it Granny! And Go Granny!* I heard a young woman yell to a friend over the din, "Amazing! Who the holy f--k is that?"

Doris was just eating the mic like she had been rapping since rapping began. She dropped it on purpose when she was finished, though she looked for her purse to drop it on safely. She could have had a new career from that night. And yes, students registered to vote at the door.

For several days after, I could hear her mumbling some ideas for new lines, but the chance to rap in a club would only come once again, as different days presented different opportunities. Her rap career was short but killer, as rap careers often are.

There was this ghostly sense to the trip so far. When Doris was on foot three years earlier, every mile brought political change. We were passing through towns now like spirits, changing so very little. Not yet. We had plans for the swing states ahead, but I could not but be amazed by the fact that it was her act of walking at her age that had made her previous passages through these same places consequential. Gandhi's Salt March would not have turned world history if he had done it from a motorhome. People listen to you when they know you are serious enough to suffer for telling you.

Asheville Ceremonies

Doris and I had spent more days in West Virginia than we planned, but Ken kept finding events and voter registration opportunities for us to attend, and of course he was running for office and liked showing off Doris.

But I wanted us to get situated in Asheville soon, so Doris and I could fly to our respective homes in time for Thanksgiving. I owed that to Maureen. I missed her, plus Lauren and Austin would be home from college.

All along, we had been driving through another West Virginia love story; this one was the love between Senator Robert Byrd and his own name. Every building and improvement and byway seemed to have his name on it.

We crossed out of West Virginia via the bridge over New River Gorge, one of the highest in America. It remains the only government structure in West Virginia not named for Robert C. Byrd. The young people of West Virginia and from a few other states gather on it each autumn to jump off it. They are celebrating Bridge Day, jumping with parachutes that usually open. We were a week late to see it.

I told Doris that we had a TV story set up, and it would require her to parachute from the bridge. She was happy that our extra time with Ken made us miss the thing. To be clear, she would have done it if I hadn't been kidding, which I certainly was.

As New River Gorge is a beautiful river canyon, some people naturally wanted to build a dam and flood it. Just as naturally, Ken organized successfully to stop them.

We also passed through White Sulphur Springs, where the old Greenbrier Resort still operates with golf and all the rest. For many years it was where the richest of America's rich came annually to drink, dine, and plan their depredations.

There are some curious grassy humps on the hotel's grounds and rather more satellite dishes and ventilation pipes than you would expect from a lawn. Inside, there are some large doors here and there—one of them is 28 tons. They lead under that lawn to a 112,000 square-foot office and living space built in 1960 as a bomb shelter to accommodate the entire U.S. Congress. It was supposedly decommissioned when its cover was blown in 1992. For a time, the hotel was giving tours of the shelter, and I went through it at that time.

A sudden turnaround in that open door policy, however, made some locals think that Vice President Cheney and the shadow government might be taking residence there after 9/11. He had, in fact, often hosted dignitaries at the resort in earlier times. We stopped for lemonade at the hotel, and I tried to see if I could get a tour for Doris. The hotel staff said they had no idea what I was talking about. The big doors were wallpapered and invisible. It was indeed back in use, but their coyness about it was laughable.

We sped onward for campus events in Charlottesville, including a mock presidential debate where Doris had to stand in for Nader, as no student was comfortable with the honor. Besides, Doris knew Ralph, and he would call her up occasionally, so she knew his vocal style and his positions. She had recently tried but failed to talk him out of running for president again.

Several times a day now through Virginia, old Rosie was smoking and stalling out. We stopped at garages along the way, but all of them wanted the vehicle for a half a week or more, and the estimates were in the thousands. I bought an extra fire extinguisher, and we kept going.

New Hampshire Charles, who had been catching up to us on and off in Doris's old car, was sure our old van was a fire hazard. He insisted we cancel the project. Instead, we sent him home via air, stashing the scout car in a Virginia storage lot.

Doris and I then rolled westward through North Carolina. I watched the edges of the hood as I drove, not wanting to see the old bus to burst into flames.

We stopped for coffee with volunteers in Chapel Hill then Charlotte, where I left Doris for two days in the company of a young woman filmmaker who wanted to interview her. I had committed to speak in Des Moines at an election reform event and so made a quick flight there and back.

The home in Charlotte included an albino python, whose cage extended the length of the living room. Doris was honestly delighted to see and pet the thing. I could only hope that she would not be a lump inside it when I returned.

After that sojourn we headed to Asheville, where I planned to find artists to pretty-up the van while Doris and I took our Thanksgiving break.

A filmmaker, Rebecca MacNeice, had been following our adventures by email and showed up at the Wal-Mart where we hoped to do sidewalk voter registration but were kicked out.

Rebecca, lanky, dark-haired, mid-20s, with her video camera tucked under her arm, stood far aside and watched the confrontation with amusement.

She led us to Asheville's artful Lexington Avenue to meet Kitty, a gallery owner, tattoo artist, and something of a mother-figure to the young artists of the district. Kitty happened to be managing a community mural project.

I gave Kitty the short version: Doris Haddock here is 93 and is going across the country getting women to register to vote. She is the woman who walked clear across the U.S. a few years ago to promote campaign finance reform.

Kitty did not look particularly impressed, but she was happy to step out to the sidewalk and look at our little motorhome. Its nondescript blandness overwhelmed her. She immediately agreed that it would be a good canvas for a mural. Fate had brought the van to her doorstep like an orphan. She would find someone to head up the project. Her protégé, Blue, a tall, tattooed, nose-ringed gay woman in her early twenties, got the assignment.

I do not think that one's gayness should be automatically mentioned in an introduction any more than one's straightness or any other ness. But Blue's gayness figures into the story.

Blue had a genius for tattoo art, and her serious attitude about health made her a natural for running a new-age tattoo parlor. Kitty was setting her up for that.

After tough years growing up, Blue was finding her place in the world, even though her arranged future on Lexington Avenue, like a marriage too young, was beginning to bother her.

Politically, like most of the young artists of the town, she knew a good deal about what was going on in the world but had little knowledge of how the gears of politics worked. Blue was curious about the gears. Many of her friends were convinced that politics was hopelessly corrupt and a waste of time. Blue wasn't so sure. She was looking for a political education and it's rather as if she manifested us.

We set up camp in filmmaker Rebecca's grand old Craftsman house surrounded by Asheville greenery. Granddaughter of English poet Louis MacNeice, who was a cohort of W.H. Auden, Rebecca came to Asheville for the whitewater rafting and stayed. Others who have come for rafting but then moved on form a network of friends across the country. Emily, Rebecca's whitewater friend and partner who had long since moved to St. Petersburg to cater from a pink castle of a beach hotel, would put us up down the road. Emily had learned her restaurant skills at the Vanderbilt home, Biltmore, an Asheville landmark. I mention this because it describes the principal way we found shelter on the roads ahead. Everybody knows tons of people. I will name any city, and I'll wager you know someone there, or a close friend who does.

With Rebecca's help we went about setting up events and visiting the newspeople and writers of the city. I met with Blue downtown and told her what we had in mind for the bus—loose specifications that would give artists plenty of creative room yet still advance our mission of encouraging working women to vote. I gave her our little brochure, which featured Norman Rockwell's Rosie the Riveter, reproduced from the cover of a World War II Saturday Evening Post.

That night, Doris and I walked around Lexington Avenue as it came alive with gallery openings, drifting cannabis smoke and open drinking. There was an artists' cooperative space, a big garage where drummers drummed and where an alternative political newspaper was buzzing into the evening. A bicycle repair co-op was piled high with spinnable donations. A daycare nursery, empty for the night, was papered with joyful drawings. In a warehouse art space, a young woman was high on a ladder, hanging colorful self-portraits of her different moods. Kitty's gallery was having a major showing, and le crème was mingling, including the mayor.

I think it was the first time Rebecca and Blue met. They would become close.

On the street, everyone was interesting and young. Blue was tall on the sidewalk, towering over the moving cluster of her friends. I pulled her aside to give her cash for the paint and supplies and to tell her where Rosie would be parked when we left town. I gave her the keys and told her about the overheating and the fire extinguishers.

The next morning, I rented a car so Doris and I could get to Raleigh-Durham for flights to our separate homes, except that Doris decided to go to D.C. for some time at her daughter's bedside, as it was likely their last Thanksgiving together.

After that holiday, I flew back to Raleigh-Durham and retrieved Doris's little car from the airport's long-term lot. I would use it to get to Ashville, then somehow get the prettied-up van and the little car down to Jacksonville, where Doris would fly from D.C. I would need to find a volunteer second driver.

It was after midnight, cold with a very light, icy rain, when I arrived in Asheville. I parked across the street from where our van was waiting, and I resolved to get some sleep before any artists arrived. In the dim light from a distant streetlight, I could see the van had been considerably transformed. It looked terrific.

Then I saw a puff of winter breath rise over the van from its far side. I imagined a fire, of course, as that was always the fear. I got out and walked briskly toward it, but as I got a better angle, I stopped.

Love and Democracy

Standing on a stepladder in the light rain, painting the bus in the dim light, was Blue.

There was no traffic on the street as I stood and watched. She didn't see or hear me—earphones were plugged into her short, dark haircut, and she was singing along to something.

The picture of Rosie the Riveter from our little brochure was now perfectly executed across the port side of the bus. The starboard side featured the historic march of women for the vote, with straw-hatted Doris in the mix. On the rear was the beginning of what would be bluebirds holding up a "Live Free or Die" banner. The colors were as stunning as the designs, even in the green tint of the streetlight.

I had a feeling that the old engine would run better now, as vehicles that look good seem to know it. Blue and her friends had done us some magic, and, as I would soon learn, she was now concerned that they had put too much into it and would not be finished in time for our departure. That's why she was painting in the icy rain.

Her usual day in Asheville included walking several miles to downtown from the old house she shared with a small group of friends. The house fronted a green acre of vegetable gardens and a wilder outback of fir and spruce where one might walk or sit or have a bonfire party, which they sometimes did. The old house was warm and well-kept, with musical instruments and computers upstairs and a monastic-vibe living room smelling of incense.

I gave her a ride to her house and picked her up there the next morning. She was happy for the ride but explained that she normally walked the long way by choice, just to be with the wild growth along the French Broad River. Her other interests were medicinal herbs and oils and scents, the movement of energy fields and peaceful living. She carried in her purse a kit of oils and scents that she displayed for me.

She explained how the French Broad flows between the Great Smokies and the Blue Ridge, making Asheville a whitewater Tahoe where kayaks hang from the ceilings of beer bars, and young, outdoorsy confidence energizes the town of artists, political progressives, the rich, and punks with knives in their big pockets. Blue had a sense of the big picture of it and a big knife in her pocket.

Money does insinuate the town. The Vanderbilt family built their great mansion, Biltmore, on the south end. To plan the garden, she told me, the Vanderbilts brought in Frederick Law Olmstead, whose other credits include the Boston Public Garden, Central Park and Golden Gate Park. It remains the largest privately owned home in America, with an entry that is more scenic highway than driveway.

Asheville has absorbed big-money families without succumbing to snobbery or the lining of its streets with the kinds of stores that usually follow money. But wherever the rich come to live, starving artists are not far behind.

Back at Rosie, Blue put me to work with a brush, filling in like paint-by-numbers after she drew the lines. People came by to watch, and everyone under thirty knew Blue by name and had some joyful gossip to share with her.

For me, it was all an indictment of the places I had known and had mistaken for cities. Real cities nurture everyone's potential, freedom and creativity. Asheville was hardly perfect, but it showed a lot of leg and hinted at what my old hero Lewis Mumford described as the city's main role regarding the magnification of life.

"Yes, Lexington Avenue is Sesame Street," Blue summarized my compliments. I'm sure that show taught urban planning to several unsuspecting generations.

Rosie was soon pretty enough to get on the road, though there were some areas Blue said were quite unfinished.

I told her not to worry because Doris and I could find other artists in Florida to finish up. Blue gave me an Oscar the Grouch frown, or perhaps more the look Vincent van Gogh would give if you said you needed the thing now and would have someone back in Paris put in the sunflowers.

My logistics problem was that we had Rosie and the little car and only one driver. I asked Blue if she knew of a U-Haul place that could rig a tow bar or anyone who might be interested in driving the little car down to Florida and flying back. I knew I would have volunteer drivers once we got to Florida. They had signed up.

"Hmmm." She painted silently for maybe a half-minute.

"I might be interested," she said. "I could finish the painting down there. The weather is probably nicer. It wouldn't take long. Kitty will be mad at me, but I need a break anyway."

After we packed up the paints and cleaned the brushes, I gave her the keys to the little car, and we made plans to meet up in Florida when Doris would also be arriving.

Jim, when I told him that I had given away his mother's car to a tattooed girl with a big knife, paused but then said he trusted my judgment with people.

"And do you trust yourself, cavorting with an interesting young woman? What does Maureen think?" he said.

191

I told him we were traveling separately, and it was just long enough for Blue to finish the art, and that she was definitively gay, and that, yes, Maureen was cool with it.

"Ok, Dennis. But there's gay and then there's gay, so keep it in your knickers."

I headed south in our beautiful bus, driving all night to Jacksonville through the coming and going of radio stations with callers from military towns talking about getting ready to go to Iraq or just coming back.

I was kept alert and awake by the occasional sputtering and stalling of Rosie, despite her fine looks. The trouble was always curable with a simple stop for coffee or a few slower miles on side roads. The trees above these lesser paths were decorated with stars showing through until pinched out by thickening draperies of Spanish moss.

The thing was, thanks to Blue and her Asheville friends, we were now wearing our warpaint. It was visual. It was zany. It was easily understood. It would make all the difference.

Love and Democracy

Florida's Mermaid Vote

Doris and I registered new voters in Jacksonville and the progressive college town of Gainesville for a couple of weeks. Blue hadn't shown up. We registered quite a few voters, promoted news coverage about registering to vote, shared tips with voter volunteers around the country via email, and met with local activists and their groups. Doris made a half-dozen speeches at little events.

Blue and the little car? Explanations arrived via email. She was in Asheville storing her belongings and raising some cash by doing some more tattoos. Was she really going to bring the car to us at all? Had it been sold for parts?

In fact, she was preparing to run away to join the circus, and we were the circus. She had borrowed a few political books from the van—Doris's and mine, and I think Hightower's latest—and had devoured them. She wanted to be the change she was seeking. She wanted to be with us long enough to get some answers about how the world works.

When she finally arrived, Doris, who had only met her briefly in Asheville, took a liking to her immediately. They both had hearty pirate laughs.

For Doris, I suspect Blue was a connection to her own avant-garde youth. For me, Blue brought back the tarot-reading circle of artists I knew when I returned to Phoenix in my early twenties. Everyone over forty or so is always trying to get back to something.

Blue did her promised painting on the van, a continuous improvement with each stop, but she was also intensely interested in the political work. She proved to be a natural with a voter registration clipboard—we were now hitting across the full spectrum of generations. In the evenings, she was pumping us for information about politics. She wanted to know everything, and she asked smart questions. She wanted to talk about our present strategy, which she thought was a little haphazard, which it was.

As for accommodations, we were still finding volunteers where Doris could have a bed, though now we asked for Blue's lodging, too. My place each night was alone in the bus, where I worked late with email campaigns and the website.

We were finding our stride with the news media, but I was anxious to get started with one of the main angles of our adventure: that Doris should trade places with working women long enough for them to go register to vote. News coverage of those events would encourage tens of thousands of viewers and readers to register, and it would pressure voting officials to provide easier locations and hours. We would need irresistible visuals for that kind of news story.

We stopped everything for a Christmas break, and I flew home.

I returned to Florida on the second day of 2004. Doris, Blue, and Nancy Brown, a volunteer from New Hampshire, were waiting and ready.

My first evening back, we joined forces with a local democracy group at a big mall where we combed the stores and hallways for new voters. Young clerks were particularly ready to sign up.

We learned some lessons. "We're bringing voter forms through the stores as a convenience to employees" got a lot more acceptance than, "Would you like to register to vote?" which was like a solicitation instead of a convenience. Carry the forms in shopping totes, not on clipboards, or you'll get kicked out too soon. We put our lessons on the website and sent an email blast to volunteers, asking them to try cruising the malls.

The next morning, we were set to register an 18-year-old named Jamie while Doris took over her job feeding the alligators of Gatorland. The job required standing in the mud and throwing huge hunks of raw meat into a snapping swarm of giant alligators two feet away. We had the main newspaper, the Sentinel, and two television stations with us as planned, but the alligators were quite a bit larger, more numerous, hungrier and closer than we expected.

Doris was a hell of a sport about it. I mean she was a sport her whole life, like driving to Alaska with four other people in a VW, or walking across the United States in delicate health, but especially on this day in Florida.

We were taken to a muddy cove in the big lagoon by Tim, an alligator wrestler, whose white mustache and khaki safari suit made him look positively British. He asked Doris if she really wanted to do this. When the cameras and reporters are standing by, you really do get the adrenaline you need. I expect even a firing squad is easier to take if there are cameras rolling.

"Of course," she said. "My, aren't they beautiful!" she said, looking worried.

"Damn, Dennis; they're big!" Blue leaned down to whisper in my ear. She was not suggesting we back out, and one of the reasons to continue might have been her immediate fascination with Jamie, t-shirt and jeans, blonde hair pulled into a ponytail and two walkie-talkies on her hips.

Doris wore her trademark walking vest with Campaign Finance Reform embroidered in a panel and festooned with meaningful little pins given her across the country. She also wore her straw hat and an elegant, white pantsuit—perfect for the mud shot.

Tim slapped the water with his big alligator stick while his Igor-like assistant lugged buckets full of ex-horse from a golf cart.

Hearing the slaps, the monsters began to boil the water into a storm heading our way. They moved up the mud bank, tails flipping, water spraying, giant jaws snapping open with huge teeth.

Doris and Tim were soon the edible attractions in this carnivorous theater-in-the-round. Tim pushed them back here and there with his stick. Some gators looked twenty feet long.

"Ok, Doris," he shouted. Try to share it around. Do it now."

After a second of hesitation that might have been a prayer, she began lobbing big hunks of meat, each the size of a pot roast, into the open jaws. It made her stagger to do so.

"No, you've already had yours," she was soon barking to individual monsters.

"He's hungry, isn't he?" she said of one getting a foot from her. Tim pushed it back a bit.

"Don't get your hands so close to their teeth, Doris! Toss it down their throats," Tim advised.

Nancy Brown and I flicked around taking pictures for the website. Tim drew our attention several times to late-arriving diners coming behind us.

TV and newspaper cameras and alligators were rolling and snapping. Blue was signing Jamie up to vote on a neon plastic clipboard, and both were sneaking glances to make sure Doris wasn't snatched by her legs and pulled into the frenzy. It would, of course, have been fabulous TV.

Jamie intervened a time or two to make sure the older, less aggressive of her friends got their fair share. She didn't want any hard feelings, as she was learning to wrestle with them in the water. Worker conditions are different in different kinds of businesses.

So, yes, a great morning! When the cameras and telegenic young TV reporters finally left, and Doris and I had spun all the voting messages we could spin, we visited with Tim and watched Jamie feed her giant tortoises.

Tim was a Vietnam vet, and looked over Jamie like a proud father, though he let her wrestle alligators. Jamie, over lunch at a chain steak house, told us all about alligator wrestling. Do you practice with little ones or with giant beanbags or what, I asked him.

"No, you just get in and do it, but you must be careful. A wrestler was hurt bad in the face not long ago. It helps if you feed 'em good first."

Jamie was commuting from her parent's home six hours a day for love of the job and animals in general. She hoped to earn a degree relating to wildlife and was planning a trip to Kenya to work with animals in the wild. She was very concerned about climate change.

We dropped her off back at the park after lunch, took farewell pictures of each other, and went into the souvenir shop to buy a small rubber alligator, which Blue wired onto Rosie as a hood ornament. She named it Tim.

The gator would prove a good kid magnet in the housing projects and slums ahead. It also gave passing motorists something to look at besides the smoke from our hood.

We drove west out of Orlando, leaving behind good newspaper and television stories about how young people and working women need to register to vote and how they can do it.

This was all in January of 2004. Attorney General Ashcroft had recently recused himself from investigating the outing of CIA agent, Valerie Plame. Kerry's campaign was doing well. Bush was in the newspapers, pushing his No Child Left Behind program, which was all about leaving children behind, at least the poorer tikes.

Doris, as usual, was digesting newspapers as we drove out of Orlando. She would often bring articles up to me to read aloud.

"Does this mean what I think it means?" she might ask, looking for the stories behind the stories and sniffing out the campaign finance angles. She had been fearlessly feeding alligators a few hours earlier. She would take a nap soon. She would be 94 in a few weeks. Her emphysema was kicking up some coughs, especially after last night's mall walk and today's heavy lifting of horse meat.

Blue was on the motor home's couch, looking through press contacts for the cities ahead. We were headed for Weeki Wachee Springs, the City of Mermaids.

Nancy was driving the scout car, but she had to get back to teaching soon, so we followed her to an airport, said goodbye, and headed west, with Blue driving the scout. We would see Nancy again when all hell broke loose in the spring. She would organize Portsmouth for us.

"Dear God," I heard Doris say an hour later. She was looking at the clipboard used that morning.

"The alligator girl, Jamie. She registered as a Republican!"

We filed those properly, of course, same as Democrats, same as everybody.

Love and Democracy

We stopped at a Waffle House along the way. We told our waitress that we could register anyone in the place to vote. Her coworkers, including her male boss, loudly argued that voting was a waste of time. Our waitress was quiet about it, just calling us Hun and serving our food. But when we left, she followed us out to the parking lot to register.

"Don't mind them. They're all registered, but sometimes I wish they wasn't." she said.

Motel maids, desk clerks, and waitresses had signed all along our way.

As late as the 1970s, Florida was the land of family auto vacations. Millions of station wagons buzzed like honeybees from one roadside attraction to the next: Marineland, Gatorland, other marine, jungle and alligator parks, rollercoaster piers, beaches, circus towns. There were over 200 major roadside attractions until Walt Disney World and Epcot changed all that, offering an oversized park in a single fly in, fly out destination.

Gatorland seemed to be surviving if not exactly prospering, perhaps because the gators were real and the people who loved and cared for them were charming.

The mermaid park ahead, on the coast north of Tampa, had suffered financially, almost fatally from the Disneyfication of Florida, but the little town around it purchased the property out of receivership and treated it as a city park with benefits—the benefits being jobs and mermaids and tourism.

The water park elements, with big slides and swimming pools, are available to the kids of the town every summer day. The adjoining City of Mermaids, maintained as a campy roadside attraction, provides youth jobs and tax revenue to the community. The underwater jobs for mermaids and mermen are a bit more fun than the McDonalds and Wendy's jobs suffered by other American teens.

The park is built over a natural spring that delivers millions of gallons daily into a huge, glass-walled theater where narrated classics such as Hans Christian Anderson's The Little Mermaid are performed in mime underwater. As the spring is the headwaters of the Weeki Wachee River, alligators sometimes pirouette into the show, and the mermaids and mermen take a break.

"Watch the little girls, especially," Barbara, a longtime mermaid sans fin, advised me seconds before the first mermaids appeared. Yes, the effect on children was electric: fingers suddenly covering their open mouths, eyes popping wide. "Murrrrmaids! Weeeel ones!" a little girl sitting near us with her family managed to utter.

Real ones? In a sense they are. The whole thing has become a lifestyle for many of the former performers. Even in their 70's, they come back monthly to swim under the waves with each other and remember who they are. They mentor the young mermaids and mermen in a true fellowship of the fin.

"Do you feel, at least in some respect, that you are a real mermaid?" I asked Barbara, the volunteer manager of the place, who sat beside me to watch the Granny D World's First Underwater Voter Registration Show.

Barbara looked down at her human feet in sandals and hid one under the other as they swung from the bench. She thought about it as she looked through the great blue window in front of us, where her young charges spun happily in the effervescence, blowing bubbly kisses to the entranced children.

"I do. I am," she said. "Honestly, Dennis, it is the best part of my life—the most meaningful part."

Love and Democracy

It was no small thing for them to take Doris into their secret rooms and no small smile on Doris's face when she came out in her iridescent mermaid suit, carried by a young hunk of a fellow who set her down in a chair in front of the great performance window. A young woman with a pink fin and a fine front was then placed beside her. Mermaids suddenly swarmed in the water on the other side of the window behind them, stretching out an American flag underwater as patriotic music played to the auditorium full of confused tourists. A dry clipboard appeared, and Doris registered the mermaid next to her.

In the water, mermaids began registering each other using grease pencils on laminated registration forms clipped to neon-colored plastic clipboards, all prepared by Blue. Two television stations and one major daily newspaper from Tampa caught it all.

Doris was, I think, a little disappointed not to have been tossed into the soup, but, for the purposes of the TV cameras, she looked every bit underwater.

The sheriff, the mayor, all the local and county dignitaries joined us for this fun, and local newspaper reporters were scribbling away. The county registrar of voters, whom we had invited, was all over the reporters with information on registration locations. She said they were going to put together some workplace voter registration events, thanks to the publicity. Home run.

Doris was happy to be carried around by that gent for as long as he ever would care to have her in his arms. Blue was in a candy store of fabulous-looking fish women.

I dreaded to think that the days ahead would not bring anything to beat this, which shows how wrong you can be.

We bought a little plastic mermaid for Rosie's dashboard and headed south where activist volunteers in

St. Petersburg were making a space for us in their offices, homes and voter plans.

We hung up some of the prop registration forms in the bus, as mermaid writing is rare. A few had signed the proper forms, too. FYI: Mermaids tend to be Democrats.

Tampa Bay is the sparkling centerpiece of the Tampa and St. Petersburg metropolis. St. Pete is the pink land of retirees and shopping on the seaward side of the bay. We were offered hospitality in the St. Pete home of Winnie and Al Foster, and office space in a nearby African American neighborhood. Winnie is a legendary organizer in Florida. She has stood up for racial fairness, voting rights, free speech and peace, and she booked us at events all over town.

I assembled a little red wagon for Doris to pull down city streets with our forms and supplies. It had a voter registration sign popping up from it, and clipboards and water bottles, sunscreen and a map. Doris crisscrossed St. Pete that way, with television and newspaper reporters occasionally in tow. She ended one walk at the University of South Florida at an outdoor voter registration rally. Here is a piece of that speech, which is the sort she made on campuses:

> *I hope you are not taking your studies here just so that you can someday be comfortably ensconced as somebody's wife, somebody's husband, somebody's employee, somebody's taxpayer. I hope you feel within your heart a spark of life that is far greater than any of that. For here, you are in a world at a time when heroes are required. You may not quite see that. It may not impress you that the polar ice lost 44% of its thickness in the last 40 years, that all the new fresh*

water in the North Atlantic from that melting is slowing down the Gulf currents that control much of our weather. When you are my age, and probably long before, there will be great dislocations of people, great famines, great epidemics on account of these changes. We are not doomed to that. We can make a difference, given the right leaders and the right civic action and our own life choices.

I am not exaggerating when I say that a heroic life is called for, and that you must rise to that call if you are to live in a good world. And this heroism begins with a simple act of faith like voting. I have voter registration forms for you today. I hope you will register now, if you have not already done so. You may need to reregister if you have changed your address as a student. I want you to double or triple your vote by taking a few extra forms for your friends who need a little arm-twist. If you will but vote and be involved in the big issues that you care about, I think you will remember this year as the beginning of a great time in your life. I ask you to rise to the joy of it.

Each evening of our St. Pete week, Blue slept on Winnie and Al's couch, Doris had a back bedroom, and I slept in Rosie under a starfruit tree that was new to me. They taste sort of like Starburst candies or Kool-Aid powder—a little treat I could harvest from the window while working the website.

Each evening, Blue would make me walk a few blocks down the street to the bay with her. She wanted to see a manatee but didn't want to go through the dark alone. We saw only the big creatures' tantalizing blurs and humps in the water and heard their distant splashes. Our conversation was usually environmental politics, though she did start telling me more about her childhood. She had a hard time growing up, saved by grandparents and by her art.

I think I was becoming a spare dad. People need to feel emotionally safe before they start asking themselves who they really are and what they are going to do with their lives. These few nights were mostly moonless and pitch black, with a great show of clear stars in the water.

We took an intermission from St. Pete to drive inland to the state's annual Citrus Festival. Doris had her picture taken with Miss Florida Citrus. Blue, who had long since perfected her young voter registration pitch she called *apathy matching*, signed up all the midway carnies to vote. They would have jumped off the Ferris wheel for her.

Apathy matching worked like this: "I know you probably think voting is a waste of time because they're all corrupt and everything, but you would be doing me a personal favor if you would register to vote anyway, just for the hell of it, just for me."

She could instinctively tell who needed to hear that, and it worked. As she was learning from us, she was also teaching. At the heart of her beliefs was, and I'm sure still is, a kind of personal responsibility and a belief in the nearly limitless power of every person to shape a loving world.

The people of the Dean campaign, mostly from their manager, Joe Trippi, were preaching that same gospel of personal power and personal responsibility. A few months down the road, Joe Trippi would instantly see that in Blue.

For now, she was unhappy that the three of us were not saving the world fast enough. She was right. We were just playing at the margins, when there were millions of unregistered women.

Love and Democracy

On a lightly scheduled Saturday, I took some time to myself to worry about that. I went for a drive through endless miles of orange groves in the scout car.

I was taking stock of our journey, wishing the Florida Democratic Party would return our phone calls, wishing the League of Women Voters hadn't turned us down. I was regretting we didn't have John Anthony, Nick Palumbo or Matt Keller involved, who were, respectively, the press, organizing, and lobbying brains behind Granny's big walk in 2000. John was in Colorado. Nick was in Minnesota, organizing for public financing of campaigns—we would catch up with him in a few months. Matt was in Rome, now the co-director of the U.N. Food Program. When he was walking through Arizona with Granny, and even when he was helping me drag a dead dog off a reservation churchyard for a Good Morning America story, I couldn't imagine him ever not being a Hill lobbyist, as he was so good at it. He knew which lawmaker was weakening, ready for a Granny visit. He would be ducking in and out of McCain's office, Feingold's office. Almost a priest early in life, he seemed to have taken reform politics as a religious vocation. Of course, world hunger certainly qualified for a heart like his.

But I missed the old band. We weren't making enough of a splash. It was just a time to feel a little pitiful.

I stopped on a red dirt road in a grove and picked an orange and ate it in the road. If I owe that orange to the Florida Orange Growers, let me say by way of payment that it was a wonderful orange, and the next time you buy some, you should buy an extra one.

It may have been a magic orange, as a little way down that same dirt road I came across an African American man under a big straw hat, selling something out of two steaming vats. He didn't have a sign, but people were stopping and going away with plastic bags full of brown goo.

"Never had a boiled peanut?" He asked me.

You might think this was an old fellow scratching out a living selling some little soulful treat. That would be the old South; this was the new. Mr. Roberts was a retired engineer, selling boiled peanuts in a little weekend partnership with his brother. About a dozen people stopped in the hour we visited, each spending about $4 for their baggie of goo.

The peanuts are boiled in the shell, swelling to twice their size like a body too long in the swamp. The two cauldrons, Regular and Cajun, were thick broths of meaty flavors. You pop them from their dripping shells right into your mouth like oversized edamame. They are wonderful, better than big, beefy, Boston baked beans.

Mr. Roberts was an angel beside the road. I have already described the fact that the necessary people appear when you are doing something worthwhile.

"Well, look, you need to be working with the churches down here. That's what you got to do," he said. "That way, they have the church committees to keep the registration goin' after you and your friends be on your way."

I had the feeling that his slight dialect came with the boiled peanuts and went away when he engineered. He was in a role and doing it.

He rattled off the names of a few pastors who weren't afraid to get political. I asked if he could call ahead for us, and he found his cell phone in a deep pocket of his overalls.

The next rainy Sunday, Doris, Blue and I were the honored guests at the Faith Pentecostal Church in Avon

Park. The music and energy as we walked in were inspirational beyond my ability to fully describe. Doris and Blue looked fabulous in their best outfits. Doris, by virtue of her age, was honored for that alone. Plus, she wore her biggest hat. We were escorted to the front pew.

The congregation members had already been told who she was and what she had done in her life, all the way back to stopping H-bombs in Alaska.

The Pentecostals, once called the Holy Rollers, know how to find divinity and joy with every clap of the present moment, with spontaneous dancing and uninhibited expressions of joy. Though we were of a different race and of different flavors of belief, the several ministers, in turn, welcomed us from the pulpit and, with voices of awesome authority, blessed our mission.

We three were asked to come up front and be blessed, which we did. Pastor Brown and his wife, both among the best speakers I have ever heard, weaved the gospel into politics, while the choir and the band found the right places to come in and make it all rise to the roof every few minutes.

"Granny D, you come up here and speak to us," the Reverend's wife called.

Doris was too moved to speak, and she pushed me forward. "Mr. Dennis, you come speak for Miss Doris," the woman called.

I don't know all that I said. I know I talked about Doris's great walk, and how, in all of that, she was instructed by Dr. King and by his five principles taken from Mr. Gandhi: that we understood that we must all bring change to the world not by making others suffer, but by suffering ourselves, as Doris has suffered joyfully for our democracy.

"That's right!" the people would interrupt me, led by Pastor Brown. The choir was building a holy background hum behind my words.

"As our Lord suffered!" Mrs. Brown added. "Hallelujah! Glory, glory!" people shouted.

And I told them we had met so many people who had given up on politics and believed that they had no representation for their needs, and there is so much despair.

"That's right!" the people called out. And the choir did something big to go along with it.

I said that things would never change until all the people used the power of the vote, the power that so many had sacrificed for, that it was always a Freedom Summer somewhere.

"That's right! That's right!" Pastor Brown moved in and took it from there, as the choir swelled. They all got to singing and dancing—it was something. Holy Rollers know how to rock as well as roll.

"Everybody here got to vote" he commanded on behalf of the Lord. Before he was done, Pastor Brown had pointed to a young lady who was going to set up the tables for registration, and she would be in charge of all that until the election.

In the back of the church after the service, it was all hugs and introductions to children and grandmothers.

The peanut man had set us right. Down the rest of the road, we would check in with the Gospel churches and sometimes it was something.

We drove back to St. Pete by way of Peace River and a calm lake where we paused to let things sink in before we went back to work. We stopped at a diner that was once the favorite gathering place and town hall of a community established by circus freaks. Blue was fully absorbed by the clippings and photos on the walls.

We went back to Winnie and Al's embrace in St. Pete. Winnie maneuvered us into the Martin Luther King Day Parade. With Rosie as a moving supply depot of handed-out registration forms, Blue at the wheel, Doris and I worked the crowds on both sides of the street, three and four people deep, all reaching out for forms. Some asked for stacks for their churches.

Doris had been hurting that morning with pain in her back and difficult breathing. Blue gave her a massage to get her ready for the long parade, which she literally ran, zipping back and forth to Rosie for more forms. She was fit as a kid by the end of the day.

Get Up! Stand Up!

Just when we were starting to plan another move down Florida, Blue said she had made a decision about her life. She said she wanted to stay with us for the long haul, if we would have her, but she wanted a clean slate back home. She needed to return to Asheville to make good on some promises, especially a mural in the kids' room of a community clinic, pledged in trade for some health training she had already received. She would take the little car, if that was all right, and then catch up with us in Miami. That was her plan.

Blue had been taking walks alone and generally looking the way people look when they're in the middle of a serious think about life.

I'm always wrong when I try to psychoanalyze people, but that never seems to stop me. Plus, Maureen helped me think through what Blue was going through—I called home every night from my bunk in the van. Blue had been on her own for some years and had fallen into a new family of sorts, meaning the traveling three of us. But she might be experiencing that as a danger as well as a comfort, in that she didn't want to be the traveling daughter. She was an adult and wanted to do things because she decided on them, just as she had decided her own name and the patterns on her skin. We were threatening her independence at the same time we were opening the world to her. It was confusing.

Going home and settling affairs would be the thing to do, as her freedom couldn't be free while she had entanglements back there. Besides, a week or two with her tattoo clients could provide her with some financial independence. She wouldn't be our daughter but a peer.

We said goodbye, worrying that she might get stuck back in her old world.

Doris and I were not finished with the area. We worked Tampa for several more days. One new idea to test was to hit fast food joints after the busy dinner hours, and, sure enough, we found plentiful 18- and 19-year-olds behind the counters who were ready and anxious to register and didn't know how. We spread that word to voter registration groups.

When making our way on foot down a Tampa sidewalk one evening, between a McDonalds and an Arby's, we passed in front of a strip joint. Doris said, "What about this place? I bet they have young workers."

"I bet they do," I said, "but if I take you in there, you'll squeal about it later. So, if you go in, you're on your own and it was your own damn idea. I'll just wait here."

"Well, they are working women, and they ought to register," she said, grabbing two clipboards and storming past the disoriented bouncer.

An hour passed as I loitered uncomfortably outside. Had they put her to work?

Finally, out she came, flanked by two fully dressed but obviously well-cast women, laughing with her and thanking her for coming. She was holding signed forms from the women inside and from some of the customers. The women had sworn to her that they would get the word to other clubs. She had been the belle of the ball and had turned down their offer to take to the stage.

The two women who came outside with her later set up ExoticWomenVote.org.

And the pirates. I should mention the pirates. In a Tampa cigar store I found myself surrounded by pirates.

Their outfits were as authentically piraty as anything Edith Head could have sewn up in Hollywood. The men seemed to be coming in for their annual supply of huge cigars. One had a live parrot on his shoulder. I naturally asked one of them what the deal was.

"We're pirates," he explained. I nodded and got my little cigar out of there.

I waved off the encounter as a statistical event: if you go into enough cigar stores, there will sooner or later be pirates. But, in a downtown elevator on our way to a radio station, the situation was soon clarified. I overheard a group of secretaries making their weekend plans. Gasparilla Days started the next Saturday. Residents celebrate the pirate heritage of Tampa Bay in an interesting way. Many belong to pirate crews. A crew might be four or forty people. They dress up, appear in the Mardi Gras-like parade, and generally party har-har-heartily.

The remarkable part, as I also learned on the elevator, is that many crews are involved in charity work year-round.

I was impressed. Yes, there is a famous amount of drinking, and some residents do escape town to avoid the whole noisy experience. But the idea of creating little groups that overcome the dehumanizing scale of the city is something that every town needs to think about in their own way. Old-line civic clubs and church groups certainly fill part of the bill, but zany civic clubs linked to the heritage of the region seem worth a good think, excepting the Klan.

In Fort Myers, after working the downtown streets and media, we parked Rosie in the middle of a housing project where we were advised by reporters not to go. We just started visiting with people hanging out on sidewalks and front patios. Veronica Shoemaker, an elder African American florist whose shop was located at the edge of the district, had given us the lay of the land as she arranged flowers. Her shop was on Veronica Shoemaker Boulevard, named for her long life of activism. Her main advice was to just go do it. Nobody was going to eat us up. It was just before Valentine's Day, so I was in her shop to send flowers home.

Hanging out in the projects, we talked to mothers about their sons who were in prison or had been. Some of the women had seen Doris on the television news that morning. The telephone grapevine quickly spread about her presence. One after another, young men came by for instructions on how to get their voting rights back. We had the special forms ready, stapled to clear instructions. We let the little kids pet Tim the Alligator on the hood and gave them a peek into Rosie, which might as well have been the Starship Enterprise.

Before we left, several mothers appointed themselves to get more forms and make sure they were submitted properly. They started brainstorming about who had recently turned 18, and who would do so before the election.

I again wondered where on earth the Democratic Party was.

Jim showed up by air in Fort Myers and showed us the way out to Sanibel Island, where we saw the most stunning sunset I've ever seen, and I'm from Arizona.

After a few more days working the region, Doris, Jim and I headed down the highway called Alligator Alley.

We rolled into Miami and found a sprawling swap-meet we had heard about. We worked the crowd with clipboards as the manager made supportive PA announcements for us.

The plan was for Blue, who had now been gone a few weeks, to find us there if she had finished her mural. She had done so and had made enough tattoo money to travel as a peer, not a kid. She had driven straight through from Asheville, not wasting her new money on a motel or shower.

At that swap-meet, Jim had his first sight of her. It took him about one second to have her in a bear hug.

"Blue, darlin', you're a tall one! You stink!" The bonding was mutual. They had talked enough on the phone to have a sense of each other's personality and humor, but they hadn't smelled each other or ruffled each other's hair until now. Their loving friendship was official.

From Jim's work with young people, he understood and cherished her feigned unruliness.

We worked the crowd for the rest of the day. Blue did the best.

In the evening, Jim left in the little car for the Florida Keys for his annual campout under the Florida sun. Without it, his skin wouldn't be right for the rest of the year. Some winters, he would camp on a platform in the Everglades, alone among the bugs and alligators, and private enough to sun himself all over without notice. This time, Libby would fly down to camp with him.

After some smashed Cuban sandwiches and Cuban coffee in Little Havana, Doris, Blue and I took the bridge across Biscayne Bay to Miami Beach, stopping in South Beach for a walk along the surf and cutting through umbrella-shaded cocktail areas where there were wonderfully tanned sights for everyone. Somewhere in all the sea breeze, Doris lost a prized eagle feather from her straw hat—punishment, she said, for our indulgent detour. A Native American man had given it to her with some ceremony in an Arizona desert.

"Didn't we plan to be in Little Haiti by now, or did you just want Blue to see South Beach?" Doris asked with some attitude. She was sometimes a little jealous of the quite innocent attention Blue got, most recently from her own son.

The pastel clubs of South Beach were opening for the evening, and I took the long way to see them, and yes, maybe so Blue could see the scene. The rich, fashionable young and the well-preserved were already gathering, talking on cell phones along every sidewalk and holding wine glasses on balconies. Cruise ships the size of the Las Vegas Strip lit up the Bay. We returned to the mainland via a long road of little humped bridges, each revealing a little Venice of homes and yachts below.

I am always amazed at the wealth of this nation. It is best appreciated when one is well dressed and arriving in a fine auto. We were clomping along in Rosie, which was trying not to embarrass us with too much smoke. Our bright graphics did catch eyes along the boulevards, and garnered the usual confused looks, waves, thumbs-up and a few honks that we took positively.

On the mainland, the scenery changed quickly. Little Haiti is not a slum, but it is a hard place compared to South Beach. The poverty is lightened by a culture of food, religion, and the music of the Caribbean. We could smell its restaurants and hear its music as we drove in.

Low, brightly painted buildings, Creole restaurants, beauty salons, music stores, and car repair shops are strung along the main streets of Little Haiti. Beyond the commercial streets are little homes and sprawling, two-story housing projects and people walking about. A

Creole language radio station blared from screened doorways and passing cars. The office of the Haitian American Society stood at the heart of the community and was one of our goals.

We found a cheap motel and settled in. Taking the bunk in the bus, I had a view of the street life long into the night. Business was carnal and prosperous. Even at dawn, when I went looking for coffee, the night was just winding down.

That morning, as usual, had me coming through the motel room door with coffee and muffins. Blue would still be asleep, cuddled like a cat and unready for bright light or humans. Doris would be bent over a book, a sheaf of Internet news from the printer in the bus, or a speech draft for later. She would have her hearing aids out, so there was nothing I could do that would not completely startle her, as she always seemed to have her back to the door.

After her big jump, she would laugh, go fishing for her hearing aids, wonder if Blue was going to sleep all day, though it was still early dawn, and then I would sneak a shower.

We found the big Catholic Church and introduced ourselves to the pastor, Father Dabus, who was a quiet Haitian man of great dignity. Earlier inquiries that morning to patrons at the coffee shop had identified him as the man to meet. He listened with suspicion and eventually warmed to us, but he had a problem.

"People had a bad time voting here last time. I don't want to put people back in harm's way," he told us. Stories of voter intimidation had followed us all over Florida, but he described police arrests in polling places and soldiers posted to keep people inside the housing projects.

"I will call Jimmy Carter and ask him to send poll watchers here for the next election," Doris offered.

"You know Carter?" Father Dabus leaned forward over his desk.

"I do," she replied.

It wasn't a stretcher, as Carter had blurbed her book in glowing terms: "Doris Haddock is a true patriot, and our nation has been blessed by her remarkable life."

We had run into him in Seattle the year before on our book tour. I was walking past a hotel meeting room when I saw a big fellow standing guard at the door. The Secret Service tip-off was the curly audio thing in his ear.

"Who's in town?" I asked him. Even as his head jerked toward the meeting room, I could hear the comforting tones of Carter's great Georgia voice at the microphone.

He and Doris visited in the hall later, with Carter introducing her all around, bragging on her great walk, her book, and the bill she got passed.

She told Father Dabus she would call her son and ask him to call Carter's sister, who had become our conduit.

Beyond our view, other, much larger efforts were underway to protect the Little Haiti vote with an army of poll watchers.

Father Dabus looked at the draft of the flier we intended to distribute around Little Haiti. The flier said that, if Haitian U.S. citizens in Miami were ever to be as powerful as the American Cubans, they must all become voters. Father Dabus liked the flier generally.

"But this should be in Creole," he suggested, sliding it back to me. Did I think I could find a good translator? No? He would send us one.

He agreed to promote voter registration from the pulpit and form a committee to register parishioners, which was another way of saying he would get every U.S. citizen in Little Haiti registered. We then met with the

Catholic Social Charities where some 500 people were served every day. They agreed to stack up the forms and our new fliers when we had them translated. They were agreeable because Father Dabus had called ahead. It was like that all day, until we took time to park under a tree so Doris could call Jim about Carter and take a nap.

While I was enjoying a little cigar under the big tree and Blue was off talking to a high school principal about planning a voter registration day for seniors, a Haitian woman in a Caribbean-bright dress approached me and said she had heard about this Granny D and would like to help us with translation. She taught both languages.

"Father Dabus sent you!" "Yes, yes! Father Dabus!" she laughed.

Later that night we had our flier, but only after an argument with her in a coffee joint near her house.

"The more I tried to do this," she said, "the more wrong I knew it was. You need to talk more about the issues of this place," she advised. She gave us a quick lesson in the hot issues of Little Haiti that could be improved with a bit more democracy. More about schools. More about the dread condition of the housing projects. And then we could use the Cuban argument for a kicker.

Now we had a flier to work the neighborhoods, housing projects, beauty salons, barber shops, laundries and little markets. One side of the flier had our main message; the other side promoted a citizenship and voting registration event on the coming Saturday, where people could try voting machines and get signed up. Most people had citizenship issues, if not for themselves then for their immigrant kin, so the citizenship information was a big draw.

The door-to-door work, especially in the housing projects, was successful, especially because we could

Love and Democracy

assure people that there would probably not be voter harassment this time. People led us to apartments where someone had just turned 18, or where someone had just become a citizen, and they often served as translators for us. The mothers always got it and became our agents throughout the projects.

In the evenings we cruised the main streets, trying to hand out the fliers to the people on streets, but they were suspicious and shied away, even after we had the Creole radio stations talking about us. Our big stacks of fliers were not thinning fast enough.

"We're just too damned white!" Doris said. We strategized during our dinner break in Rosie, parked at a little strip mall. Doris had cooked a wonderful soup.

After dinner I ducked into a used record store right in front of where we parked and talked to the young clerk, explaining our mission. What is the best music that says liberation, political freedom? He didn't have to think. "You mean Marley?" I thought he might say Marley, but I was afraid to suggest him, as it might just be my whiteness jumping to stereotypes—maybe a rap artist would be his hipper advice? Nope. Nobody hipper than Marley.

"Marley. Yes, Marley is who the people listen to and believe, because he speaks for people, you know. He is the man, you know. It's still Marley. Always Marley, you know?"

I got out my wallet to buy the Marley CD he picked as the best one for us.

"Keep your money!" he smiled.

We rigged our public address system, used normally for speeches at rallies, to blare from the high windows of Rosie's sleeping loft. While Blue was finishing the wiring, I went into another little shop in the same strip. It had a selection of musical instruments and furniture and a few Republic of Haiti flags in the window. It was dark but the door was half-open. Inside, candles were burning in a circle on the cement floor, and an old woman was clearly in the middle of something with other women, no doubt relating to the old religion of the islands.

I apologized.

"No worries. Why do you want a flag?" she said.

I hadn't said I wanted a flag; she just knew. I told her why we were in town. She stood up and went into the back, returning with a folded flag—her largest, she said.

"I give it to you free, because you are trying to do a good thing."

I tied it so it would flow from the rear of the bus. Then we rolled out again into the evening.

Blue hung out the passenger window and Doris out the dinette window with handfuls of fliers as we now cruised slowly to blaring Bob Marley.

Wake up and live--wake up and live!...There's work to be done...All together now...Wake up and live now, y'all!

The same crowds who an hour or so earlier had viewed us with confusion and suspicion now began to move, to dance and smile, rocking up to Rosie to get the fliers. Creole language! They noticed it instantly on the flier: "Very nice, very nice!" The headline was "*Poukisa Ayisyen dwe Vote?*" --why should Haitians vote?

"Mama be jammin' tonight!" a man sang as he danced up to take fliers from Doris. Blue would give extra copies with instructions to go take some over to that man standing over there, those ladies over there, that beauty shop, and all would obey, dancing away.

Flee from hate, mischief and jealousy!... Don't bury your thoughts; put your dream to reality, yeah!...W'all together now...Wake up and live...

Many didn't know much English, but they had known the English of Marley all their lives:

Get up stand up, stand up for your rights!...Get up, stand up! Life is your right! Don't give up the fight!

The bright yellow buildings turned neon green under the streetlights. The air was cool and scented with foods. Smiling faces kept coming out of the dark for fliers. The bigger-than-life faces of Martin Luther King and Aristide loomed large on murals painted in unexpected places. We cruised until the fliers were gone, sometimes stopping so Blue could run a stack into a market or another beauty salon where customers stared and smiled from windows. Three young men walking under a freeway bridge changed their walk to dance as we approached and as the music filled the space. Fists flew up as they turned and smiled: "We registered, Mama!" one shouted to us as we passed. By the end of the evening, Little Haiti was ready for Saturday, which was a great day with hundreds attending.

For the remainder of our few days and nights there, we could not cruse the streets without people waving fists in the air and smiling and shouting, *Mama!* as we passed.

If the Democratic Party had storefronts in such places, learning about and advocating for the needs of the communities, America would be a different political world. We couldn't find the party anywhere in Little Haiti, except in the person of Jacques Despinosse, Vice Mayor of North Miami, who let us set up office in his own law office.

We wanted to connect with as many community groups as possible, mostly to be sure there would be a continuing registration effort after we left. He was the political man of Little Haiti, well dressed, highly educated, with a front office filled with plaques and photos of his connections. People waited to talk to him as the godfather of the district.

Toward the end of the afternoon on Wednesday, February 25, there was a strange mood in the office. People were talking excitedly in Creole on the phone and leaving early. Looking out the window, I could see little clusters of people gathering on the street.

"What is going on?" I asked Jacques' secretary.

"Aristide!" she said as she rushed into the big man's closed office.

We stopped our work for the evening, as Aristide was all anyone wanted to talk about. We were on the sidewalk when Jacques came storming out of the office and headed across the street.

"Come!" he shouted back at us. "History!" he said

Directly across were the offices of the Haitian American Society and its meeting room that quickly filled with the leaders of Little Haiti. We stayed in an anteroom, watching through glass doors as they entered for some kind of great consideration. Jacques could be seen making wide gestures, his gold-rimmed glasses and big gold wristwatch catching the invading last rays of the day. He jabbed his little finger to nail down point after point.

Between the coming and going of English and Creole, we gathered that Jean-Bertrand Aristide, the popularly elected, ex-Catholic priest and President of Haiti, had been overthrown by the CIA. Little Haiti had strong pro-

and anti-Aristide factions, but that seemed not quite the issue. It was more immediate. The CIA had done this?

"It is always the CIA in such matters," a man huddling with us in the anteroom explained. He stared at tall Blue, wearing her sunglasses.

"You CIA?" he asked her, kidding.

"I could tell you, but then..." she said.

"I understand," he replied.

I was afraid it might not be the right moment for that joke, but she had read his eyebrows correctly, and he became our translator for the next hour.

The meeting was about the community needing to speak with one voice, not two. Yes, peacekeepers should be sent immediately—that should be demanded, but perhaps not American peacekeepers. What is our position?

Men and a few women shuttled in and out of the room, making cell calls from the sidewalk and huddling in twos and threes, then returning to the meeting. What are the facts? There seemed to have been a call from the Miami captain of the U.S. Coastguard a few minutes after 5, an hour earlier. It was something about a ship in Miami Harbor. Some of the individuals on the ship were armed, it was said. The Coast Guard was approaching the ship. Was it Aristide, or a ship of partisans leaving Miami for Haiti? Or all a rumor? What are the facts? What is our position?

Calls were made by people who knew people. Is Aristide coming to Miami? How will we care for him? Where? Then long, careful arguments and agreements negotiated in Creole. Within the hour, something had been resolved, information had been received. Jacques finally emerged, quickly telling us that he was late to teach his class at a nearby college and that all had been resolved.

There would be a press conference in the morning. One voice.

Popularly elected Aristide had, in fact, been kidnapped by the CIA and by U.S. troops at gunpoint and was on his way to Africa. He was becoming too democratic and liberal in his reforms. The Bush White House called the report of Aristide's kidnapping "utter nonsense," despite credible accounts in the weeks following.

Haiti has not been the same—has not been peaceful—since that day.

In the fog of uncertainty, the Haitian community had done the one thing it could do: it embraced unity and stood up for democracy.

Doris and Blue and I were especially outsiders this night, and so we went away to let them be Haitians while we cased the African American neighborhoods closer to downtown, and where we had a meeting set for the next morning.

Triangulation

Breakfast found us in Overtown, an African American neighborhood in central Miami. We were breaking bread with the head of a group of ex-gang members who were into a new thing: voting. Brian Dennis, of Brothers of the Same Mind, had interesting things to tell us about why the Democrats had been losing elections. Two members of the Miami Heat basketball team were eating at the next table. Bootleg music and movies were on sale at the side of the room.

"You got the bad voting machines and the purging of Blacks from the voting lists and you got that bitch, what's her name, as Secretary of State," Brian said, looking at the NBA guys instead of us as he talked. "But you also had Clinton in there. He was so busy triangulating to look conservative that he messed up everything. Triangulation was a noose for us and for the Democratic Party. He put a hundred thousand extra cops on the streets, right? That made the cities safer, right? Well, maybe it did. But it also meant every brother driving down any street with a cracked taillight or a twisted license plate was pulled over, and anybody with anything in their cars, like a little weed or the wrong size pocketknife was going to get hauled in. Some of them were hauled in so often that the third time became a felony, and I don't know how many tens of thousands of young men lost their right to vote, but they were sure as hell Democrats. They were enough, just them in this one city, to turn the 2000 presidential election. So that's what you get for trying to look Republican," he said. "And probably just as bad in other states, too."

A better way to reduce crime would have been jobs and good schools and easier college loans, which was his next point.

Brian told us who to talk to in Overtown. As a result, we got accepted into a street fair for the following day. In the meantime, we pulled the little red wagon through the neighborhoods and into the old downtown area's shaded archways, family stores, and restaurants.

For the street fair, Blue bought a stack of poster boards and a big box of colored markers. We set up a table and let kids make their own "vote for me" posters. That drew in their parents and their older siblings, and we did a good business registering voters. Blue also bought a bag of plastic jewels and let kids glue them onto Rosie's hood, outlining the flames that she had painted all over the fenders and hood at an earlier stop. Rosie had become a rolling art project.

Before heading out of Miami, we decided to hit the Keys, where Jim and Libby were camping on Bahia Honda. Before meeting up with them, we thought we should do some voter registration in Key West. Traveling there with us was Baltimore activist Mike Eisner, who flew to Miami to help for a few days.

There wasn't a spare motel room or RV space anywhere in Key West, so we camped on a beach off the highway. We had whiskey at sunset, then with flashlights watched little octopi and other creatures in the tide. It was a starry night, balmy and beautiful.

After breakfast we tied a pirate flag to Rosie's stern and started cruising the neighborhoods of Key West. Some old boaters with leathery faces came up and signed. One fellow said he had dropped out of voting years ago but knew he needed to get back in "Before they ruin the planet," he said.

Love and Democracy

Mike and I worked the wharf area with voter registration forms while Blue and Doris worked a street of massage parlors. In early evening we rolled out to find Jim and Libby.

Mike and Blue and I were standing with Jim in the water, talking about our adventures to date and strategizing the road ahead when I noticed three sharks not too far away, circling closer. We were up to our chests. I mentioned the creatures to Jim, but he waved them off and continued the discussion.

Jim finally agreed that they were getting a bit close, so we took our leave. Jim was never one to panic.

We dropped Mike off at a friend's house in Miami and sped northward, to the extent that Rosie could speed. We would be without the scout car for the rest of the trip, as Jim would drive it home to New Hampshire after taking Libby to the Miami airport.

On Leap Day, 2004, a Sunday, we were limping northward after several stops to let the engine cool and a few hours for Doris to visit her Florida sister. We arrived in Daytona Beach without knowing in advance that it was the beginning of the 64th Annual Daytona Beach Bike Week. Down every street were Harleys and other beautiful bikes—six-hundred thousand of them.

The roar covered the city with a constant roar. At every stoplight we were surrounded. Should we keep going or try to do something with this? We found an inexpensive motel right on the beach, thanks to a whole bike club that had canceled on account of a funeral.

Maureen had been an editor in Daytona Beach for years, so I called to tell her we had stumbled into Bike Week and were thinking of skipping the town. She said Bike Week was too fun to miss, and that we should think of an angle.

We mixed in on the sidewalks, asking people if they wanted to register to vote. We might as well have been selling Bibles.

"Think of something," Doris said, echoing Maureen. After we dined on Chinese take-out in the room, Blue and Doris went for a walk on the beach, and I climbed into Rosie to adapt. I reserved "Bikersvote.com" and put up a quick website that had all the links to on-line voter registration. I designed a little folding palm card that we could give out to promote voting and promote the site. It was something they could spread around to bikers back home, wherever they lived.

When the walkers returned, Blue penned tattoo-style biker art for the cover of the little folder. We found a 24-hour copy shop and ordered five thousand.

Over breakfast, Doris loved the ad hoc plan, but not all of it, because Blue had spotted a silk screen shop across the street and had a sweatshirt made for Doris. The back had an American flag flowing through a skull. The front had a skull and a simple message: "Register to Vote, Motherf--ers!"

Doris just stared at it.

"All right, but no photos," she said, "Jim would kill me," and she pulled it on with a laugh.

Morning crowds formed circles around her and took our fliers and took selfies with her. Florida natives among them signed the voter forms on our clipboards.

We worried that we might be registering crowds that would vote against the stream of our own thinking, but we soon learned otherwise. Bikers like freedom, and, while they weren't crazy about Kerry or Dean, many were angrily opposed to Bush. Bikers include about every kind of American, despite what you might think. A group of lesbian bikers passed Rosie one evening, shouting, "Anybody but Bush!"

After a long day on sidewalks lined with booths, we retired to print up more handouts. Blue insisted we attend a women's wrestling event that took place on a huge pile of coleslaw. Even with so much more to look at, people at that event were anxious to talk to Doris, have their pictures taken with her, agree to spread around our BikersVote palm cards, and buy us beers. Blue ran into some tattooed friends from back home and had a grand time. For me, it was all just very Salvador Dali.

I was taking a picture of Doris with one of the winning wrestlers when the woman asked, "Flash?" I replied *Yes*, thinking she wanted to make sure the camera flash was on, as it was dusk. That was not what she meant at all. Another photo that Jim must never see.

As ferociously loud as those few days were, they were great fun—a politically incorrect carnival of freedom, really. Driving around town, seeing all these tough guys and chicks on incredibly beautiful machines made you think, gee, you'd hate to ever have to invade this country. Our military is redundant. Inside the head scarves and leathers are a lot of lawyers and accountants on fantasy weekends, but even so, if the Iraqis invaded Boca Raton, the bikes would be on their way, and it would all be over by Miller Time.

We woke up on March 4th on an organic farm near Ocala. Pauline Copello was misting her vegetables when I stumbled out of the bus to go wake Doris and Blue in the house. Pauline's husband, Joel, and their four-year-old, Anthony, were busy with chores here and there. Pauline's parents, Beth and Tony Ehrlich, were indoors fixing us a farm breakfast. They had all sold their homes in Daytona and Ormand Beach a year earlier to move out where Pauline now had land enough for her vegetables and where Beth and Tony could grow old. Joel sells things at antique shows and Pauline has a delivery route for her organic vegetables.

We talked about basil that morning, their most reliable cash crop. There are dozens of varieties, and some are so perishable you must eat them immediately upon picking. Later in the morning, Doris was in a chair under a tree practicing a speech and I was working on the website and communicating with voter volunteers. I looked around and thought that this is the kind of America, with sustainability as a core value, that Maureen and I need to find our way into.

Dennis Kucinich, the greenest of the mainline Dem candidates, was going to speak that evening in Gainesville, and Doris was set to meet with him. We had been pressuring him and Dean to join forces after the coming convention, as progressives were now split by the two campaigns. We wanted to get a promise out of both before the Boston convention, and Kucinich had agreed to meet about it.

Halfway back to Gainesville for that rendezvous, old Rosie died dead and would not restart. It would need a major cool-down, and we didn't have the extra time for that if Doris were to make the meeting with Kucinich.

So, Blue and Doris hitched a ride together into Gainesville while I cooled down the machine with bags of ice from a convenience store. Tiny Doris in her signature straw hat and Blue in her now signature blue fedora were quite a picture with their thumbs out. The first vehicle to come by stopped in a screech. It was a woman in a red pickup truck who then drove forty miles out of her way to get them to the church on time. I arrived toward the end of the event. Kucinich had agreed to call Dean and get talks going. I caught up with them as Kucinich was getting in the back of a car, saying, "OK, Doris, okay. I will call him. I said I would," as if he were promising to clean his room.

Long months later, just after the close of the Democratic Convention and while everybody was still in Boston, Dean and Kucinich did hold a unity rally.

It was 2 a.m. when we limped back to the farm in Ocala after the Kucinich meeting. We didn't want to wake the family, so Blue and Doris bunked in the bus, and I took a tarp out under a tree. In the distance I could hear the deep hum of motorcycles on Route 40, still flowing in and out of Daytona Beach for the last weekend of Bike Week.

The next morning, we were off to register the senior class at a high school and head one more time into Gainesville for a big outdoor Democracy Fest with candidates speaking, plus a stem-winder from Doris. She made it rain, as was often the case with a particularly good speech. It happened too often to not notice with wonder.

After Gainesville, we worked Jacksonville one more time, staying the night on the outskirts in the home of a carpenter, Mark Rothermel. He had read about us on the Internet and caught up with us on the streets of downtown Jacksonville. His old farm was a restful place, though Doris got up before the rest of us the next morning and got lost on her morning walk. A woman with a cell phone, and Doris's good memory for phone numbers, saved the day. She was miles away in a confusing tangle of looped streets and woods.

The woman quite literally dropped her jaw when I drove up in the bejeweled, alligator-ornamented, multicolored dream bus.

"My ride,' Doris said.

I suppose we had stopped at twenty repair garages by this time. Mechanics are nice fellows who look off into the distance when you describe an engine problem. There is a high angle where their eyes and thoughts go when they are diagnosing things mechanical.

"No, we already had that replaced," I would say with regret.

"Are you registered to vote?" Blue or Doris might add.

As we moved westward along the Panhandle, it occurred to me that Rosie never overheated in the rain. We stopped at a hardware store and bought about thirty feet of half-inch, clear plastic tubing. We duct-taped one end to the spout of the kitchen faucet and stuck the other end out a wind wing and into the front grill, held in place by the jaws of Tim the Alligator. The next time the engine started to stall and smoke, Doris or Blue turned on the kitchen tap, spraying a mist of water into the front grill. The engine would smooth out and not stall. It worked for the many miles ahead.

Also, if you have ever asked yourself which Hindu God should be prayed to for better engine performance or finding good parking places, Ganesha is your best pick, according to Blue. Elephant-faced Ganesha is a friendly god who will do endless favors and keep things going, if you will only be kind enough to ask. A small Ganesha medallion had long swung from Rosie's rearview mirror. Blue said it was to be rubbed if the engine was having a hard time starting, or sputtering, stalling or smoking, or if a parking space was needed. I am not Hindu, but I'll take help from anybody's heaven.

Love and Democracy

Doris's health was another matter. She was now 94 and this was a tough road. Blue and I were keeping an eye on her energy and health. She had her low days, but not many. Blue gave her muscle massages and used magic oils and scents. Blue was like a fight manager in Doris's corner. Doris would nap on the narrow couch as we drove, sometimes waking with little screams when her legs started to cramp.

"Keep going!" she would shout if I started to pull over.

The home of Susie Caplowe and Dan Hendrickson in Tallahassee is very nice and quite what you might expect of a normal American home until you open the door from the laundry room into what used to be a two-car garage. Computers, voting precinct maps, file cabinets and bins of clippings, reports and plans stretch out before you. This was the town's progressive headquarters.

Susie and Dan briefed us on the blow-by-blow of the 2000 debacle. The thugs who came in from Washington to physically stop the vote counting by means of belly-bouncing intimidation were a white-hot memory fueling their voter work.

They set us up with events and press interviews. Over the next few days, we did two television stories, a newspaper story, a public radio story that ran statewide and another that ran nationally on NPR. The message was always the same: working women need to find the time to register to vote.

We worked outside grocery stores in African American neighborhoods with the help of volunteers that Susie recruited. The evenings were filled with rallies and coordination meetings of voter groups. Gayle White of the Atlanta Journal-Constitution traveled with us and wrote a good story.

In Tallahassee we finally connected with the National Organization of Women, and at a NOW event ran into the state chair of the ghostly Florida Democratic Party. He would only talk to me if I walked with him from the event to his car. I pitched him on what we had been doing in Florida and what the party could do to follow up, especially in housing projects and Black churches. He looked at me, turned to his flunky, and said I could call the flunky. The flunky gave me a card but never returned my calls. It was sort of the perfect last experience with the party in Florida. You could tell they were pulling out all the stops to lose another one for America, which they did.

We had earlier crashed a meeting of the North Florida Democratic Club where I introduced Doris. They were pleased to meet her and had lovely cookies. They looked confused and a little disturbed when Doris mentioned we had been through their low-income neighborhoods and everyone we signed up to vote claimed to never have seen anyone from the Democratic Party in the neighborhood before. They were happy for the next speaker and more cookies.

Susie and Dan took us to a big union barbeque at the fairgrounds and to a student march at the state capitol, wherever potential new voters might be found.

Susie was deep into environmental issues and was defending ocean manatees against bills in the state legislature that would destroy them. She had worked with the actor John Lithgow on a children's book about the creatures. Blue had been a manatee fan since St. Pete and was full of questions for Susie.

Dan had personal history in Kentucky coalfields, and he taught me a great deal about the strikes and violence there.

Love and Democracy

When we pulled away from their house, Susie, I am told, had a new little tattoo somewhere to remember us by.

We had done Florida. It was the first time I had ever been in the state, which is three or four states, really, and I loved them all. From time to time, Doris, Blue and I talked about the global weather changes coming, the sea rise and the hurricanes ahead. I hoped we hadn't seen Florida at its final best.

Life on the Mississippi

Paulette is a poet, a literature professor at Loyola of New Orleans, a refined woman who has shared a drink or two with Tennessee Williams and André Codrescu at Molly's in the French Quarter. She had the useful brutality of a literature professor. I say that because I did have a few poems of my own in my bag and showed them to her at one point. She shuffled through them and found one: "Well, this one's all right," she said.

She had been following our adventures and invited us to stay with her when we came into New Orleans. She put Doris and Blue up in her extra bedrooms, let me sleep in the driveway—probably for lack of better poems—took us to the shipyards and ferry stations where people might need to register, and helped us register people all along Canal Street.

Paulette then arranged for Doris to take over the job of a young woman bartender at Molly's. Doris had no trouble mixing drinks. She was a bit short for the bar but was otherwise darling, holding her own in funny conversations with drunks and other artists and writers.

We later set up a table and banner on a corner in the Ninth Ward and did a good business of registering voters. There is a fatalism that goes with Louisiana politics, so we didn't expect to stir up much excitement, but we were welcomed warmly everywhere.

Paulette and her son were Rock the Vote organizers, which connected us with several voter projects and with the upstart League of Independent Voters, known informally at the time as the League of Pissed-Off Voters, which attracted Blue instantly. We offered several groups our expertise on ex-felon voting, as they had been turning away many people who in fact could register.

A Republican family that lived across the road from Paulette, snug under a levee, stopped when they saw Blue painting on Rosie one morning and just had to know all about our adventure. They invited us to dinner, which was a one-act Southern play of accents and attitudes, generational stresses between mother and strange son, and conversations in their garden that charmed us back a century or more. The home and its gardens could have been a set for a Tennessee Williams play, and we were on stage with brilliant actors who knew every New Orleans affect.

The next night, our intended departure night, they invited us up to their friend's apartment in the Quarter, a luxuriously overstuffed place where we overlooked Bourbon Street from an iron balcony as the ladies kept filling our glasses. They were beautiful and well-informed people and were particularly concerned about the loss of wetlands protecting New Orleans.

Their teen daughter, Taylor, had the statistics in her head: eleven football fields-worth of wetlands were lost each year between New Orleans and the Gulf. She said one big hurricane could now swamp the city. Those on the balcony were also concerned about the mess in Iraq, and we seemed to have many other shared concerns. How they could get from those concerns to their support for Bush was as mysterious to us as our liberal views were to them. But, like many Republicans, what they liked most in a leader was authenticity. It was, and remains, more important than issues. It didn't matter to them that Doris was an old Democrat. She was an authentic and the ladies kept her glass filled.

The light of the balcony was somehow just right for Doris. She looked like she was born for this place. But for poor Blue, the early spring pollen was a thick blanket upon the town, and she could hardly breathe. Despite her excitement in discovering Voodoo shops and talking with interesting people including neon-feathered Indians, and despite her travels down jazz-filled streets and her adventure late at night with Doris to visit and photograph graveyards and crypts, she needed to get away from the city to breathe.

The ladies of the balcony, temptation incarnate, insisted we stay the night. There was so much more to discuss over drinks yet to be served. The French Quarter was a glory of human interest and neon below us. But Blue stared at me fiercely. She needed out of the city.

After Hurricane Katrina, we checked on Paulette. She had resigned her post at Loyola so that younger faculty members with kids could keep their jobs. She moved to Rochester to live with her daughter. The ladies of the balcony all survived, and the family across the way, at the foot of the levee, had moved back to rebuild.

Driving at night to avoid overheating, we charged up Louisiana and into Mississippi, stopping in the dawn for breakfast and a few loads of laundry. We found signs life for the Democratic Party there: a laundry attendant in Canton gave us a good report on party organizing and registration in the area.

We were heading to Memphis and a date with the Hip Hop Summit voter project, sponsored by rap promoter Russell Simmons. Also, Doris was going to be a featured speaker for the 35th anniversary of Dr. King's death in Memphis. She would speak from the Lorraine Motel balcony, where he was killed. She didn't know if she would be able to do that without getting too emotional, even though she had spoken there during her long walk.

She did very well this second time, too. Kids climbed trees to get a better look at her over the heads of the big crowd.

Doris and Blue later went inside Graceland while I sent an update from the bus in the parking lot. They came back greatly amused by the décor of the place. From there, we did voter registration in the housing projects along Vance Boulevard. Kids in the projects posed with Tim the Alligator and Rosie generally. We did good registration business with their parents and older brothers and sisters.

One of the defects of our journey was that our best television and newspaper stories often appeared just as we were on our way out of town. We were driving out of Memphis when a big television story finally ran. We went back to take advantage of it by registering some more housing projects—the notoriety made a difference. We had to dash to the Shelby County Election Commission to get more forms, but they made it as hard as possible, wanting to give us only ten forms per visit. They relented when we threatened to bring in TV cameras. We had run into that same problem in some Florida cities.

Thereafter, we always tried to connect with a town's top voting officials and get them into publicity shots as soon as we hit town. That's what we did in the next big town, St. Louis.

Upon arriving, we drove an hour through central St. Louis without finding a breakfast joint. We dared look in Rosie's little museum of foods that was its refrigerator. It still had strange, oriental, curdy things that Jim had left and that we had never dared handle. Blue was about to serve up something awful from Jim's stash when I spotted a brunch place, tables on the sidewalk and everything lovely, so we were saved. We might have died.

We registered as visitors in the St. Louis housing projects and walked with reporters from the St. Louis Post-Dispatch and the Riverfront Times. We hung out in an area between the big hospital and the lunch joints, registering nurses. Doris went into the hospital cafeteria and learned sad life stories which she shared with us that night over dinner. We worked with ACORN and Rock the Vote volunteers, going door-to-door in areas that looked like Germany after the war.

We got lost in a big park one morning and parked to figure out the map. We were in sight of a freeway, where a woman driver saw us. She exited and parked beside us. She had heard we were in town and invited us to a women's art event. Julia Butterfly Hill, the woman who had saved a stand of old-growth trees in the Northwest by parking herself in one, would be there. Granny D would make it perfect, she said. Julia had in fact been trying to get in touch with us, we later learned.

Blue turned the bus into the centerpiece art project of the event, adding bright, new features as the other artists gawked and commended her. It was tremendously affirming to her as an artist, and she made at least one very good friend, judging by the fact that she didn't come back until the next morning. She was also knocked out by Julia, someone her own height and age and just as stylish in a black jacket—another model for using joyful sacrifice to make a difference in the world.

There was less work for Rosie's plastic cooling tube and Ganesha as we moved into cooler latitudes. We arrived in Des Moines early one Monday after a trouble-free, all-night drive.

In terms of our political mission, we declared victory in Iowa the minute we crossed the state line, for Iowa, being Iowa, was already 96% registered to vote.

The Iowa Caucus had taken place in mid-January; it was now April. Dean had screamed his scream and was gone. The progressives were still in mourning. Some were blaming the media for making too much of a rally whoop, which is undeniable. Others were blaming his campaign for not having a backup strategy and backup money after losing Iowa, but Dean and Trippi had figured it correctly that they had to win Iowa. If they had done so, millions of new dollars would have come their way. If they lost, no reserve fund would have been enough to repair the damage. It had made sense to bet the farm in the farm state. The scream thing really didn't matter—it was a death scream, as he was politically dead, and Kerry was sailing to the convention without serious competition. Kerry was politically dead, too, but nobody understood that until election night—it was his Iraq War authorization vote and more death screams than Dean's.

Before Iowa, Kerry had saved his failing campaign by mortgaging his house on Beacon Hill, which sent a conga line of his wife's Heinz money into his own account. Campaign finance laws limit what another person can donate to a campaign. But the law allows candidates to spend unlimited amounts of their own money.

John McCain would do much the same thing when he ran for president, also with a rich wife's house. While voter registration was our current mission, Doris and I were still interested in watching the money move through politics, and we provided Blue with color commentary on the rising campaign season.

As Iowa voters were already registered, we could instead do some good with the campaign finance issue.

Doris and I had been encouraging the work of a community action group, Iowa Citizens for Community Improvement, or Iowa CCI, for several years. They had a history of deep organizing, meaning they taught people to speak for themselves. They had done that with the predatory lending issue, factory farms ruining family farming and the environment, and other issues. They understood that, until they got the fat cat checks out of the Iowa Legislature, they were always going to be fighting on uneven ground. As I was deeply involved in getting Arizona's public campaign financing system passed, they had asked me to come up and share ideas a couple of times. Doris had spoken at their state convention.

They were known as a Saul Alinsky kind of shop. Their fearless tactics had given them an edgy reputation that made it hard for them to form coalitions with the more genteel groups like the League of Women Voters. We made it our business to use Doris's visit an opportunity to broker a coalition or at least a first date. We also helped them gather some good press stories boosting their bill in the legislature for public campaign funding. We jointed them making rounds through the Iowa state house and the offices of Iowa's Members of Congress.

Driving through Des Moines toward the end of our stay, I asked Blue and Doris if they more enjoyed driving into a new town or leaving it after a job well done. Doris said, "Are you kidding?" I looked and she was teary-eyed. "You meet such wonderful new friends and then you just have to drive away. It is awfully sad for me. You two may see them all again, but it may be different for me."

This whole project sometimes struck her as a farewell tour of a great nation and of life itself. It wasn't quite that, but it was getting close.

Maureen was in Iowa at that same time, as her mother was dying. We went to the farm in Perry, where I would stay behind to be with Maureen and her family for a bit. I would catch up later with Doris and Blue in Minneapolis via a Greyhound Bus.

Minneapolis has a perfect picture spot to talk to TV reporters about working women. It's Nicollet Avenue, a pedestrian and trolley street where a bronze Mary Tyler Moore tosses up her bronze beret. After working the town, we headed to Madison and our 20th state.

Just as Rochester is the home of the Abolition Movement, so Madison is the home of American progressive reform. I had always wanted to tread the streets once walked by Fighting Bob Lafollette, the man behind nearly every reform Teddy Roosevelt gets credit for. It's the region where farmers rebelled against big banks, big railroad and corrupt politics.

With university president Charles Van Hise as his cohort, Governor Lafollette turned Madison, the state capitol, into a city-wide think tank, engaging experts at the University of Wisconsin with the state government in a problem-solving co-op. The direct election of U.S. senators, the workers' compensation system, citizen ballot initiatives, and many other reforms came out of that happy arrangement, which continues today. The best thing a state can do is to have its capital in a medium-sized university town where everybody runs into everybody over coffee, and ideas can be cross-pollinated. Accordingly, Texas has no excuse for its legislature, as it's located in wonderful Austin. But maybe Texas would be even worse if not for that grace.

We worked cities as far up as Duluth, where there was something of a parade and rally for Doris and where cliffs of glacial blue ice lined the upper roads. We then turned south to Illinois.

In Chicago, the concrete stairwells of Cabrini Green were stained with bloody handprints. Blue was appalled but fascinated. She took pictures of the unintended art. Steel shutters secured every window, and the big, brown eyes of little children often peeked through the slits when we knocked—and we knocked on every door. Many of the apartment interiors, against our expectations, were clean and lively. Many of the children were nicely dressed and courteous. Because of its reputation for being the most violent housing project in America, most of the towers have been taken down; only a few remain. The towers stare down on empty parking lots, for few residents can afford cars. Rosie was the only vehicle in the lot, far below us as we worked from the top floors down.

"Would you like to register to vote? On election day, you can vote right across the parking lot at the school."

The doors would open wide. "Yes, please. How do I do it?"

Most people claimed to have never met anyone doing voter work in the buildings. We were as welcome as if we were handing out chocolates.

One of the most amazing organizers in the country was with us, along with volunteers she had recruited. Andrea Raila, a tax consultant, had followed Granny's big walk and our recent travels via the web and had promised to have Chicago ready for us, which she did. Andrea moved us through Cabrini with a forceful spirit.

The next day we covered the Le Claire projects with a Tribune reporter in tow. Andrea was again our organizer, using our red wagon to pull her two younger kids down the streets. We also spent a day with her downtown under the El, registering students at Harold Washington College.

Love and Democracy

Andrea's second child is an adoptee from China. When the little girl became sad one night that there was nobody else in the family quite like herself, Andrea and her husband said, okay, let's go to China and get you a sister, and they did. There seems to be no sadness in the world that they will not happily jump into to make right.

Chicago's Heartland Cafe was at that time a Garrison Keilloresque restaurant and radio studio that flavored its Lunt Avenue neighborhood with the kind of local democracy that should be a part of every American town. On two Saturday mornings, Granny D's voter registration project was the big show, broadcast city-wide.

The Green Mill, a famous speakeasy frequented by Capone during Prohibition, is still a working bar with good music. On a chilly evening in that early May, Andrea stole me away from her busy houseful to show me the place and sit down for a drink and a visit. Naturally, I took the occasion to find out what had turned her into an activist.

Chicago-born, one of eight kids raised by a divorced mother who moved them to Louisiana. Her mom worked long hours to support them. An African American woman, Elmira, took care of them in the daytime hours. Vietnam and the Civil Rights Movement were rocking the nation, and Andrea watched it closely. She was six years old in 1965 when King was on the march. Elmira's son was murdered by the KKK and dragged down the street. When Andrea moved back to Chicago at the age of 15, she was already changed, "overwhelmed and outraged by all that blatant racism," she said.

"I learned cooking, cleaning, fighting, spitting and cussing from Elmira. I learned compassion, fairness, and bravery from her. She was a single mother, poor, uneducated and world-wise. I idolized her."

In Chicago, Andrea joined a student movement in support of democracy in Iran. The CIA at that time was installing the Shah, who commenced a regime of torture against the people while he opened the door to U.S. oil companies. All that would of course end in the popular revolution that installed Islamic fundamentalism.

Andrea was arrested twice for supporting the candidacy of Chicago's 1st African American mayor. Like Winnie in St. Pete, Sue and Dan in Tallahassee, Paulette in New Orleans, the folks in Iowa and Minnesota and other places, Andrea was a human storm of energy and high spirits.

Some activists act from anger, leaving their own lives and their own families behind. Andrea, and the organizers we had been getting to know, seemed angry on the surface but deeply joyful inside. Most of them knew enough about themselves to know their origin story as an activist.

Andrea had used her activist courage to beat cancer.

"You get all the facts, you demand action, and you never say die," she said.

How interesting this life! Here we were at a little table in the dark den of Al Capone, talking about Martin Luther King and other good people, making our plans against the Bush syndicate. You can never know what this country is up to. We drank to that.

It was spring. The flower boxes down the middle of Michigan Avenue knocked me out. Chicago is a beautiful town, Cabrini and all. The sun on the Lake makes the whole city sparkle. We had registered voters on State Street, that great street; we had hoisted the Polish flag from Rosie in the Polish Day Parade. Andrea had made the town ours.

Doris had been crying from time to time in Chicago, trying to get through Jonathan Kozol's book about the education system and the poor. In Cabrini it had been all around us. Cabrini was the place, Doris reminded me, where a young boy was dangled from his heels and dropped to his death for refusing to sell drugs. The reality of being there overwhelmed her.

I asked her if she could deal with the poverty of Detroit, still ahead. She said she could. "We need to go there," she said. We did.

We pulled into a metered parking spot on 9 Mile Road in Ferndale, a town within the Detroit metropolis. We had contacts for the days ahead, but not for this first night, getting in so late. We had taken extra time in Battle Creek when we discovered Sojourner Truth's grave was there. It somehow seemed like a place we had to stop to pay respects.

The first night in the Detroit area was one of the few nights all three of us needed to bunk in the bus: Blue in the loft over the front seats, Doris on the narrow bench seat, and me on the floor.

There was a knock on the front window at daybreak. I was sure we were being rousted by the constabulary, having parked at a two-hour meter.

No, it was the city manager of Ferndale, with a box of coffees for us. The folks at the Greenhouse, a progressive activist center just upstairs from our accidental parking place, had spotted us and notified friends in City Hall. It was going to be like that. The mayor told us that the parking meter did not apply to us, and that the police had been so informed. He invited Doris to come to the city council meeting that evening and receive a key to the city. Doris was delighted—he had a collection of oversized city keys back home.

We were given an office in the Greenhouse, where activists were at the time working on instant runoff voting as their next reform. That is where you rank your choice of candidates, a much more sensible way to vote than with primaries and generals and runoffs. They would win that reform. They also were about to launch a community radio station, without the required FCC permit because the Bush Administration had let organizations like Clear Channel buy up all available licenses. The interesting thing about this pirate station was that its backers included the mayor and some council members. It was a modest revolution, and the connections were the reason we later met Pete Seeger at a pirate radio conference he organized.

We quickly connected with Kathy Gauthier-Grogan and her mother, Irene, who ran a health and therapeutic massage center in their big new building. This was exactly the medicine Doris now needed, and Blue went into her student mode each evening with Kathy and Irene. By day, we combed the housing projects of Detroit.

Blue discovered the magic of colored chalk. In the housing projects, she would begin by writing her name in stylized letters on the sidewalk. There would soon be a dozen or more children writing their names and drawing butterflies and a thousand other things. The mothers would then come out to see. The clipboards and voter registration forms would come out next.

We identified the natural leaders of each housing project and tried to connect them with volunteers who would stay in touch with them and help them. We asked them to host election day barbecue parties for voters—no *I Voted* sticker, no entry.

When Doris bragged to one mother that I had originated those stickers, the woman said to me, "Oh my, you must be very rich." I explained that you can write a two- or three-word best-seller without making a dime.

On the way out of Detroit we went across the water to Windsor, Ontario to get a breath of Canadian air. I had asked someone in Detroit if we needed passports, and they had assured us that people run across for lunch or dinner all the time. Wrong.

It took some explaining to get back into the U.S. Our subversive-looking van was also a problem. We were ushered into the security building through a door marked "personal search" and were turned over to a young man in uniform. Sternly, he asked all about us and our journey. He disappeared for quite a long time into a back room. I finally saw him coming toward us down the hall, a serious look on his mug.

"Nice website," he said. He walked us out to Rosie and asked how he could become more involved. He gave us his email address and sent us on our way.

Doris was getting tired. We all three were getting irritable. It was almost time to consider the eastern swing states as finished, at least as finished as we could do.

Doris was often getting off message, talking to reporters more about campaign finance reform than about the need for working women to vote. I was getting irritable about that. I never gave her much slack for being 94, but she usually appreciated that. But not now.

"I don't think you like me anymore," she said one morning. I told her I loved her.

"Of course you love me. But I don't think you like me. I am always messing up the interviews you work so hard to get for me. I say the wrong things, and I see you pulling out your hair."

This conversation was in a breakfast diner south of Detroit, in a booth of cracked vinyl. Blue scooted in and immediately understood the situation. She hugged Doris, who had tears in her eyes because I didn't like her. Blue glanced a dagger or two my way.

"We need a break," Blue said.

We decided to pick up Ohio on our swing westward after our scheduled rest. Besides, we were invited to Heartwood, a Forest Council conference. The activist retreat in the deep woods of Virginia sounded like a good place to recharge. Woody Harrelson had invited Doris. She had rather liked him when she met him a year earlier at the same event, and he had given her something to smoke, via what's called a shotgun breath. After a while and a few more inhales she said she just didn't feel it. Woody asked her why, then, was she giggling? And she was and now couldn't stop.

After our second Heartwood we headed to Asheville. Before we got there, Blue insisted we take a swim together in a pond she knew in the Great Smoky Mountains National Park. She said we needed that. We needed to reconnect with the earth and wash away the toxins. We did that. Then, like three bad pennies, we were in Rebecca MacNeice's Asheville driveway again.

They were beautiful days. Blue reconnected with friends. Doris got a ride around Asheville on the back of Rebecca's candy-red Vespa. She said it reminded her of a ride in 1930 with a young man from Harvard. She took Rebecca's Lhasa Apso, Henry, for his morning walks. She caught up on the latest political books.

We stood with an anti-war demonstration downtown, and met with Jimmy Massey, a Marine who came home from Iraq, refusing to participate in any more civilian killings. We met Clare Hanrahan who spent six months in federal prison for protesting the torture school at Fort Benning. Like so many others, she was anxiously asking herself what she might do to make a difference in the coming election.

When Clare was in prison, Asheville peace activists put a new kitchen floor in her little house.

That community response reminded me of how our friend Randy Kellior was arrested for tax resistance some years ago in Massachusetts, as his way of resisting illegal wars. When the feds came to take him away, he was playing the piano in his home, with his family around him. He asked if he could finish the piece, which they allowed. When they put his home up for sale, no one in the Massachusetts community would buy it, so his family did get it back. Randy pretty much invented the idea of public financing of elections, which passed first in Maine before we stole the idea in Arizona.

On our way out of North Carolina we stopped at Blue's grandparents' house. Its big screen porch looks over a meadow. Two of her uncles got out their guitars and we had some very good porch time. They hardly recognized Blue at first. She was now a confident, respected, salaried organizer, ducking out to take cell phone calls from important people. It was great to let her family see her in this new light. She had already seen far more of the world than they had.

It was a particularly good day for her, as she had received an email that day from Julia Butterfly Hill, asking for political advice and comparing notes for the campaign season ahead.

After a few days at a Forest Council conference deep in the green trees of the Shenandoah Valley, we headed back to New England. Blue split off with Marlo Poras, a filmmaker who had traveled with us off and on since Chicago, to go see New York City for her first time. She fell in love with the place, of course. She would catch a ride north to New Hampshire a few days later.

On we rolled until Doris started recognizing the trees of her own woods. It was June 4, 2004. We had logged 23,000 miles and had done business in all the swing states east of the Mississippi except Ohio. The plan was to relax for a week, restock, raise a few dollars, and head for the western swing states.

Doris was delighted to get back to her big bathtub and her rows of good books and all her clothes and her own kitchen and her Tuesday Morning Academy friends and Scrabble. She settled in for a week or two of real rest.

I said I would fly home for a few days. Doris stood in her doorway and asked if I was really coming back.

"You seem to be taking all your things," she said. I gave her a kiss and said of course I would. In truth, I thought it might be too much for her to continue.

Back in Phoenix, I was raiding our refrigerator when Jim called. I had a sense of dread when I saw the call was from him. Doris had looked so worn out when I left her that I suddenly feared I had killed her.

"Mom's running for the U.S. Senate," he said. "She has the New Hampshire Democratic Party's nomination if she wants it. Their regular candidate dropped out because his manager stole all the funds, and they need a candidate right now, as the filing deadline is in four days. Otherwise, Judd Gregg will run unopposed."

Doris got on the line.

"Doris, are you really up for this?" I asked.

"I can't win against Judd Gregg because he always wins, of course, and I'm not going to take PAC money,

Love and Democracy

but we can round up a lot of votes for Mr. Kerry on the presidential side, and we can talk a little bit about campaign finance reform. You really must come, Dennis. It will be fun. Won't it be fun? Blue got here last night. Won't she be perfect for getting younger voters?"

You couldn't leave them alone for two days?

Annoying Seatmate

So, I'm flying from Arizona to New Hampshire, having put in calls to my son and my Arizona crew for some campaign advice. Everyone agreed that it was important to pin down Judd Gregg with an opponent, as he was George Bush's college buddy, his sparring partner for the presidential debates, and Bush's most effective surrogate on the campaign trail. Even a 94-year-old candidate might keep him on the defense in his home state.

Let's pretend you are in the seat next to me on the plane. Obviously, you're interesting so I have grilled you for two hours about your situation, your family, everything. Then you ask me how I got to be a liberal. At the Green Mill in Chicago, Andrea had asked me that same question, but I spared you my answer in that chapter to keep the story moving. But we now have a few minutes. This will be short, not much more than text for a dust jacket, if this were, say, a big coffee table book.

I already mentioned the Army general who wanted the Vietnam War to last a little longer for the sake of his offshore oil leases there. That did radicalize my politics a bit. This is the rest of the story.

In the bloody year 1968 I was in college in L.A., loading and unloading baggage at night for Delta Airlines at LAX.

The tragedies in the news hung over us all—first JFK and then Vietnam. At Delta, the ugly world came to us nearly every night, in the form of cardboard coffins filled with young soldiers being sent home as freight.

Love and Democracy

One foggy April night, after unloading a flight, a buddy and I were leaning against the baggage conveyor belt, catching our breath. A figure appeared through the fog, walking under the wing of the plane parked at the next gate. We first just saw the silhouette of a tall, powerfully built man, but then could see a woman walking with him, almost inside his coat. As they came closer, we recognized them. It was Harry Belafonte with his arm and raincoat protecting Coretta Scott King. They had come off the rear of the plane next to ours—a flight from Atlanta—via a roll-up stairway and were finding their way into the terminal through the service area to avoid public notice. Martin Luther King had been assassinated just a few days earlier. His widow bravely insisted on coming to Los Angeles to speak at a civil rights event planned months earlier by Belafonte.

There was no romance in the view of this pair, just the drama of it, coming in a moment of our national despair over the killing of another great leader—one I had defended many times against my father's dinner table opinions, where my mother repeatedly begged, "Please, gentlemen, no politics at dinner."

We took off our Delta caps and nodded. Belafonte nodded back. Coretta seemed fully sheltered within the safe embrace of her towering friend. When they disappeared into a waiting doorway, my coworker and I had nothing to say to each other. I saw tears in his eyes, and he saw them in mine.

Bobby Kennedy would be shot two months later. I saw him on his way to victory at the Ambassador Hotel—I waved from a Santa Monica corner—waved as a future voter who still believed in the possibility of leaders who could quote Aeschylus at will and lead us toward our aspirations—and he waved back. That night he became another wax statue in the sad diorama of America's violent history—another lost opportunity to bend the arc of history toward peace and justice.

Five years before that, when his brother was killed, I had just come back from lunch at my high school. I saw clusters of students leaning into the windows of parked cars, listening to the radios. We would all soon be marched into chapel for the news about the nation's first Catholic president, who had been alive in third period and now, in fourth, was not.

I traveled the East Coast alone at seventeen, thanks to some conference in Indiana and parents so Western that they thought I might as well see New York and Washington, as long as I was in the area. In New York I saw the desperation of the Bowery, and it broke my heart—there was nothing like that in Phoenix at that time, though it is everywhere now, because white boys just a few years older than me had destroyed all the affordable urban hotels in the name of city planning.

On that teen trip to Manhattan, I happened to mention to an elderly cab driver that his job must be interesting, meeting so many different people. Before that, I had asked him a few questions about the men sleeping on the sidewalks.

"You got a lot of questions, kid. You really want to know?"

I said sure, and he pulled over near the dock where I was going to see Admiral Byrd's famous ship. For nearly an hour with the meter off, he told me all about his life, looking at me only through his mirror. He concluded by finally turning around and telling me that it had all been hard work, and that he was tired now but could not afford to retire. He would just keep going for as long as God would let him.

In that moment I came to deeply and unforgettably understand that everyone deserves a decent life, not just those who win the longshot chance for the brass ring.

I had seen poverty before. Our Jesuit high school teachers made us all volunteer in rough parts of town, stuccoing and painting houses that were no places to live. Dirty children who must have thought we'd come from Outer Space watched us as they sat beside their dogs and told us, without even meaning to, about their lives and struggles and those of their parents and grandparents. Their stories and their faces have always stayed with me. I have seen them all over the world since.

Democracy is about listening carefully to other people's stories and giving a damn. It's about seeing what you can do to make their situations a little better, whether through your own deeds or through your church or your government. I think democracy requires that we nurture our own imaginations and our children's imaginations because it is the essential ingredient of empathy—you must be able to imagine what it is like to be in another person's situation, whether or not they're your own daughter or son. I think a liberal education is needed for that. Liberal education means an education so full of literature and science and history that it liberates your mind to think beyond your immediate influences. I was fortunate to have a great liberal education. We need everyone to have one if we're to ever have our best democracy.

A liberal education does not necessarily produce political liberals, though the truth has a well-known liberal bias. There is also a need for society to urge people to take care of themselves and their families through hard work and good character. Even so, the rich who profess the primacy of individual effort over the village, ought to look around at the villages responsible for their own successes. Only a fool thinks his success is his own. I use only the male gender in that statement because women tend to get it, which is why we wanted to get them all registered.

While some of my influences were accidental, like seeing those two almost divine figures walking in the airport fog, some others were intentional. The Jesuits knew what they were doing when they put us down in those hard neighborhoods to lend our hands. Father Tom Allender, who died recently, knew what he was doing when he made us read and take apart The Red Badge of Courage in a year when the Vietnam War was blazing and extending its bloody finger of recruitment. From good books and well-nurtured imaginations, we knew enough about war to stay away from it if we could. Most of us were privileged enough to manage.

I grew up the son of a Goldwater Republican. When I was 13, Dad took me and my sister to a Christian Anti-Communist Crusade rally at Montgomery Stadium in Phoenix. It was funded by the same Knox Berry Jam money that would fuel Goldwater and Reagan. The prime excuse given for the unequal distribution of wealth by the Republicans and the far-right was that, yes there is poverty, but anyone in America, and of any color, can make it to the top if they will just try. I mean, take Sidney Portier!

There was something else happening back then and still now: Family businesses, including Dad's, were under attack by corporations that were extending their chains and banks from state to state like pandemics targeting the middle class. A plan of misdirection, still underway, was aimed at Dad and others: Make the beleaguered middle class blame the government, which was trying to protect them from monopolies and other abuses. The campaign of misdirection kept my father and others from blaming the corporations that were buying up and shutting down Main Street, paving it over in favor of ever-wider streets and freeways to suburbs and their malls—where you could finally find the parking spaces stolen from Main Street businesses.

Big corporate money poured into the accounts of buffoons like Rush Limbaugh to convince Dad and millions of others that only the Republican Party could save them from the Big Bad Wolf of government. Anti-government messaging flowed from Limbaugh and later O'Reilly and Hannity and from pretty blondes on Fox selling poison apples.

The Democratic Party was nowhere to be seen in countering this. The Party could have broken that hypnosis with explanatory campaigns. They still don't and they still should. The rest of us should have been doing more with posters and graffiti and we still should.

In that Manhattan cab, the white-stuccoed bullshit of the Far Right fell away from me in one piece, though it had been loosened by what I'd seen and felt in the poorest neighborhoods. It was long gone before that foggy airport night in Los Angeles. By then, I knew who I was and what I needed to do.

We're landing in Manchester. It's going to be freezing.

The Candidate

Blue gave me a happy cartoon smile when I walked into Doris's home in Dublin, a short hike from Peterborough. She was already doing something on her computer to round up local volunteers. Jim was on the phone to the Democratic Party in Concord. Doris was fixing bowls of ice cream. When she saw me, she came with joyfully tiny steps for a hug.

"Oh, Dennis! What fun!"

Given her long fight against big money in politics, there was no way she could accept PAC money; we would have to rely on small contributions. There were outfits like the Dean machine, Emily's List, and MoveOn who could get out the word and encourage progressives to contribute, but they would never do so, I suppose because of Doris's age, which should not have mattered under the circumstances. They did have tighter races to fund.

Doris needed an announcement event at the state capitol:

> "I pledge to run for only one term. Judd Gregg pledged the same, several terms ago. I happen to have the biological ability to guarantee my pledge."

Her living room, its huge windows overlooking forest and creek, filled with used computers and telephones on long tables. A satellite dish was installed on the roof. The conversation pit around the fireplace filled with sleeping bags. I bought tents and cots from the Big Lots in town and set up a volunteers' camp in the forest clearing across the creek, even building a little bridge over the water from wood timbers found in the town dump.

We scouted Manchester and Concord for a headquarters office, unsure if we really needed one. Maybe an office down the hill in Peterborough would be enough—which is what we finally decided. For the first weeks, the forest camp would be it.

Experts in key issue arrived to help us lay out important positions on the economy, terror, Iraq, veterans, health, all of it. It was time to test our own opinions for realism and accuracy. Some of the experts took up temporary residence in the tent camp while they wrote their summaries and briefed the candidate: Fran and her daughter from Tallahassee, Kathleen from Washington—an expert who worked with Congressional committees; David from Boston—a top Pentagon consultant on defense and veterans' issues. The porch deck, the kitchen and the big living room were constantly busy.

We began the search for a campaign manager, as I figured I probably didn't know how to do that. It was late in the campaign season and most the good people were already engaged. But after the Democratic Convention in Boston, when the many campaigns would be whittled to a few, there would undoubtedly be some good people available, thought that would be late in the game.

Right in Peterborough was an ideal press secretary, Maude Salinger. She was a public relations pro, experienced in politics, and she instinctively understood Granny's appeal and her narrative story. Maude was the niece of Pierre Salinger, JFK's press secretary, which was somehow cool.

We wouldn't have the money for a lot of advertising. We needed to instead generate a flood of town-by-town news coverage, and that meant that Doris had to walk the state. She demanded a good route so she could get started immediately. Every day she was not out there, she said, was a wasted day.

A neighbor up the hill brought some maps of the historic postal roads through New Hampshire. They were still maintained as two-lane roads, looping through hundreds of towns and the major cities. That would give us multiple hits with the state's few television and daily papers.

Doris warmed up by walking around Dublin and then in the local town day parades that pepper New Hampshire each spring.

The day before the first parade, in the picturesque town of Wilton, Jim was up at the community farm, gathering food for the troops. Leslie, a fellow co-op member, asked if Doris might need a marching band. That was the beginning of a good thing, as Fred and Leslie and their musician friends would be with Doris constantly: Fred on the trombone, Leslie on accordion, and friends with drums, trumpets and tuba. They took "Just a Closer Walk with Thee," cranked it up to Dixieland, added new lyrics, and "Just a Walk with Granny D" started rocking the main streets and town squares of New Hampshire. With the town day parades, the campaign was off to a cheering start. Even Republicans with Bush buttons stood up along the parades and cheered as she passed.

Our relationship with the state party was rocky. They didn't take her seriously as a candidate, even though they had invited her to step into the candidacy and even as we started to attract big news stories, tremendous word-of-mouth, and good poll numbers. She was by rights the head of the New Hampshire delegation to the Democratic National Convention, being the candidate for the highest office, yet the New Hampshire party didn't even invite her to the Boston Convention.

So, we crashed it and its cocktail parties. A friend in Boston who worked for the printing company that had provided the official tickets to the Convention floor sent me a spare box.

On the first night of the Convention, I got a call from a blogger who had been following our campaign. Would Granny and her friends like to attend the Bloggers' Ball, a side-event of the convention?

We did. Doris and Blue arrived in the bar to some applause. Joe Trippi, late of Howard Dean's campaign, was there. He knew all about Doris, and we sat down for a drink. He said he would be willing to advise our campaign, gratis.

Nicco Melle was there, one of the new superstars of political web-based organizing, and someone I had known from Common Cause and the campaign finance reform fight. He said he would help, too.

Dean's campaign staff had already been snatched up by Kerry. The Kucinich people were up for grabs but were a bit like the relatives you hope don't show up for the reunion. They weren't my first choice, but ours would be a grassroots campaign, and that's what Kucinich's campaign had been all about—though they had lost badly.

At that Dean-Kucinich joint rally that Doris had encouraged, I cornered Kucinich's campaign manager. She had a reputation for running an efficient organization. Add a little Trippi and other experts, and maybe we could patch it together. But, no, she wanted only to go home and forget about politics. She had someone on her team, however, who would be perfect for us, she said.

Before leaving Boston and the convention, Doris gave a moving speech in historic Faneuil Hall. It began:

Feel this place under you and around you. Know where you are. All the world knows the story of how the Americans became a free people, how they declared their independence, how they devised a constitution that is still an engine of fairness, of improvement, of justice and freedom. But the story seems remote sometimes. So, feel this place under you. Know where you are. Remember who we are.

This room, these walls, echoed the words of Sam Adams as he stood in this place and reminded Americans who they were and what they must do. In this very room we Americans heard George Washington and Daniel Webster shape the new Republic.

In this room William Lloyd Garrison helped define an American value system that could no longer admit of human slavery, and he defined nonviolent resistance in a way that was persuasive with Ruskin in England and Tolstoy in Russia and Gandhi in South Africa and India — and from Gandhi back to Martin Luther King in America. From this room.

And here spoke Susan B. Anthony to move our engine of equality forward again. And here spoke John Kennedy and so many other Americans who loved freedom and justice and who pushed us to be a better people, moving ever along and up the Freedom Trail.

Feel this place. Remember who you are and why you are here. Understand that all of them and all of us are of one mind and sometimes are of one place. We are in this room. And perhaps those who have come before us are in this room yet, to see their work continue and be the real spirits of our inspiration.

Feel this neighborhood around you: The street corner of the Boston Massacre is but a few steps behind me; The Tea Party was but a few steps behind you. Revere's house, the Old North Church, are but across the way, still there, still living containers for our aspirations and our shared courage. Remember who we are and how we rise up when our liberty is threatened!

We are not a people to be trifled with, Mr. President. We are not to be trifled with, ye corporations who press down upon us like a plague of King Georges, turning our middle class into greeters and our lives into the credit card indentured!

We shall have our freedom, and we shall have our democracy as it was given us, made better by our own sacrifices.

We are here. Our revolution needs defending in this moment. We are come back to our room where we devise strategies and double our courage. We are in this room. We breathe its air. We hear its soft assent.

After the speech, we returned to New Hampshire and the remainder of her campaign. We hired the manager suggested by the Kucinich manager the next week over tea at a New Hampshire farm.

Doris's New Hampshire walks were getting good press. We made friends with key reporters who were falling in love with her. Roads filled with honking and thumbs-up wherever Doris walked. Judd Gregg was taking her seriously enough to start attacking her.

In speeches at the end of daily walks, she talked about Judd and the influence of special interest money, but mostly she slammed Bush's attacks on peace, on Social Security, and on true homeland security. She claimed that all the advances made by The Greatest Generation were being wasted. People were listening. A lot of people were deciding that the 94-year-old woman with the worsening cough might be too old for six years in the Senate, but she was dead right about Bush.

Trippi called to arrange a first meeting over dinner. Doris was far across the state, but he was happy to meet with me and Blue—especially Blue, I think, because he knew that young people, the young vote, was becoming the most important thing in politics.

My first question to him was *how hard should we hit old Judd for his voting record, and when should we begin?*

"See that guy coming in right now?" Trippi nodded toward a man just outside the restaurant. "Let's say that's you, Dennis. Let's say I just met Blue here, and she tells me, watch out Joe, here comes the biggest jerk in town. Well, let's say you and I have known each other for many years, Dennis, and I think you're a reasonably okay guy. I just met Blue a few minutes ago. What am I going to think? I'm going to think Blue is the jerk."

We got it. Despite her age and a lifetime in New Hampshire, Doris was the newcomer to most voters. They had known Judd Gregg for years. They weren't going to change their opinion of him by anything Doris said. Any harsh claims would just reflect badly on her.

Good advice is always obvious after you hear it.

Then what could Doris say?

"Doris should look into the camera—and it really must be a TV campaign because time is already up, and say, look, Judd is a fine politician. His father was a fine politician before him. If you're happy with politics just the way it is in Washington, by all means send him back. But if you want to send a message to him about politics today, if you want to scare him into cleaning up the campaign finance bribery system, vote for me."

That simple. For the first time, I could see it. She was offering herself again as a human monkey wrench for the K Street bribe machine, and her age said she wasn't doing it for herself or a career. She wasn't even saying she would or could win, but that votes for her would be a truth-to-power demand for change. It was certainly clear that McCain-Feingold had not been enough, and more reforms were needed.

Blue pumped Joe for advice on using the Internet to organize and fundraise nationally, his area of fame. He believed that the Internet had the ability to turn politics upside down. Traditional politics begins with a few wealthy backers, some black-tie dinners. It then trickles down to the grassroots. With the Internet, as he had proven with the Dean campaign, the black ties could be made to come running to catch up with their checkbooks. That was exactly what his new book was about, and it would be one of the blueprints of the coming Obama Campaign.

Everything you might have liked about the Dean campaign was mostly Trippi. One day toward the end of their partnership, they arrived at a rally where thousands of people were cheering with Dean signs. Dean said, "Oh, God," meaning he would have to put up with the crowds again. Trippi loved the crowds and loved the idea of popular politics, and Dean's reaction at that moment was kind of the end of the road between them. That and Iowa and the scream.

Our new manager arrived from the ruins of the Kucinich campaign, assistant in tow, and they started in. They would cancel the website and hire folks she knew in Oregon to do a new one from scratch. It would never get as many hits as the old one. Her associate would waste the next critical weeks reloading the new site with the information from the old one. I was in shock.

Even more oddly, she would cancel the walk, as it put Doris out of the big cities too many days a week. Yes, but that's how we are getting big, state-wide media coverage: they were following her walks as news events. The AP bureau wanted daily walking schedules.

I thought I was pressing my case firmly but professionally. You do have arguments in campaigns, and this had the potential to be a very important presidential swing state campaign. My resolve was reinforced when Maureen came out for a visit, saw what the new folks were doing, and immediately started arguing with them for their stupid moves. She never, ever did that sort of thing. More importantly, as a seasoned newspaper woman, she saw how they were wasting the message and misusing Granny's appeal.

Blue wasn't upset by anything except the enmity that was brewing inside the little campaign. She said I was creating a negative environment with my criticism, instead of adopting an attitude of love and cooperation.

"Blue, I can't post issue updates on the website. They won't give me the codes to the new site!" I tried to show her a stack of emails that I had sent, courteously making suggestions and receiving curt or no replies. My evidence didn't wash with Blue.

The thing is, Blue believes that everyone has almost unlimited power to shape the world with love and that I wasn't even trying. She would close her eyes and breathe out deeply in some sort of Buddhist way when she said that sort of thing.

It came down to a big staff meeting in the living room. The manager said she was going to resign. Blue said she was going to leave. I argued against both ideas. The manager had capitulated on the idea of Doris walking, so we were now back in the groove and back in the press, but that defeat had cut deeply into the manager's feelings. She was becoming a nervous wreck, she said, and Blue thought it was pretty much my fault.

When Blue said she was leaving, Jane LaPointe, a management consultant who worked in New York City but who lived in Peterborough and helped us run our meetings and keep on track, had tears in her eyes.

"Then that's it for the campaign," she said in a whisper. Jane understood that thing that I also got, that Granny's courage and common sense were the engines of the campaign, but Blue somehow carried the soul of the enterprise, maybe because she was the future, maybe because she believed in a better world that was way beyond what the rest of us could still imagine.

When it all seemed lost for a long, silent moment, the manager said maybe she would stay. There were only, I think, about three or four weeks left. I was torn, of course, as it was too late to find another manager and I did not want to do it myself—not at all my specialty. I just wanted her to do more sensible things with the campaign's time and energy. I was backseat driving, a wrong thing to do and a no-win situation for anyone.

A thin breeze of grace and love moved through the room. Blue said she would stay, too. She had attacked me hard in that meeting, and it really hurt. It was like a family argument.

Nick Palumbo from Minneapolis had come to New Hampshire to be the field organizer. He was down on me, too. He had booked Doris to speak to a retirement home on the proviso that she does not make a political speech. Well, this was a political campaign, and I didn't think it was reasonable for the retirement home manager to make that kind of condition, so I advised Doris to treat them like the voters they were. Nick felt I had undercut his honor by suggesting Doris make it political, and he wouldn't talk to me for several days. He was in Blue's camp.

My little basement office no longer had traffic from the people who had started out as my friends. I had also argued with Nick about his plan to host house parties. That's the way he knew to organize, and I was saying that campaigning like that was for candidates who had the luxury of time, while we had come in at the last minute and couldn't afford to preach to the choir of progressives who would go to such events. Besides, Dean's showing in Iowa had proven that such gatherings are feel-good therapy, not campaigning. I wanted Doris speaking in Veteran halls and town halls talking about the Iraq war, Bush's cuts in vet benefits, and Gregg's complicity. I wanted her talking about the bribery of the government they had risked their lives for. So, we argued.

In these pages I can only give my side, so you may think I was right, but I probably wasn't. Not all the time, anyway. And I was putting Doris in the middle.

During all this, the campaign rolled on. Jim drove Doris to the far corners of the state to walk the postal roads, and her brass band and her banners made a splash. We had hand-made "Burma Shave" signs posted all over the state. They were collections of four or five signs along the two-lanes, with a dozen different messages I had penned:

Her Campaign Cash / Is Fat-Cat Free / She'll Represent / Just You and Me! / Doris Granny D Haddock for US Senate

And:

When Will Congress / Work for Me? / I'm Sending In / My Granny D!

Judd's fans were tearing the signs down about as fast as we could put them up, but we had a factory of volunteers making and installing them. Maury Geiger, a volunteer from Maine who was a major force working for humanitarian conditions in Haiti, arrived to manage the sign campaign. He slept on the floor of our little campaign headquarters in Peterborough, waking at dawn to oversee another crew of sign makers.

The people of Peterborough piled into the office to gather up the signs and drive them to locations across the state. They also brought in food, hosted barbecues and even a barn dance.

It was real democracy right out of Our Town, which Peterborough historically was. Doris was indefatigable. Jim was indefatigable. The volunteers were joyful elves all over the place, day and night.

Looming ahead had always been the live television candidate debate. Doris was petrified by the thought of it, and so were we all. If she didn't hear the questions well, or if she got flustered and couldn't think of what to say, it would be deeply embarrassing to her.

Jim drove her to the TV studio in Manchester for the debate. They were barely out of her driveway when she demanded he turn around and go back to the house. Jim told her to be brave, that she couldn't back out now. She laughed and said that wasn't it; she had forgotten her teeth.

She did amazingly well. She made Judd Gregg answer to his campaign donor conflicts and his support for disastrous Bush policies. The high moment was when Gregg was waxing eloquent about standing in a New Hampshire stream and catching a fish, and Doris said, "I hope you didn't eat that fish, Senatah." She then attacked him for the levels of mercury in New Hampshire streams, largely a product of the Bush Administrations loosening of environmental regulations on coal-fired power plants upwind in Appalachia. She also whacked him for warrantless wiretapping allowed by Bush's Patriot Act, which the Senator erroneously denied.

When the moderator asked for her position on gay marriage, her reply was, "I'm for love."

The debate was a big moment for her. Here she was, all alone to face Goliath, and she knocked him out. Polls taken of viewers said as much.

We were down to the final two weeks, and poll numbers came out that said we hadn't budged since the arrival of the campaign manager. We were at a sickening 20%. That would be an embarrassment if we didn't improve it. We were really in it, of course, to move Kerry ahead of Bush, and we may have been doing that. Blue was organizing new voters on the state's campuses. Doris was getting retired people in retirement homes to remember their duties as citizens.

I was trying to be good in the back seat, but I thought I owed it to Doris to force a meeting with the manager and ask her for an end game. We met on the back porch, and I said I thought the Haddocks had a right to know where they would be financially on the day after election. And I thought they had a right to know what the plan was to get some TV going to punch up the numbers.

I could still imagine Joe Trippi's suggested TV ads. We could do very well if we could get them on the air. Rebecca MacNeice, the Asheville filmmaker, had come up with a crew to shoot the spots and they were great. But no air budget. The manager had Rebecca shoot and produce a DVD to use in Nick's house parties, as if we were a year away from the election.

I suggested that it might be time to go to an all-volunteer staff for the last two weeks, allowing some budget for TV. I suggested, in other words, that the manager fire her friends and buy some media.

The manager said that she would not fire anyone, and that there would be money for last minute TV, but that the Haddocks would have to raise money after the campaign to clear the debt. I argued that we weren't that kind of campaign, and that Doris would not be able to clear big debts. Donors bail out a lost campaign only when the candidate will likely run again.

Just the same, that was our manager's plan. I threw up my hands. I told Jim and Doris that I wasn't going to stick around and watch that happen, and I wanted out. I said I was going back to Arizona.

I packed my bag and was smoking a little cigar in the basement doorway that looked out into her woods. Blue pounced behind me like her old pirate self and put a very sharp butcher knife to my neck. I have mentioned that she's a head taller than me and it seemed about to be two heads taller.

"If you go, I'm going to kill you," she said.

My only real fear was that I knew she liked to do the unexpected.

"Why are you so afraid to be in charge?" she said, finally taking the blade away.

That was a good question. The victories I had been associated with, the clean elections campaign and the redistricting reform campaign in Arizona, and the grassroots element of McCain-Feingold, were not campaigns I had managed, really. I had assembled teams, experts, financing. I had encouraged people, developed messages and strategies, but had always been the introvert in the background. I didn't trust my ability to lead the charge from the front line.

A moment later, Jim came down to the basement.

"Mom and I just let the manager go," he said. "We have two weeks to make this work. Are you in? We need a manager."

Doris, Jim, Blue and I had some ice cream. Maury Geiger came in and said he was delighted, that the change was long overdue. He had some ice cream, too. Blue said she was happy, but she wasn't doing any good around headquarters, and she wanted to take old Rosie out to more of the colleges around the state. She had been making friends with the college-age organizers and would have lots of volunteers. They could sweep all the colleges and recruit for the get-out-the-vote moment.

I booked the little TV we could afford. We used Doris's remaining speaking engagements to hit Bush harder on his attacks on the middle class, on veterans and the elderly. Maury went into overdrive with more Burma Shave signs.

There was no way to go from 20% to 51% with the few dollars we had.

Fred and Leslie kept the band playing behind Doris and we hit the downtown sidewalks all over the state. It was great fun, really—back in the joy business, as red and gold leaves swirled around. We went from a fifth of the vote to, on election night, a third, which was respectable, and was double what the pundits had predicted. We won in the markets where we advertised, Portsmouth and Keene, especially.

Granny had used the campaign to talk more about Bush than Gregg. New Hampshire became the only swing state carried by Bush to swing to Kerry that night. It swung by 9,000 votes. Doris may have made that difference. It wasn't enough to give the nation the new leadership it needed, but we had done something—everything we could. On election night, as we watched New Hampshire swing blue on the television, we were ecstatic. It was a victory party.

That party was in a big room in the Peterborough building where we had our headquarters, an old mill on the river. Just outside its great windows, under a three-quarter moon, water flowed over the mill dam like black silk. It carried a carpet of a billion red and gold leaves.

Through the evening, townspeople arrived with food and joy. Doris danced with Jim, as Fred and Leslie and their band played a hundred songs. Blue arrived from the seacoast where she had been shuttling students to the polls. More than that, she had led rallies. When Kerry was late for a rally in a Manchester airport hangar, Blue was ushered to the stage. She spoke from the heart, describing her journey from apathy to engagement. She said she had now taken responsibility for her country, and that she wanted to feel her democracy under her like a motorcycle as we moved into the future. The crowd roared and stomped. She raised the roof of that great hangar. When Kerry finally arrived, I am told, it was an anticlimax.

As I walked out into the dark later that night, Blue, jacked up even taller on platform shoes and wearing her blue fedora, was entering the building with a new girlfriend. Blue was in a daze that made it hard for her to do more than give me a goofy smile. She nudged her friend past us like a gangster guiding his girlfriend past the luckless droolers at the bar. I had heard what had happened in the Manchester hangar and was incredibly proud of her.

It would take a couple of weeks to take down the campaign, return equipment, clear signs, pay bills. Blue gave me a tattoo of a little blue bird on the back of my left shoulder. It was one of the birds from the back of the bus—a bird to whisper in my ear when I needed a little joy and wisdom.

Doris started the long job of sending letters to everyone who donated an hour or a dollar to the campaign. It would take her a year, but she wanted to do each one personally. Then she started going around the country again, supporting the activists who were working for campaign finance reform and peace.

Blue would stay in New Hampshire for a few months to help Doris thin out her home from campaign materials and make it beautiful again.

Rebecca MacNeice, the filmmaker, would move on to make other films. If you watch daredevil filmmaking, such as *Ice Road Truckers* or *Deadliest Catch,* it is likely Rebecca fearlessly hanging over the edge of something to get the shots.

I went home to Arizona. Blue eventually went back to Asheville. She came through Phoenix on her way to get a first look at California with a new girlfriend. They had blown an engine and four old tires getting here. They camped in the mud of Louisiana and skinny-dipped in the New Mexico hot springs where Doris had done the same.

She said the bayou outside of Baton Rouge was "amazing, so full of God and freedom." She said she was going to get into an art college in California, which she did.

Maureen asked if she wanted to stay involved in politics.

"Well, you can have a good political system, but if bad people are in it, it still doesn't work. I want to work on the idea that people should be awake and feel their own power and take responsibility for it." She flexed her arm to make the point. She had a new tattoo, a bold arrow design, on her arm. She was Artemis, I realized, goddess of the hunt and the moon.

"How did you like her new girlfriend?" Maureen asked me when the two women pulled away from our curb. I said I thought she was great.

"Do you think she gets' Blue?" she asked.

Maureen understood that there was much to get about Blue.

Shortly before Doris died in 2010, at the age of 100, the governor of New Hampshire gave her a birthday party in his office. The only thing about it that was not joyful was that the Supreme Court had, three days earlier in the Citizens United Decision, undone the McCain-Feingold reform she had walked the nation to get enacted. She knew that our politics were about to suffer a tsunami of money from the new class of American oligarchs. But she told this story at that party in the Governor's office:

People have been asking me how I feel about the recent decision by the Supreme Court to strike down some of the campaign finance reforms that I walked for and have been working on for a dozen or so years.

When I was a young woman, my husband and I were having dinner at the Dundee home of a friend, Max Foster, when a young couple rushed through the door breathless to say that they had accidentally burned down the guest cabin, down by the river. Max stood up from his meal. He set his napkin down. He smiled at the young couple, and he said,

"That's wonderful. We have wanted to build something special down there on the river, and this will give us a chance to do that without feeling guilty about getting rid of that old cabin. I'll get a crew down there tomorrow to lay it out. Now eat, and we'll get you some bunks up here."

Well, I guess the Supreme Court has burned down our little cabin, but truth be told, it was pretty drafty anyway. We had not really solved the problem of too much money in politics, and now we have an opportunity to start clean and build a system of reforms that really will do the trick. So, let's get a crew down there in the morning to lay it out.

The point of that is that democracy will always win, because it's what people need and want, and they will keep at it until they have it. The game is never over if you keep playing. If you lose it, you just start playing again until you have it again. Authoritarians don't live forever, but the democracy fighter does, always there, like Tom Joad, I suppose.

And what else might she say to us now? I'm quite sure she would remind us to keep our chins up and keep going, because we will always win in the long run. We will win because democracy, which is the plural word for freedom, is the natural inclination of modern people.

She died in Jim and Libby's home a short time after her 100th birthday. She had been walking three miles a day with me in Arizona only the week before.

She died bravely. She was having a hard time breathing after a coughing fit in bed. It was the old emphysema. A bad attack.

Jim sat beside the bed. He asked if he should call the paramedics.

"Or is this the one, Ma?"

She nodded yes. She would let this be the one. She squeezed his hand.

But as far as I'm concerned, she's with us as ever before.

And Scene

I've been writing this book off and on for too long. But Maureen recently died of leukemia, and I have needed this writing to dissolve into. After an unthinkable loss, the people who love you, their heavy hands upon your shoulder, tell you to avoid big decisions for at least a year. Don't move to a new city, even across town. Don't change jobs or careers or friends—you've had enough change for now.

But you do have to do something, especially people like you and me. And because you believe politics may have something to do with the future of your children and grandchildren and others, you can't just be a sad statue of yourself. I have needed to be doing something more useful than standing at my window drinking yesterday's coffee and watching the long-married pair of neighborhood pigeons, Midge and Walter, as they clean the last bits from the cat's patio dish. I resent that they are outliving the one I loved. The Egyptians had it right: Bury everything and everyone along with the loved one, because it's monstrously unfair for them keep going when the one who mattered is not here to dance in the living room, prune the roses, pet the cat, murmur encouragements, plan lovely trips, smile curiously and then courageously.

The Egyptians and I suppose the Vikings would be disgusted to know that, in our culturally strip-mined wasteland, the mortuary men come and just carry away your love, draped over like unwanted furniture. They take her out to a nondescript van and drive her away, not even going slowly past the walkway roses she loved and cared for so dearly over the years. It is hardly the way to leave home for the last time—no fanfare, just a hollow man standing in the driveway, making a small pathetic wave and not wanting in the least to step back into the house to a life without her.

But four wonderful people were waiting inside. I asked them to take coffee on the patio and spare Maureen's spirit the indignity of her body's unceremonious exit. Hours earlier, we all had pulled up chairs at the end of the bed, Maureen's rosary wrapped around her cooling hands. I read Millay's *Dirge Without Music*, which is not a proper prayer but does express the moment. Those present with me were Maureen's sister Ann; Maureen's friend from newspaper days Christine; my sister, Kathleen; and our neighbor Barbara, who had brought a treat or a card of encouragement to Maureen every day for over a year. I can't imagine how widows and widowers get through those first hours without such people around them.

But then it's the night and the next day and the next. A sort of long seasickness is the way of it. People want to remind you that life goes on, but you take that as a wrongful acceptance of the Great Injustice. "Life goes on," might be the harshest thing people say to you when the only right words are, "there are no words." It is particularly difficult for those of us who have never been good at facing reality.

And you can't help but feel some guilt—not just the survivor thing, but guilty for every lost opportunity to show your love more, to have been kinder. She could have and should have found a better mate. You think that. She had choices—many candidates. I got her vote, a great blessing for me. But she could have done better. Truly.

People adapt. It's what we do. Months pass. I renamed the automatic floor vacuum Wilson, and we now have a pretty good relationship—it gets lost and stuck, but I rather like that it needs me.

However the days begin, they usually end with bedtime television lectures on quantum physics or consciousness that I love but don't understand, and other charming shows filled with misinformation verified by ancient alien experts and crystal skull researchers.

On Fridays I launder the bedsheets and straighten the place as if someone who has been away on a trip might just walk in. It is cargo-cult behavior.

Maureen and I used to walk down to the sandwich shop at the end of our street once or twice a week and split a veggie sub for lunch. Now I overeat there for two. The weeks and now months fold up precisely the same, like little origami pigeons. I have isolated myself from the chaos and excitement of the larger world, though that is where we find life's color and joy. I'll get there. In the meantime, I am in this small house with hardwood floors that Maureen installed when I was off on a voter registration adventure some years ago. I think of the place as a little yacht rather than a small house, with the green yard in back as a little sea, and as if I'm on a long sail around the Milky Way, which I am.

I have tried attending grieving sessions hosted by the hospice organization, but on nights when I miss her most desperately, no meetings are scheduled—or they are nights for people grieving pet loss. That did give me an idea for a short story that I'm certainly not going to write, but if you're interested, it would be about a new widow so hungry for human contact that she goes to that kind of gathering, pretending to have lost a dog named Ralph—her late husband's actual name. It works fine for her until the second or third time around the circle, when she forgets where she is and admits to really missing sex with Ralph. The others are appalled, of course, except for one woman who says she knows exactly what she means. So, that made me laugh a bit on what would have been a tough night.

Sometimes you can't prop it all up and it's just the void. When Teddy Roosevelt's wife and mother died on the same Valentine's Day, he wrote in his journal, "The light has gone out of my life." It's like that. It's obvious that new memories and adventures will gradually fill the emptiness, but even that seems somehow tragic and disloyal. Sometimes I take a moment to put my palms skyward, just to be that little bit closer to her. You do a lot of things privately that others would think silly or overdramatic unless they've been there.

Life does go on, and the guilt of not doing something worthwhile is building in me. I don't know what to do. I have not made any big decisions, except to do nothing. It's time to get a bit active, and I'm writing this because it helps, as I said. Any kind of art is alchemy for the transmutation of leaden pain into beauty. That works for me in the hours I write, as a decent paragraph can make me happy.

I don't want to be one of those sad widowers who can't manage to stay alive for even a year or two on their own. I was driving down a street in Phoenix many years ago and I saw the remains of a dove in the center of the road—a pile of white feathers. The bird's sad mate stood next to it, oblivious to traffic. I was on a short errand. When I returned, there were two piles of white feathers. I don't want to be so melodramatic and predictable as that.

Writing about Maureen will help keep her present. One of the worst things about grieving is the feeling that her presence is evaporating. You cut up her credit cards over a trash bin and each snip is a painful burial at sea. You find a bobby pin or a mint wrapper in an unexpected place, and the little surprise hits your chest, and your face twists. You don't mind the junk mail and catalogs that continue to come in her name, as mailing lists will remember us longer than even our families. She received an ad in the mail recently from a company called Eternal Health and my thought was, *Christ, they never give up.*

I keep her cell phone around because so much of what she knew and loved and wrote to others, and what they wrote back to her, and what she read and what she saw through her own eyes and then captured in photos are dormant seeds of life inside that little black monolith. I also keep her perfume, Chanel Chance, on a high shelf in the medicine cabinet, though I'm rarely strong enough to put the bottle to my nose.

You try to escape by watching movies or shows, but they will all somehow just happen to be about a wife contracting leukemia. Years ago, my father took a new movie over to cheer up our closest family friends who were grieving the loss of their five-year-old child, killed by the snap of a chain as the boy's father tried to uproot a tree stump with a truck. But, as my parents sat with all of them watching, the movie unexpectedly had almost that exact death scene in it, as if tragedies have echoes.

I have come to see religion differently. And romance. I used to compartmentalize romance as one of life's elements among others—as an ornamental episode that shows in the giving of rings and jewels, fine dining, slow-dancing to Sinatra, untying tuxedo bowties, etcetera.

But romance is hardly just that. Some years ago, Maureen and I visited a Marc Chagall exhibit in Paris that moved us both deeply—mostly the brides flying in the embrace of their grooms and in the company of other creatures of nature. The exhibit described Chagall's family history of suffering under Russian pogroms and his need to document the beautiful community and traditions of his Jewish youth before they disappeared under the violent heel of history.

We had seen prints of those paintings forever, even on the walls of one of our favorite Phoenix restaurants, but it's different when you're standing as close to the paintings as the breathing artist once stood. His brides in the sky, held by their mates, is an image that keeps coming to me now. It gives me a new understanding that romance is not a part of life but is its everything. We fall through this existence and the only thing that makes it bearable and beautiful is to fall through it in the shared embrace of another who loves us—the soulmate, if you will.

I always resisted that term, soulmate, but I now think it's a real thing. I know what Jung writes about regarding the anima and animus, driving us into each other's arms, but that's just the mechanics of it, not the experience of it. My parents were registered soulmates—how lovely that was to watch and now remember—their gravestone says *"Inseparable."*

I learned to be Maureen's soulmate. You might think I have that wrong, that soulmates have a timeless connection, not something learned. Well, it can be learned, and leukemia is a good school for it. She cared about the idea of soulmates. I ducked it several times when she brought it up, but I did finally come to tell her we were soulmates, no question. I told that to her spirit as recently as this morning.

On that same Paris trip, we went to the tip-top of the Eiffel Tower. Maureen was fine with the grand balcony halfway up, where we had champagne and looked through a brass telescope, but she wasn't keen on taking the narrow little elevator the rest of the way up. But she knew I wanted to go, and it was my birthday. As the elevator shot heavenward, she hugged me, and I held her Chagall-like as the rattling tower narrowed around us. I whispered *brave little girl* as many times as it took to get to the top. It was something I would say again on her last evening, and she smiled to remember that previous trip heavenward—that rehearsal, perhaps. I would say it like a mantra in the hour after her departure, before friends arrived. Who knows how long new spirits can hear us?

I now better understand why Doris needed to do something worth the memory and spirit of the people she loved and lost—to do something for democracy, which is the love of life through the respectful sharing of freedom.

With friends and our handmade signs, I have been going to the protests, contributing to candidates who understand democracy and empathy. I am writing.

I'll see you on the streets. We gather under the sky to remind other Americans who we are and why our grandfathers waded ashore in Normandy. We awaken our neighbors to what America is. It is the mass dream for a better world.

What we do from here isn't about getting back to some ideal. It's about getting someplace new and better and sustainable and just and free and healthy and universally kind. That's a long way to march, but so many great spirits walk with us.

Remember: democracy always wins. If we haven't won yet, it's just because we're not finished fighting.

Love and Democracy

Appendix

The Orange Revolution

Before Putin attacked Ukraine, back when U.S. presidents supported democracy, Ukraine had a nonviolent revolution to get rid of a dictator. We should take lessons and encouragement from how they did it.

In 2004, Ukraine's president and prime minister were longtime Putin puppets. In that year the president announced he would step down and support the prime minister for president in the fall election.

The president, Leonid Kuchma, whose official residence had gold-plated bad taste throughout, had held power in the ways that dictators backed by oligarchs always do. Ukraine was in a delicate moment, as many people felt more a part of Western Europe than of Russia, and the values of democracy were in ascendency. The repressions and infinite corruptions of the regime, all for the financial benefit of Kuchma and his choir of oligarchs, were facing more resistance.

If you were outspoken, you would need to look behind you when you walked on the street. Many people were followed, and phones were tapped. But breaking points invariably happen. For Ukraine, a big one was in 2000 when reporter Georgiy Gongadze dared ask hardball questions about corruption to Kuchma on live TV. The reporter was privately warned that he was "playing a deadly game," but he persisted. Then he disappeared.

His wife, US-born Myroslava expected him to return to their apartment every evening. When walking down a street, she expected him to appear around every next corner.

But six weeks after his disappearance, his headless body was found in a shallow grave. That was perhaps the last straw precipitating an uprising that would take four years to mature.

After that murder, some journalists were more emboldened than cowed. "The most they can do is kill you," Olena Prytula, editor of Ukrainska Pravda, later told a documentary filmmaker.

When some people are bravely outspoken, others follow. A member of parliament released an audio recording where Kuchma says: "Before I forget, there is this guy named Gongadze. He is the worst possible bastard, Gongadze. Well, the Chechens should kidnap him and take him to Chechnya."

When autocrats call members of the Press enemies of the people, their henchmen eventually and invariably commit violence. When violence happens, freedom lovers must respond by doubling whatever the victims were doing to offend the regime. Americans should take that as the first lesson.

Gongadze's murder energized the pro-Western reform elements in the parliamentary elections of 2002. The reformist bloc, "Our Ukraine," received double the votes of the pro-Kuchma bloc, pushing charismatic reformer Viktor Yushchenko into position as Ukraine's most popular politician in parliament. He had earlier served as Prime Minister during an especially prosperous time for Ukraine, 2000 and 2001.

When the presidential campaign came in 2004, Viktor Yushchenko was the clear favorite for reformers, opposing the regime's man—and be prepared for the confusing similarity of names—Viktor Yanukovych. I will save you some trouble in the paragraphs below by referring to them as "Good Viktor" Yushchenko and "Bad Viktor" Yanukovych, who had two criminal convictions. Americans can relate.

Good Viktor's anti-corruption campaign posters featured bright orange. "Tak" (yes) was his slogan. There is a lesson for us in his campaign's use of the word *Yes*, because the belief that a better future is possible and at hand is the only thing that can overcome the lethargic surrender intentionally imposed by autocrats. His campaign was about freedom and the rule of law that comes with real democracy, but it focused solely on corruption, the part of Ukrainian life that was most aggravating to most people. Corruption in a society or an economy starts at the top. A corrupt head of state creates an ecosystem of corruption that floods everywhere, even to clerks and butchers. Do you want to pass your driver's test? A bribe is necessary. A passport? Admission to school? Have surgery scheduled? Also, the man who robbed your apartment is free on the street because police and judges are also for sale. There is freedom in such a society if you have lots of money. For most Ukrainians, ubiquitous corruption was the concern.

> *Harris and Walz lost the 2024 US election largely because they didn't sufficiently understand that people vote for the problems right in front of them. If you live hand-to-mouth and with difficulty, you are not among the "elites" who can afford to vote for egghead issues like democracy. Our resistance movements now should not make the same mistake. Another lesson might be this: Resistance campaigns are essentially "No!" campaigns, while "Yes" is energizing for the long haul and points to a better future. A third lesson here might be that Good Viktor's campaign did not specify issues. It simply claimed to be "the people," which set it against the corruption of the regime. A campaign of, by and for*

"free people," might be more powerful than a campaign to preserve federal agencies and values of governance.

The 2004 Ukrainian presidential campaign was rough. Good Viktor's ads were not allowed in most newspapers or on most TV and radio channels. His campaign plane was sometimes denied landing at airports. Supporters were beaten. Everyone was followed. Supporters could not get train tickets to rallies. For the regime's candidate and his supporters, trains were free.

Credible opinion polls showed Good Viktor leading by landslide numbers. The regime decided to take him out. Two months before election day, the first symptoms of his poisoning appeared. Vomiting. Pain throughout his body. He was taken to a hospital on September 10 for treatment and surgery.

Campaign surrogates took to the stage at rallies. Government TV claimed that he had not been poisoned, that it was all a campaign lie. A doctor was produced who said it was likely food poisoning from one of his own events or alcohol abuse.

Good Viktor Yushchenko finally was able to show up at a rally on September 18, thanking the doctors and all who supported him. He was sweating and in great pain, with a pain catheter in his spine, but he spoke powerfully for two hours, warning the regime that they would not poison the movement, as it was millions of people.

The scarring of his face from the poison would continue, making powerful speeches difficult for him. His rallies were therefore mostly rock music and mass singing of traditional Ukrainian songs. Rock music kept the young people coming and excited. They became the energy of the campaign. That's a lesson.

On September 24, the regime lamely tried to even the PR score. Bad Victor stepped out of a campaign bus and collapsed into the arms of his aids. His campaign claimed he was hit with a heavy blunt object in an assassination attempt. He made a video statement from a hospital room, blaming his opponent.

A cameraman who got away before his videotape could be confiscated released the tape to a reform-friendly TV station. The weapon was a single egg thrown at Bad Viktor's chest. A brave woman in the Interior Ministry acknowledged that fact before her statement was retracted in favor of the official assassination claim. The egg was thrown by a first-year college student, Dmytro Romaniuk. I include his name for no reason, except to show that not every Ukrainian man is a Viktor.

> *A lesson here is that any violence, even a thrown egg, will be used by an autocrat to further clamp down.*

Good Viktor repeatedly warned his crowds not to believe polls that said the race was close. It was not close, and the regime was obviously using false polls to prepare for a dishonest count. He quotes Stalin from 1936: "It doesn't matter how you vote; it only matters how you count them."

Two days before election day, Vladimir Putin came to Kyiv for a state visit and to watch a military parade. It was several things: don't think you can mess with the present regime, your neighbor has your autocrat's back, and nice little country you got here—careful how you vote.

October 31, 2004, election day. Exit polls show Good Viktor with a modest but healthy lead. Nevertheless, the count went to Bad Viktor. As there was no majority winner, a runoff was scheduled. The dishonest count was a clear warning to Good Viktor's campaign that the next count would be even more corrupt. They began to prepare the physical logistics—everything but bullets—for what would become known as the Orange Revolution.

> *Some of Bad Viktor's voters were beginning to come over to Good Viktor, as the first round was such an insult to all citizens. It was helpful that the Good Viktor campaign had been about the people, not about issues other than corruption. No one had to cross an ideological line to join the crowds already forming in Maidan Nezalezhnosti (Independence Plaza). The regime's former voters had not been demonized. That's a big lesson for opponents of autocrats.*

November 21-22, 2004, runoff election night. Even before polls closed on the day of the runoff election, the Good Viktor campaign had filled Independence Plaza with supporters, starting at 9 am with about five-hundred people. By 11am, 30,000. By noon, 80,000, growing continuously as people streamed in from Ukraine's western regions. The crowd would swell to half a million.

(Good) Viktor Yushchenko at the Independence Plaza mic:

> *"What I want to say and what I want all Ukraine to hear: we will protect the rights of the voters, and we will defend Ukrainian laws. The time has come my friends all across this plaza to raise the tent city and to prepare for acts of protest. We should show, dear friends, that together with us in the capital all regions of Ukraine are acting together. This unity exists in every region. In every province there should be a tent city with opposition activists."*

His running mate, Yulia Tymoshenko, always wearing her signature strawberry braids like a crown, said they must prepare for lay siege to the criminal regime.

A very important student movement, PORA, accounted for an important part of the crowd. Could the crowd keep the voting counting honest? It would not. Good Viktor took the microphone to urge people not to go home. He said that he had information that the Plaza would be cleared by the military at 3 am otherwise.

Exit polls of 30,000 voters from 500 polling locations showed Good Viktor with a 10 or 11% advantage. Another exit poll showed him with only a 5% lead, but still healthy.

More than 1.2 million ballots appeared unexpectedly from Donetsk, the most Russia-friendly province of Ukraine. In some polling places, acid was poured into ballot boxes. At 2 am, the Election Commission announced that a third of the votes had been counted and Bad Viktor was ahead by 4%. That was enough of an alarm bell: After conferring with experts on the vote count, Good Viktor called on all his supporters to come to Independence Plaza if they wanted to save their democracy.

The Regime was also busy. Armored vehicles flanked the Elections Commission. Several thousand troops and special forces then also surrounded the Presidential Administration.

By that time, Good Viktor's campaign had turned Independence Plaza into more than a crowd. Preparations had begun even before the first round of elections. Tents, sleeping bags, portable kitchens, portable toilets, and an army's worth of food donated from wholesale food companies had been secured, and now it all moved into the Plaza. Almost all the funding had come from the people. Large companies, tired of corrupt business-by-oligarch, had been the first to donate. That encouraged smaller companies and individuals to donate—supplies and money for more supplies. The first 200 tents went up in the early evening as the second-round ballots were still being counted.

From a properly permitted stage, patriotic songs were sung and broadcast through loudspeakers continuously. Then rock groups came on, and two dancing eggs in Sesame Street-worthy costumes to make jokes like, "Do you know why nobody ever found a heavy blunt object at the scene of the crime?" No, why? "Because they picked him up by his arms and carried him away!" Giant television screens showed the show and the reported election results to the far ends of the crowds, which were orange with flags and scarves.

Putin was already congratulating Bad Viktor, but leaders of the city councils of four large cities in Western Ukraine were congratulating Good Viktor. A lesson here is to have such statements ready in advance to build momentum at critical times.

Good Viktor, covered by the friendly television channels, called for more people to come to the Plaza. His running mate called for mass strikes in industries, transportation, schools and more.

The United States weighed in: Senator Richard Lugar, chair of the U.S. Senate Foreign Relations Committee, issued a statement condemning the falsification of the results. Elmar Brok of the European Parliament issued something similar, threatening financial sanctions. The U.S. Secretary of State's office summoned Russian Ambassador Yuri Ushakov to appear for a scolding regarding Putin's statement.

The crowds in Ukraine were urged to contact their friends to come after work and stay as long as necessary through the days ahead. They did. While it was not advertised as a general strike, the economy was nevertheless at a standstill. That is the one condition a corrupt regime cannot survive or abide.

Yulia Tymoshenko, the running mate, announced on her own that a march to the presidential administration was planned for the second day. Other campaign leaders, including Good Viktor, thought this would result in violence that would turn many Ukrainians against them, but did not argue publicly.

The crowd continued to grow, as people streamed into Kyiv. The march to the Presidential Administration took place. The marchers stopped at a thick line of riot police standing with their shields. Yulia Tymoshenko approached the police and asked them to step aside, saying they represented the people of Ukraine. Protesters attached yellow ribbons and flowers to the barricade between their numbers and the police.

Tymoshenko had not been clear about the purpose of the march. Some supporters thought they were there to storm and occupy the buildings. Those people were held back by others, who recognized that any violence would be a tactical mistake and a bloodbath.

General Oleksandr Savchenko, Commander of the Kyiv Police, sympathetic to the marchers and the cause, told the organizers that if he let the demonstrators through his line, the federal police guarding the federal buildings would kill them.

This sobered up the more aggressive demonstrators long enough for Good Viktor's people to turn the rhetoric toward a peaceful blockade. This was in line with the candidate's intention, which was "maximum participation and maximum peacefulness." He was quoted to say, "Even one person's life is worth more than my future presidency."

It was snowing but the crowds stayed. Schoolteachers and parents brought their kids out to see democracy defended. Back in the Plaza, speeches, rock music, patriotic songs known by all in the crowds continued. Supporters of the other side also flowed into the city.

Love and Democracy

By the third day, November 24, Good Viktor was urging unions and other workers to engage in a general strike, and to come to the Plaza instead of to work. Blockades were paralyzing the city and the government.

That day, the Central Election Commission announced that Bad Viktor had won with 49.46% and Good Viktor with 46.61%. One member of the commission left in protest.

When a state-friendly television station announced the results, a sign-language interpreter in the corner of the screen did not translate the official announcement quite correctly. Nataliya Dmytruk, 46, signed: "I am addressing everybody who is deaf in Ukraine. Our new president is Viktor Yushchenko. Do not trust the results of the Central Election Committee. They are all lies, and I am too ashamed to translate such lies to you. Maybe (or maybe not) you will see me again."

Her courage prompted 250 news colleagues to confront the network's owners, chanting, "No more lies!" The network changed almost immediately to fair reporting, as did other news outlets.

Nataliya Dmytruk's red line had been crossed. The television station had become an organ of a corrupt government—think Fox News. The people who worked there knew it. When they saw Nataliya's courage, they had to join her.

A Bad Viktor supporter on the street, celebrating his candidate's supposed win, was confronted by a Good Viktor supporter who said there were falsifications. The drunk young man said, "You go ask President Bush. Were there falsifications? Did he have falsifications? Did he really win the election?" If that was a reference to the "swift boating" of John Kerry, vote-switching voting machines or other stories, it shows how election misdeeds in America give people around the world permission to accept unethical practices as a normal part of winning. But a young woman on the street pushed back: "If there is no fairness in the country, there is no democracy!" she said.

Crowds were now perhaps 600,000 for Good Viktor. More rock music. Laser lights. Songs about "Our Future, Our lives!" The weather was 10-degrees, and the crowds were staying.

On November 25, the Ukrainian Supreme Court heard arguments. The crowds held their ground for days.

The regime was under tremendous pressure from Russia and from the oligarchs to clear the streets. As many as 10,000 troops were on the outskirts of the city, heading in. They did not want to come. Communications between Good Viktor's campaign and the military paid off. The general bringing in the troops said he would not continue if there were a blockade to prevent them. Good Viktor's campaign sent one car and a few people to block the highway. That was enough for the general.

A great effort was also made to not provoke individual police officers. The police with shields would change guard every half hour, giving the protestors the opportunity to help the retiring ones with good marching music like "When the Saints Go Marching In," and welcoming the new police with friendly hellos and welcomes. "Good evening! The police are with the People!" And then the national anthem.

The city police were coming over to the people's side. The Police Chief made a speech to the crowd: "We are convinced that no policeman wants the future president to be a person who was convicted of premeditated crimes in the past. We believe that solidarity of the police with the Ukrainian people will lead to complete victory over this criminal government."

Cheers went up: "The Police are with the People!"

The federal police were another matter, but the city Police Chief addressed the phalanx of riot-shielded federal police: "Think about what you are doing. These are our parents, our sisters standing over there, freezing. And you are standing here. Who did you take an oath to? To the people of Ukraine! You haven't fulfilled your oath… Who are you protecting? You're young, they'll take off, and you'll be left here to live with the people. How will you look each other in the eye then? Think about it. Serve your people. Glory to Ukraine."

Some of the young federal police seemed on the verge of crying. Their top officers told President Kuchma's office that they would attack the crowd only upon explicit orders signed by Kuchma. In fact, Kuchma saw the writing on the wall and did not want to risk that paper trail. People remember the fate of Mussolini. According to his advisors interviewed later, the fact that protesters were before his residence convinced Kuchma that the nation was no longer under his control.

Good Viktor's campaign manager gave his personal word to the Minister of the Interior that the crowd would not enter any government building if the federal police would withdraw. That assurance, as it was between men who knew and trusted each other, was enough to prevent bloody action. The federal police withdrew into buses as the people chanted "You're our guys! You're our guys!"

Noisy steel drum music was played by the crowds outside the presidential residence. Organizers with bullhorns repeatedly reminded the people to remain peaceful—at least in all things other than making noise. Graffiti was prohibited and a self-imposed distance of two meters from the fence was enforced, giving the police no excuse to react. "Behave like civilized people!" organized repeated to the crowds. "We will let everyone through!"

Offers were made to let Good Viktor be President of Ukraine, if Russia could have some of the eastern areas. The offer was refused.

December 3, 2004. The Ukrainian Supreme Court orders a new election. Everyone knows that Good Viktor will win, which he did, though not without another great effort to fight the efforts of the corrupt regime.

Ukraine has continued to fight its fight, dealing with the long-lasting poison of corruption set in motion by the autocrats they ousted. and then dealing with Putin and his friend Donald Trump.

Love and Democracy

Three Notes

1. Doris "Granny D" Haddock's political activism is carried on by Open Democracy in New Hampshire. They are worth your support. They get mine!

   > Open Democracy
   > 4 Park Street, Suite 301
   > Concord, NH 03301
   > Opendemocracynh.org
   > info@opendemocracy.me
   > (603) 715-8197

2. A good collection of Doris Haddock's speeches can be found in the book, "The Politics of Joy." It also includes many photos from her adventures.

3. Note to the DNC: You don't seem to know what your product is in this environment. Your candidates, of course, need your support. But your main product now is democracy itself, something we could once take as a given. You now need the best ideas from the best marketing professionals and the biggest dollars to sell the idea and the requirements of democracy. Frank Capra did it during World War II. Can you do it today? Much depends on this. Let's see beautiful, deeply moving ads that outshine the Fox gaslight.

www.ingramcontent.com/pod-product-compliance
Lightning Source LLC
Chambersburg PA
CBHW011318080526
44589CB00020B/2740